Self Studies

SELF STUDIES

The Psychology of
Self and Identity

Karl E. Scheibe

PRAEGER

Westport, Connecticut
London

Library of Congress Cataloging-in-Publication Data

Scheibe, Karl E.
    Self studies : the psychology of self and identity / Karl E.
Scheibe.
      p. cm.
    Includes bibliographical references and index.
    ISBN 0–275–94538–3 (alk. paper)
    1. Social psychology. 2. Group identity. 3. Identity
(Psychology). 4. Self. I. Title.
HM251.S2984 1995
155.2—dc20   94–40037

British Library Cataloguing in Publication Data is available.

Library of Congress Catalog Card Number: 94–40037

ISBN: 0–275–94538–3

First published in 1995

Praeger Publishers, 88 Post Road West, Westport, CT 06881
An imprint of Greenwood Publishing Group, Inc.

Printed in the United States of America

The paper used in this book complies with the
Permanent Paper Standard issued by the National
Information Standards Organization (Z39.48–1984).

10 9 8 7 6 5 4 3 2

For Ted Sarbin,
mentor and friend

Contents

Preface

The fundamental purpose of all writers, no matter how elevated or grand their pretensions, is illustrated by the famous graffiti of World War II, "Kilroy was here." To etch a signature that will linger after one's ephemeral passage by the wall is to provide evidence of a living self, and not just any self, but one that is identified just so—"Kilroy." Writing asserts and extends the self. What then of the other ostensible reasons for writing—the purposeful recording of revelation, truth, and beauty, or the provision of instruction for others? These are secondary purposes and often false pretensions. Even if "Kilroy" is code for who I really am, or even if I write anonymously, the etched trace is mine—an identifiable result of a little explosion of movement—willed and made by my self. While Freud thought he was founding and promulgating the new science of psychoanalysis, his writing is interpretable in another way—he was extending and preserving a part of his self, an identifiable self, Sigmund Freud. In this way, he is like every other writer. But in the endurance of his signature, he is superior to most authors, including me, and I bow to his incisiveness.

The self exists only in the present, but it is interested in its past and future. Nabokov (1979) evokes an image in his autobiographical memoir of someone viewing a movie taken a few weeks before his birth, in which his brand-new but empty carriage appears. "The cradle rocks above an abyss, and common sense tells us that our existence is but a brief crack of light between two eternities of darkness" (p. 6). Once we were not yet, now we are, and then we shall no longer be. The self strives toward extension—this simple axiom has broad application—and since extension into the past is not an easy option, extension into the future presents a challenge that can be assumed. So we write and make pictures, recordings, and replicas of various sorts, bringing traces of the self forward from the past and making new traces to be carried into the future—always with some emotional ambiguity to be sure, for we sense the danger presented by having our likeness and our tracings lying about for public view. As Ortega y Gassett noted, "Plotinus could never make up his mind to have his portrait made because this was, according to him, to bequeath to the world the shadow of a shadow" (1961, p. 124).

This book of essays about the psychology of self and identity involves some tricks of time. All but one of the chapters have been published in preliminary form in other sources, though all of the material has been updated and revised for this book. Chapter 1, "Psyche and the Socius: Being and being-in-place" was written for this volume and has not been published elsewhere in any form.

My own thinking and exposition about the psychology of self and identity began in my first year of graduate school at Berkeley. Julian Rotter was a visiting professor in 1959–60, and I was assigned in the spring term to be a reader for his undergraduate course in personality. Rotter had to miss one class meeting midway through the term because of a speaking engagement elsewhere. He asked me to give a lecture on the self. When I expressed uneasiness about lecturing on the topic he said, "Everyone has to blow a certain number of lectures—so if what you say is worthless, don't worry about it." And so I assiduously prepared my first lecture ever, relying heavily on William James to inform my discourse on the self. I remember little of what I said, but I survived the experience and the undergraduates neither departed nor fell asleep. This assignment started me thinking about self and identity and I have continued this line of thinking since.

Later at Berkeley I came to study with Ted Sarbin and students known as the Tuesday Morning Group, after our custom of meeting in his home on Tuesday mornings for informal discussions of psychological topics. Sarbin was then and is now an advocate of role theory. His theoretical view provided a new basis for thinking about self and identity. It accounts, among other things, for my having become so interested in self and identity in the first place; after all, it was an assigned role, with a great deal of required involvement. Erving Goffman was also at Berkeley at this time, and while I did not study directly with him, our group read his books (*Presentation of self in everyday life, Asylums,* and *Stigma*) with interest and appreciation.

Several years after graduate school, Rolf Kroger and I had the opportunity to spend the summer with Ted Sarbin, working intensively on a set of research projects having to do with self and identity. During this summer, the basic elements of the theoretical model which is presented in chapter 4 of this book were developed. The social and political context within which these ideas developed is worth noting. The year was 1965—the year of the Beatles, riots in Watts, the aftermath of the Berkeley Free Speech Movement, Timothy Leary and the International Federation for Freedom, Ken Kesey and the Merry Pranksters, and the development of a conspicuous counter-culture in the United States. Social identities, it seemed to us, were being transformed in radical ways all around. "Make love, not war!" "Tune in, turn on, drop out!"

As psychologists, we bent to the task of developing a theoretical model which would somehow render a coherent and systematic account of how social identities can be radically changed. Since the social winds were blowing with such force in this period, it became patently obvious that in order for any model of social identity to have value, it must be fundamentally and not just secondarily contextual. Goffman had offered the radical contention that apart from its presentation the self did not exist. Sarbin similarly gave emphasis to the self-in-social-commerce, drawing upon the Cooley-Mead tradition within social psychology.

At Wesleyan, I came eventually to offer courses on the psychology of self and identity. When questioned about the distinction between self and identity, I must say that I had no clear answer for several years—but would refer to one or another wobbly convention that had been established in the tradition of writing on this subject. I think in retrospect that my course used the dual terms self and identity largely for reasons of euphony—it sounded better than either term by itself, and seemed to cover more ground.

A strain appeared in my course which seemed to have little relation to my graduate education or to my theoretical convictions. Sarbin and Goffman appeared in my course, to be sure. But so did Carl Jung. As an undergraduate, I wrote an honors thesis on Jung, for I found his writings full of fascination. This fascination found absolutely no resonance in graduate school, so Jung was put away in favor of more empirically tractable approaches to psychology. But then I came to find Jung's perspective not just fascinating but in fact quite essential to my course on the psychology of self and identity. I came to think of Jung's fundamental interest in the self as vertical—of the meaning of one's existence in relation to the earth and the cosmos; and of the social psychological perspective in which I had been schooled as horizontal—where the meaning of one's identity is taken from relations to the socius. Looking back at James, I discovered what I should have remembered—that among James' empirical selves was the spiritual self as well as the social self and the material self. James didn't use the geometric coordinates which I found myself employing, but he had the same ideas in mind.

Now I began to have some conviction about a meaningful distinction between self and identity. In chapter 1 I shall set forth this distinction and its accompanying justification for the reader's appraisal and possible appreciation. By way of preface, I merely note here that the vertical and horizontal perspectives on self and identity are complementary and mutually confirming, and that either perspective by itself is psychologically empty.

Many excellent books about the psychology of self and identity have been written, despite a long hiatus in the middle of this century. Within the last few years, studies and books on this topic are appearing at a great rate. I note, for example, *The saturated self,* in which Gergen (1991) attempts to situate our understanding of the self in the terms of postmodernism, deconstructionism, and related current intellectual movements. In *The remembered self,* Singer and Salovey (1993) call upon script theory and the narrative approach in psychology to couch their view of self. Hermans and Kempen (1993) in *The dialogical self* draw upon Bakhtin's idea of multiple voices to present a conception of self which is at once philosophically sophisticated and psychologically relevant. Similarly, Sampson's (1993) *Celebrating the other* draws upon Bakhtin's dialogic theory to show that the notion of a contained and separate self is a pernicious fiction, yet one which psychology cannot easily escape. A rich series of empirical studies is presented in *Social psychology of identity and the self concept,* edited by Breakwell (1992). Freeman (1993), in *Rewriting the self: History, memory, narrative,* provides a thoughtful and challenging application of theories of the self to actual lives, weaving together literary, philosophical, and psychological perspectives through the common device of narrative. Indeed, the thought occurs that if one has a novel idea about the psychology of self and identity, it would be more economical to find that idea expressed elsewhere in recent books and journals, or to have the patience to wait a little while for the next raft of publications on the topic to appear.

But of course, such a passive and equable attitude toward the search for truth will not do, for my graffiti-writing demon will not be quelled. I have an epigram from my Wesleyan colleague, Paul Horgan, pinned to my wall. It is this: "Everything has been said, but not everything has been said superbly, and even if it has been, everything must be said freshly over and over again."

Only blind conceit would keep one from recognizing the truth of this as it applies to the psychology of self and identity. Ours is a science whose frontiers must continually be rediscovered in the light of each new day, in the terms of our current historical circumstances, which despite all our sayings, have never been before. My claim for the reader's taxed attention is that at least some of what appears in the chapters that follow is well said and will have the value of freshness.

The psychology of self and identity is potentially and often practically as boring and abstract as the poet's fabled "Ode to Elbowroom." My experience in teaching this topic, however, instructs me of the potential for electric excitement as well. We all have selves and we all have identities. These essays are meant to provide illumination on who and what we are.

They have served that function for me. Now I expose their glimmer for others to see.

Also, I would like to thank a set of Wesleyan students who worked with me, tirelessly and well, on the preparation of this manuscript. They are Joy Rhoden, Laura Rappold, Scott Berry, Chris Miciek, Sandy Nichols, and Debra Drisko.

Self Studies

Chapter 1

Psyche and the Socius: Being and Being-in-Place

God said to Moses, I am who I am.

—Exodus 3:14

I am not who I am.

—Iago, in *Othello*

I am myself plus my circumstance.

—Ortega y Gassett[1]

I am a self who has an identity. This statement could be made by anyone and it would be true. Once I specify an identity—fifty-seven years old, male, Professor of Psychology at Wesleyan University, married, father of two children, about-to-be-grandfather, named Karl Scheibe—an identity is owned and true of only one self in the world. Some of these identity characteristics remain more or less permanently fixed—sex and name— while others—age, kinship relations—change gradually. Surely by the time this is published, I shall *be* a grandfather. Much matter-of-fact and tedious detail is not here recited. Identity markers serve as provisional coordinates for locating one's self in the flux of changing circumstance, rather like gradual shifts in the surrounding terrain as we travel down a stream. The effectiveness of these coordinates in identifying me to anyone else depends upon that person's familiarity with the description coordinates I have chosen to use here.[2] If one knows nothing of psychology or colleges or of kinship customs in our culture, the information I have provided about myself would be minimally useful in telling that person of my current identity. The number of possible coordinates for the present me is indefinitely large, and I, out of consideration, will choose to articulate markers to a potential audience or conversational partner in such a way as to maximize easy identifications, imagining, as I do now, that I am among friends—that the amorphous, silent, now-nameless readers of this passage do not bear me hostile intent.

But it can be otherwise. The presentation of self, allowing as it does for contrived as well as guessed or assumed identification, requires wariness. We size each other up out of primordial habit as friend or foe, as harmless or potential threat. Identifications, on occasion, are falsely claimed—a common practice among spies or confidence men in order to avoid the penalties of discovery. So my self can dictate that false claims for identity be made and claim ratification from surrounding others.

The self is in the flow, and circumstances change—now friendly, now hostile; but more than that, circumstances determine the varying salience of the indefinitely large number of identity claims that can be made. My Ph.D. is important as a qualification to be a teacher, scholar, or therapist; it is of no importance in participating in a local road race (my claimed identity as an athlete has just the opposite relevance for these roles). The presented self is always presented *as* something, never as whole or entire. It is always presented by means of these more or less shifting coordinates provided by the surround. Thus is the self identified, on the presumption that it is an abstraction continuous in time.[3] The body might be seen as the bubble of matter within which we have our being, and thus the body itself becomes part of the shifting and aging surround, itself in the flow and part of the flow. Again, the self is an abstraction which is not knowable to itself or to outsiders in detail, but which is readily identified by virtue of staying more or less constantly within certain identifying markers, the body being one of them.

UNEASY IDENTITIES

I present now three instructive cases in which the apparently easy commerce of the self and its surroundings is rendered problematic. Circumstances are concrete, the self is abstract, and commerce refers to an act of identification—a connection between circumstance and self. It takes human beings some years to say who they are, so it should not be presumed that this process is simple and easy. Yet in adults, self-report does seem simple and easy, masking the complexity of the achievement. The self is always presented ambiguously and incompletely in its identifications, and the process is inherently difficult. The problematic cases here presented will help to illustrate the complexity of what is going on in self-presentation. I claim that this complexity is present for everyone, though it is usually not obvious.

The Suffocating Self in the Closet

The late writer Paul Monette (1992) describes his life as a gay man growing up in a world hostile to homosexuality. From early boyhood, he was conscious of his sexual attraction to men, and aware as well that he could not allow himself to be identified by his parents, his schoolmates, his friends, as queer without risking total rejection.

Everybody else had a childhood. . . . [T]here they were coaxed and coached and taught all the shorthand. Or that is how it always seemed to me, eavesdropping my way through twenty-five years, filling in the stories of straight men's lives. First they had their shining boyhood, which made them strong and psyched them up for the real leap across the chasm to adolescence, where the real rites of manhood began. . . . And every year they leaped further ahead, leaving me in the dust with all my doors closed, and each with a new and better deadbolt. Until I was twenty-five, I was the only man I knew who had no story at all. I'd long since accepted the fact that nothing had ever happened to me and nothing ever would. That's how the closet feels, once you've made your nest in it and learned to call it home. Self-pity becomes your oxygen. (Monette 1992, p. 1)

So his tortured psyche tried through various maneuvers to survive and to maintain appearances—by pretending to like girls, by psychotherapy directed to normalizing his sexual appetite, by forced sexual experimentation with women—all forlorn attempts to reconcile that which could not be reconciled. He found himself admiring and attaching to straight men— wanting to be like them. "Although I hadn't the analytic skills to know it then, I'd already begun the process of 'de-selfing'—my own word for the craziness that's turned my life into a minefield, this wanting to be someone else instead of me" (Monette, 1992, p. 118).

Monette was somehow formed gay, and this formation of his psyche could in no way be reformed by therapeutic exercises. Monette found acceptance of his gay identity in his sexual partners and in the gay demimonde of his New England environment. But the open proclamation of his gay identity had to await the more tolerant social climate of the 1980s.

His autobiography, *Becoming a man: Half a life story* recounts his struggle—a self pretending to an alien essence—furtive, fugitive, guilt-laden, confused, and yet somehow strong and resolute. Now breaking into daylight, Monette discovered a tragic and dooming feature of his identity. He had AIDS and had to accept the prospect of early death.

Floating down life's stream, one may perceive oneself to be in hostile territory—so that if one exhibits oneself clearly, one might be attacked and destroyed by the surrounding social host. So we might live in deeply secret domains, coming out only selectively and cautiously. Meanwhile, one tries to take on the condition of normal selves, knowing that it is but camouflage. In the case of Paul Monette, the camouflage was finally shucked off, with the splendid discovery that the world around him had become sufficiently tolerant to make an honest presentation of self sustainable. Alas, his body along the way had lost its intolerance of disease.

Autism and the Encapsulated Self

The condition of autism presents particularly dramatic cases of a disjunction between what is in the self and what appears at the presentation of that
self to a world of others who seem hopelessly distant. Oliver Sacks remarks
that,

[I]n some autistic people this sense of radical and ineradicable difference is so
profound as to lead them to regard themselves, half-jokingly, almost as members of
another species." (1993/1994, p.118)

The very word *autism* suggests the encapsulation of the self—of being
cut off from the multifarious connections, understandings, cue transfers,
and implicit knowings by which most of us maintain our bearings most of
the time. Sacks presents an analysis of a remarkable case of autism, that of
Temple Grandin, who has provided a rare self-description of autism in her
autobiography *Emergence: Labeled autistic* (1986). Grandin has a Ph.D. in
animal sciences, has published over 100 papers in her field, and is autistic.

She appears emotionally cut off from much human experience but is
tuned in directly to the moods of animals—cows and pigs, for example:

I was struck by the enormous difference, the gulf between Temple's immediate
intuitive recognition of animal moods and signs and her extraordinary difficulties
understanding human beings, their codes and signals, the way they conducted
themselves. One could not say that she was devoid of feeling or had a fundamental
lack of sympathy. On the contrary, her sense of animals' moods and feelings was so
strong that those almost took possession of her, overwhelmed her at times. She feels
she can have sympathy for what is physical or physiological—for an animal's pain
or terror—but lacks empathy for people's states of mind and perspectives. When
she was younger, she was hardly able to interpret even the simplest expressions of
emotion; she learned to "decode" them later, without necessarily feeling them.
(Sacks 1993/1994, p.116)

It is as if the large fund of implicit or tacit knowledge which most of us
accumulate through our sympathetic encounters with others has somehow
been denied to this person—cutting her off from the currents of immediate
understandings which allow us to experience the pains, the joys, the long-
ings, the loves, and the agonies of other human beings. Temple just couldn't
"get" *Romeo and Juliet*, and *Hamlet* bewildered her. She has enormous
powers of concentration and visualization and a prodigious memory, but
she has one difficulty: She is cut off from most of human feeling.

And yet she has self-acceptance: "If I could snap my fingers and be
non-autistic, I would not—because then I wouldn't be me. Autism is part
of who I am" (Sacks 1993/1994, p.124).

The Fugitive Returns to Her Self

For twenty-three years, Katherine Anne Power lived as a fugitive, eventually settling down in Oregon as Alice Metzinger. Her life as a fugitive began when she was twenty-one, when she served as a getaway car driver for a gang involved in a fatal shooting of a policeman in Brighton, Massachusetts, as part of a bank holdup conducted to provide funds for antiwar causes.

At the time of her arrest, Katherine Anne Power had spent more of her life as a fugitive than not. In her new life in Oregon, she had a loving husband, a son, a successful career in the restaurant business, a home, and many friends. And yet she felt a constant sense of falseness, of a strain of separation from her "real" family and "real" self.

For twenty-three years, I dreamt I would accidentally sign my real name. Well, when I surrendered, I lived my nightmare. For the first time, I signed, "Katherine Anne Power"—and I had to do it over and over, on these legal documents. It was like some insane, drug-induced experience. (Franks 1994, p. 41)

She described herself at the time as feeling, "Buoyantly light, disentangled at last from the heavy net of lies, aliases, and invented selves" (ibid.).

When the fundaments of the self are laid down, what is initially arbitrary becomes essential. Katherine Anne Power is a product of her upbringing—a Catholic girl from a large family in Denver, who did well in school and went to Brandeis on a scholarship. All of this happenstance came to be incorporated as a real identity owned by a real self. Now, when a newly fabricated identity was assumed out of the necessity of avoiding capture and punishment as a fugitive, it was not "real" for her, even though she passed as real for her many friends and business associates.

I was really this hidden, broken person and I just couldn't go on. . . . It's not for ego, it's not for money or greed or status. It's not because you want to spend more time with somebody else. It's because you have to do it to be alive—you have to quit living this sick-making life. (Franks 1994, pp. 57–58)

The false identity she had assumed was taken as real by those around her, including her son. Even after her surrender, and the resumption of her true name, her husband and her friends continued to call her Alice, not Katherine.

This provides an example in the second order of how the arbitrary becomes essential, of how what is merely created or constructed out of nothing becomes an essential reality.

Power sat down to tell her son she was not the person she had pretended to be. "It was so hard for me. I began to talk in euphemisms—I think what disturbed Jamie the most was that Alice Metzinger was not my real name. I could see something pass over his face, like a small earthquake inside him. You see, he is Jamie Metzinger. I knew he was thinking, Am I real if you are not? And then the alarm was gone, as though he had shaken it out of his head. He asked, 'Can I go play now?'" (Franks 1994, p. 58)

Jamie Metzinger is really Jamie Metzinger, no matter that his name came from a completely adventitious circumstance created by the need of his mother to be a fugitive and the availability of a birth certificate for a real person, now dead, whose real name was Alice Metzinger. The psychological reality of the given self is no less compelling for its having been made up as a product of a fleeting and highly improbable convergence of matter and nomenclature.

Summary of Cases: The Arbitrarily Constructed Self Becomes Essential

Paul Monette did not choose to become homosexual. In fact, he tried hard to choose not to be, but failed miserably in trying to be straight. Despite the cost, he finally owned his identity as a gay man. Even though he knew he was dying of AIDS, one has the sense in reading his autobiography of an attained authenticity—of a harmonized self and identity.

So too with Temple Grandin. Despite her autistic isolation and her lack of easy empathy with her fellows, she has a self and identity in harmony with each other, even with her continuing sense of strangeness with respect to her human companions. Her intuitions work better with other animals, whose understanding she seems to share.

Despite the pain of prison, the anger and the perceived injustice of authorities, and the anguish of separation from her family, Katherine Anne Power has now resolved a dissonance between her real self and her put-on identity—an identity which proved, in time, to be a torture for her far worse than prison.

All of these cases illustrate the curious but compelling transformation of that which is arbitrarily given in the self into something which must be validated and affirmed in life's more transient identifications. A dissonance between the abstraction which is the self and the concertizing reality which is one's transient identity can become unendurable.[4] We are something before we have knowledge of anything at all, either internal or external. We are called by our real names before we know of names, ours or others. Through the assimilation of reflections given back to us by people and other mirrors, we develop concurrently our capacity for knowledge and the comfort of self-knowledge. Out of the mists of our early lives, the self is provisionally formed, and self-knowledge as well. The markers of identification are only loosely connected to our physical form—one can tell age, race, stature, and gender—but the body does not tell its name, its talents, its preferences, its intelligences.

These cases also illustrate what is meant by personal authenticity—something that has to do with the harmony between the initially given self and its continuing identifications as it passes through and down the social flux.

WHY A PSYCHOLOGY OF SELF AND IDENTITY IS IMPORTANT

From these specific cases, it is now appropriate to return to more general and universal themes about self and identity. In doing this, I propose to set about the positive task of demonstrating why a psychology of self and identity is important and deserves attention both from within psychology and from without.

The three epigraphs at the head of this chapter provide a useful point of departure. All begin with the same two words: I am—the same two words which stand as the conclusion to Descartes' argument for existence. Yet the existential forms asserted in these three propositions are radically different—the divine, the diabolical, and the human.

God's assertion to Moses is in response to a question Moses poses about the identity of his interlocutor, present in the form of a burning bush. The response is an assertion of an absolute self—not identified by name or other referent. No coordinates are given for locating the other party in this theophany. This conception of an absolute being has rich psychological consequences, for such a being can easily be endowed with properties such as omniscience, omnipresence, omnipotence—so that mortals consider it possible to communicate at will with the great I AM by unmediated praying at any time or circumstance. Mortals might also live in fear of such a disembodied essence, for the vulnerability is on one side only. Of course, a major identity question for human beings arises from this condition: Namely, who am I in relation to the Absolute? William James considered this to be the root of the most general human malaise—that we feel in our natural condition somehow not at one with the Absolute.[5] We feel cut off, not recognized, not included, not blessed. The lives of great psychologists are often characterized by periods of profound despair and depression—Fechner, Jung, and James come to mind immediately, and in all of these cases the despair is hinged to the question of "Who am I in relation to the universal?" In Sarbin's (1982a) terms, human beings try to locate themselves in the cosmological ecology, and the lack of proper location in this ecology can be the occasion for profound despair, particularly as one contemplates the possibility of death.

A different set of psychological issues is suggested by Iago's negative assertion. Here is the prospect not just of isolation but of experience with pure evil. Iago is the great deceiver—fluent of tongue, far ahead of lesser mortals in plotting and in knowing by acute cunning what reactions to expect in response to his contrived appearances. Iago's acumen is superhuman, as is his resolve. After his nefarious actions have been exposed, he refuses to speak another word, denying his mortal accusers a show of either confession or contrition.

Iago's motives have puzzled critics. Why did he destroy the great Othello by driving him into blind, jealous, murderous rage? What are the Devil's motives? They are no more to be questioned than the motives of God—for they are as irreducible as they are universal. But the Devil is an inverse of God even so. Iago is the principle of evil—of destruction for destruction's sake, of death for death's sake, of exercise of malignant power to bring down the proud, the beautiful, and the good merely in order to exercise that power. Evil is the Devil's function. It is what he does. The Devil supplies symmetry to the moral order, the negative downward pole—Jung's Shadow, Dante's *Inferno*, Conrad's *Heart of darkness*—the terrible, the unspeakable, the horrific—lacking which, now psychologically speaking, the world of good and Godly things is flat and dull. Without Iago, Othello is not a story. With him, the stage is set for the fullness of human tragedy.

The book of Job relates a contest between God and the Devil, with Job the human player strung between the I AM and the I AM NOT, the object of their curiosity and play. The Devil bets that Job will renounce and curse God if he is stripped of his earthly treasures and pleasures. Job objects to being treated unfairly, but he does not renounce God. He retains his human position after all the struggle, and in the end it becomes clear that the human lot is ever to be defined as struggle.

In MacLeish's (1956) modern version of the tale, *J.B.*, one of the Comforters offers an argument for J.B.'s relief from guilt:

> "We have surmounted guilt. It's quite,
> Quite different, isn't it? You see the difference.
> Science knows now that the sentient spirit
> Floats like the chambered nautilus on a sea
> That drifts in under skies that drive:
> Beneath, the sea of subconscious;
> Above, the winds that wind the world.
> Caught between that sky, that sea,
> Self has no will, cannot be guilty.
> The sea drifts. The sky drives.
> The tiny, shining bladder of the soul
> Washes with wind and wave or shudders
> Shattered between them."

And later,

> "There is no guilt, my man. We all are
> Victims of our guilt, not guilty.
> We kill the king in ignorance: the voice

Reveals: we blind ourselves. At our
Beginning, in the inmost room,
Each one of us, disgusting monster
Changed by the chilling moon to child,
Violates his mother. Are we guilty?
Our guilt is underneath the Sybil's
Stone: not known."

And yet J.B. will not accept this passive innocence. He reacts violently to his Comforter.

"I'd rather suffer
Every unspeakable suffering God sends,
Knowing it was I that suffered,
That I earned the need to suffer,
I that acted, I that chose,
Than wash my hands with yours in that
Defiling innocence. Can we be men
And make an irresponsible ignorance
Responsible for everything? I will not
Listen to you!" (pp.122–123)

And so the human voice asserts its vote for its own humanity. "I am myself plus my circumstance"—an absolute I incorporated in a particular body in a particular place at a particular time with a particular history, a particular set of Others located on a level with me, with whom I may converse and reflect, and who tell me of my identity just as I tell them of theirs. Every I has a circle drawn around it—a circumstance. The center of this circle, let us say, is constant, but the objects, structures, places, images, events, persons, institutions, concerns, themes, and shadows comprising the periphery of our self-circles do not remain constant but are in continual flux—the flowing stream of thought, to borrow James' metaphor; the person in a differentiated and animated Life-Space, in the language of Lewin (1951/1975).

Freud and Skinner after him have said that our freedom is an illusion, that we are enslaved fatally to circumstances. That is their vote. We can say, with J.B., "I will not listen to you." When this is called resistance, we must remember that Freud and Skinner have no more authority on this matter than anyone else, and that we are free, like James, to vote that we are free.[6] Our freedom to choose may, after all, be an illusion. If so, our subscription to the proposition that we are free cannot be an object of reproach, for if it is an illusion to which we are compelled by the sea below and the wind above, then there is no alternative to our believing the illusion. But as a matter of taste and preference we can assert our freedom as real and no illusion, protesting at least partial responsibility for our own positioning in our circumstances.

The philosophical question of freedom of the will is touched upon here because of its psychological significance. The great and enduring interest in this topic derives, I argue, from its psychological importance. James' (1896/1984) philosophical essay on "The will to believe" ultimately turns on a psychological point—namely the aesthetic unacceptability of a fully determined universe. The psychology of self and identity is important, in turn, because it produces the impetus for interest in the topic of freedom. It matters greatly to us as human beings to know whether we can control our circumstances and to what degree this is possible. Seligman (1993) has argued, most recently in his book, *What you can change and what you can't,* that depression in human beings derives in large part from their learned helplessness, their resignation to fatalism, their belief that they have no effective vote in controlling their circumstances. Whether such a sense of helplessness is cause or consequence of depression, there can be no doubt of its profoundly negative experiential character. If I am not an agent in the human drama, then I am a helpless cipher. The massive literature on the locus of control variable in personality research also reinforces this point. A belief in an internal locus of control is consistent with psychological health, well-being, and satisfaction with self (Rotter 1966; Hersch and Scheibe 1967; Lefcourt 1966).

A psychology of self and identity can serve as a point of departure for understanding and even treating such problems as depression. But depression is only one of a vast range of issues which might be illuminated from this perspective. One might argue that communism has failed as a system of governance because it is based on an implicit psychology of self and identity which is at odds with human requirements—specifically, the requirement that individual selves be granted recognition and status apart from the political collectivities of which they are a part—that individuals be allowed loyalties to family, to religion, to clan, to tribe, to nation. Universal class solidarity has turned out in practice to be psychologically unworkable. If everyone is my brother or sister, then no one is a special relation to me, and I can claim no specific identity from my relationships.

The issues of ethnic and racial pluralism are also intelligible as problems of self and identity. Scholars and intellectuals have tended to be universalists, as in the case of Marx who derided the 'idiocy of village life.' Ties to blood and soil have been viewed as atavisms, throwbacks to more primitive, less enlightened forms of civilized human existence. Yet the conflicts of our times must be seen as attempts by the human inhabitants of this planet to claim or reclaim distinctive identities and to have those identities respected with full legitimacy. The Serbs and Croats and Bosnians in the former Yugoslavia are not willing to forget their ethnic roots, no matter how long they were submerged or suppressed. The Protestants and Catholics in Northern Ireland are similarly unwilling to merge into an undifferentiated identity. The massacres in Rwanda or in Turkey or in Cambodia are based not on ideological conflict but on simple tribal and ethnic loyalties and identifications. The about-to-be victims of a genocidal campaign are not first interviewed about what their views are; it is enough to be identified, rightly or wrongly, as being one of the enemy.

Colleges and universities are full of individuals who have gained liberation from forms of religious, familial, and ethnic identifications which seemed tremendously confining. A devotion to Science, to Truth, or to Humanity is sufficient for a community of scholars. But such wispy identity coordinates are not sufficient outside the academy.

An ethnic imperative, an ineffable bond that Professor Harold Isaacs terms "basic group identity," governs our lives and is the taproot of our authentic identities. The ethnic bond is primordial, molding us from our earliest hours. So pervasive is it that, because of it, selfhood is finally inseparable from group; even values such as individuality, strong though they might seem, are imposed from without upon the far more natural ethnic identity. America is thus a pluralistic society composed of discreet ethnic groups, and not at all what the myth of the melting pot would have us believe. No limits, finally, can be set to the empire of ethnicity; it is part and parcel of one's self and soul, a heritage one carries through life, imparted from the cradle if not indeed the genes. (Stein and Hill 1987, pp. 181–182)

A psychology of self and identity provides a perspective from which to bring intelligibility to acts and conditions which are otherwise quite baffling. An anthropologist colleague wondered how he could possibly understand a citizen of Bosnia who from one day to the next was transformed from a peaceful neighbor into a deadly sniper, with former neighbors fixed in his sights. The Sandinistas in Nicaragua were disappointed that the Miskito Indians did not wish to give up their backward culture in favor of joining the revolution. A student of mine spends years trying to locate her real birth parents, despite a completely satisfactory and loving relationship with her adoptive parents. Another student explores the particular difficulties encountered by young people who, like herself, come from biracial backgrounds. In all of these cases, intelligibility is restored only from the standpoint of a psychology of self and identity.

A consideration of self and identity enlarges the framework typically employed within psychology. Instead of asking how we learn and know— the typical problems for cognition—we must also ask who is learning and knowing and how that learning and knowing play a role in the development of a person's life story. Similarly, our understanding of the motivational substrate of behavior must include a person's particular reasons and purposes, and these are only to be found in that person's particular construction of their own life story. A psychology of self and identity must necessarily be large and embracing. It is about human beings, not merely about the nice but limited problems to which psychologists have been mostly attracted in recent history.

CROSSING SELF AND IDENTITY: PRESENT AND ABSENT

The Presence or Absence of Self

A living person is a living self, is conscious and knowing—as Descartes knew that he was a thinking self and no illusion to himself created by some demon. One can, of course, be phenomenologically irresponsible and philosophically mischievous and pretend not to be a self. Before the advent of behaviorism in psychology, no one would have thought this to be a move forward. After behaviorism, many psychologists acted and wrote as if human beings were merely complex automata, if perhaps reserving an implicit exception for themselves, as analysts from an advantaged position of the behavior of lower organisms.[7]

I wish now to pose a question that will seem naive but which is absolutely fundamental: How do we know, for any aggregation of matter, whether there is a self present in it or not?

One may argue about what the criteria might be for making a diagnosis of the existence of self for any other. Can one carry on a conversation? Does the other appear to be like me, and therefore, by analogy, have a self like mine? The Turing machine problem comes to mind, wherein this challenge is posed: Is it possible to distinguish unequivocally, by means of an exchange of questions and replies, between a living Other and a computer which is programmed to behave as if it were another living person?[8] Virtual reality is an attempt to create in a person a series of sensations which replicate exactly the sensations one would have in an experience such as sailing a boat, riding a horse, or conversing with another person, with the difference that the sensations are supplied not by ordinary reality but by a computer-driven simulation of real sensations. For now, the enormous technical problems involved in these simulations can safely be ignored. Of interest only is the notion that we routinely make, in practice, diagnostic judgments about whether a self is present or absent in objects.

Differences in the mode and manner of this judging are of great interest. One may treat pets, stones, plants, animals, images and effigies as if they have selves or some semblance of self. Animism, which science has traditionally regarded as a primitive mistake in thinking, is a psychological fact requiring an accounting in terms of causes and consequences. The controversy over abortion rights devolves to a question about when matter is to be viewed as having a self, deserving of protection under the charter of human rights which sentient beings merit. That there is no scientific answer to this question does not mean that individuals will not produce their own answers, functionally serviceable for them. The deeply emotional controversy over animal rights has similar roots. If creatures have something like selves, they deserve humane protection. If they do not, then the same rules of conscience do not apply. We may put old Fido to sleep, but not suffering Grandpa. Again, this is not a scientific question for which an empirical answer may be produced, for the diacritica for diagnosing the existence of self in some other object are nowhere specified; and more, I make the claim that such diacritica cannot in principle be specified in a way that will command universal assent. Some will continue to worship dead bodies as if they contained living selves. Some will continue to regard real and living people as no more than animals, and thus as not deserving of ordinary human compassion. Our object here is not to worry about diagnostic criteria or to attempt an account of how individuals determine the existence or lack of it of self. Rather, the point is to emphasize that self is either present or absent, and that for every case but one—that of the subjective I where the presence of self is a given—the determination of this presence is at least marginally problematic.

The Presence or Absence of Identity

A similar question can be posed about identity. Does something have an identity or does it not? As it applies to human beings, this question implies a segregation of all people into those who are known and those not known. Hamlet has an identity. He is a young male, Prince of Denmark, troubled of mind, friend of Horatio, and he dies untimely. One can certainly talk about Hamlet, fictional character though he may be.

Before written history, multitudes of human beings are presumed to have existed who have no identity for us, nor left a trace of any kind. A fragment of bone may be found and here and there a tracing on the wall of a cave. Oral tradition passes on epic tales of prehistoric figures, their identities so distorted through the serial repetition and elaboration of story as to bear, certainly, little resemblance to an original presented self. Fictional characters have identity for us: Sir Gawain, Ulysses, Galahad, Sherlock Holmes, Robin Hood. Others are liminal; Jesus, Homer, Shakespeare. We believe they existed because of the product and consequence attributed to them, but countable and direct evidence is scant.

History is, among other things, the storying of matter. Tales are told. By this means the remote and foreign is brought into our ken and acquires an identity. Pluto has been an object, let us now conjecture, since the origins of our solar system billions of years ago. But it was not identified and brought into the human ken until 1930. The number of elements in the periodic table seems now to have stabilized at 103, but the number and identity of the elements was a different matter a generation ago. No one can tell the precise number of animal or plant species on this planet, and doubtless thousands of species have come and gone without leaving a trace and hence have no identity. This is not to suggest, as some have, that science is just an arbitrary business of saying things are thus and so—that everything is a construction out of the heads of scientists. Science is about discovery, and as discovery proceeds, new identities are assumed by the objects of nature, entirely new objects appear, and some objects which appeared formerly to have a legitimate identity are cast into outer darkness (phlogiston, for example, or Piltdown Man), surviving only as empty names.

"In the beginning was the word," says the Book of John. But the beginning here invoked is not the creation of the universe, surely. Rather, with the word it becomes possible to name things, to identify things, to say what they are, to begin the process of human reflection and the extension of human understanding which comes as a unique possibility to us as a species because we have language. With the word we have the capacity to represent nature symbolically; and more, to create by means of words and other symbols perfectly imaginary but entirely coherent systems of thought, such as mathematics, and to create and appreciate artistic forms, such as music.

The universe of human understanding is extended in several ways, and as it is extended, so is the identity of the person who participates in this understanding enriched and extended. Science is the enterprise of pushing at the frontier of unknown nature, bringing ever more of it into view. Science reveals more and more of how things work in nature, offering us the possibility of intervening meaningfully and usefully in the natural world. History is the enterprise of revivifying the past, of telling and retelling that which once was. Hermes, the messenger, brings and takes information and knowledge from one locus to another, offering as he does, the possibility of indefinitely large numbers of interpretive perspectives. The arts, literature, drama, as well as mathematics and music, create imaginary worlds which are perfectly intelligible and psychologically real, even if they were created out of nothing.

Self and Identity: The Four Possible Combinations

If we may consider both self and identity to be either present or absent in any given instance, four combinations are conceptually possible. These are represented in Table 1.1.

In teaching "The Psychology of Self and Identity," I have often assigned readings from Carl Jung and from Erving Goffman in successive parts of the course. It is a violent conjunction, for Jung asserts, "In the end the only events worth telling are those when the imperishable world irrupted into this transitory one" (1965, p. 4). Goffman, on the other hand, eschewed inner life in favor of human interactions, devoting his encompassing attention to "the little interactions that are forgotten about as soon as they occur. . . . what serious students of society never collect, . . . the slop of social life" (1971, p. 138).[9]

Jung provides a metaphor which enables both of these perspectives to be combined:

Life has always seemed to me like a plant that lives on its rhizome. Its true life is invisible, hidden in the rhizome. The part that appears above the ground lasts only a single summer. Then it withers away—an ephemeral apparition. When we think

Table 1.1
Absence and Presence of Self and Identity

	Identity Absent	Identity Present
Self Absent	The unknown universe	Mapped territory
	Undiscovered or disappeared species, never known	Historical, nonliving persons
	The foreign hull	Fictional characters
	Nirvana	Imaginative constructions, including mathematics
	Nothingness	Texts, poems, works of literature and art
	Persons who lived and died without a trace or memory	Recorded history
		Scientific knowledge
	No connections	Horizontal connection
Self Present	God	Living human beings
	Atman	Extant communities
	Spirit	Coordinate being-in-place, Horizontal and vertical connection
	Vertical connection	
	Being	

of the unending growth and decay of life and civilizations, we cannot escape the impression of absolute nullity. Yet I have never lost a sense of something that lives and endures underneath the eternal flux. What we see is the blossom, which passes. The rhizome remains. (1965, p. 4)

The interaction order which Goffman so assiduously studied is based upon horizontal commerce among contemporary human beings—the talk, gestures, postures, transactions, games, political struggles, fights, and ro-mances that take place among people on the level. During the season of life, living selves, all of them emerging from a common and enduring genetic stuff, commune with each other in these ways. Retiring from the meeting or the marketplace, the individual alone can reflect upon, reminisce about, and rehearse human interactions—much thought is directed horizontally. Or, like Jung, one might contemplate vertical connections—one's place between heaven and earth. One cannot know the inner life of another directly, only one's own. But by inference one can sense that others have an inner life also, and more, that their vertical connections are in some funda-mental way like ours. Communication enables communion—the celebra-tion with beings on the same plane of a shared identity, and more, a commemoration of a vital and common connection to forces and powers above and below, which are somehow out of time and place.

Table 1.1 presents the fundamental concepts of the psychology of self and identity by considering these horizontal and vertical dimensions of connection conjointly. The point of departure for these conceptions is psychological—not metaphysical, ethical, religious, or positivistic. A descriptive psychology must take into account the distinction between the unknown and the known, while hedging on the question of who or what does the knowing. One may speak of Columbus having discovered the New World and speak truly from a Eurocentric point of view, even while realizing that the world he discovered was already known by civilizations which were also unknown to him and other Europeans at the time. Similarly, to suggest, with Jung, that a timeless and collective spirit exists to which we are all somehow connected will strike some people as nonsense. However, a descriptive psychology must be inclusive of the religious experience. A sense of transcendence is not to be denied because it is not an easy problem for empirical research. "The total world of which the philosopher must account," said James, "is thus composed of the realities plus the fancies and illusions" (1890, p. 291).

The upper left quadrant of Table 1.1 represents that which is without self or identity—that which is unknown, foreign, alien, unnamed, and without spirit. Certainly human beings—though ones not known to us—are in this quadrant. A substantial segment of human beings have died unstoried, without a trace of memory or physical remnant. Recently, I visited a cemetery at a large, old state mental hospital. The graves there are unmarked with name or date. Only numbers appear, perhaps coded to names in some remote and decaying archive, giving no clue as to the identities of those formerly sentient human beings whose bodily remains lie below. Archaeologists and social historians make it part of their business to explore territories where people might have existed, pushing back the frontiers of ignorance, just as scientists explore unknown parts of nature, and cartographers give identity and shape to that which was formerly inchoate—*unbekannt*. This is the uncharted part of the universe, the history never recorded. The library contains no section corresponding to this quadrant.

Another cemetery in the same community moves us to the upper-right quadrant of Table 1.1, where identity is present while self is absent. Here are names proudly carved in granite and marble, along with dates, sayings, epitaphs, Biblical quotations, ornamentation, flourishes of design, family plots providing kinship relations, size of monument giving a notion of earthly wealth and position—all of this providing some characterization of the deceased. Moving to the biography section of the library, one encounters fully identified lives, verging into fiction, to be sure. Moving to the fiction and drama sections of the library, one encounters lives with identities just as real, just as complete, perhaps even more vivid than those whose stories are based on a once-living self. Here is where our ancestors are to be located, and the stories told about them contribute to the content of our own identities.

The lower left quadrant of Table 1.1 is even more mysterious than the one above it, because even without a specific and located identity, self is present.[10] Again, we recall theophany, wherein God declares only being, not being-in-place. Here is Jung's timeless vertical dimension. In his autobiographical reflections, Jung (1965) describes himself sitting on a rock near a lake, contemplating whether the spirit of the rock is aware of him sitting on it. The vertical dimension is again and again invoked by Jung, together with the qualities of the eternal and spiritual vitality. Atman is the Hindu version of universal presence. Breath is a physical stand-in for Atman, for Psyche, for anima, for spirit. In the library, we must turn to theology, religion, metaphysics and cosmology to find references corresponding to this quadrant. For iconography, we turn to religious art of the Renaissance, and in particular, look upward to the ceiling of the Sistine chapel, where we might perceive Michelangelo's version of the connection between God and the human species.

The lower right quadrant of Table 1.1 represents known and living human beings—the combination of both self and identity. Here is connectivity in both dimensions. The horizontal dimension is Goffman's interaction order, where the most fundamental human act is conversation. The vertical dimension is Jung's connection to the rhizome or collective unconscious, where the most fundamental act is meditation. Together, these two dimensions provide coordinates for living.[11] Psyche is the inner sense of self, James' Pure Ego, the sense of timeless continuity. Reciprocal interaction with the socius provides social identity, the developing, ever-changing being-in-place.

Living and known persons have Psyche and participate with the Socius; they are beings-in-place.[12] When they die, self is lost, while their identity is merely modified, not obliterated, unless all who know them or remember them perish simultaneously. In fact, after death, one's identity might continue to undergo a variety of interesting changes. Melville was not a literary lion while alive. Lincoln and Kennedy became martyrs, undergoing fantastic transformations of identity long after death. As for Jesus of Nazareth, magnificent and multiple transformations of identity have taken place since his crucifixion, and continue to take place as religious and historical thought and research progress. No one's identity is fixed forever, not even by death.

THE GIVING OF GIFTS AND THE IDEA OF SINGULARITY

A genetic endowment is laid down for the individual at the moment of conception. At the time of birth, other gifts are customarily rained upon the infant—a name, a family, a nationality, a religion, a community, a nation, a given position in society, and objects for maintenance, for symbolic designation of status, and for play. All of this is inchoate in the infant, let us imagine, though none of us can guess how things really seem to the preverbal child.[13]

Epigenesis is the idea that the process of development is dialectical through its course. Initially given and quite particular stuff is at once exposed to a circumstance, which shapes it in some way, so that at the next stage of circumstance, the inherited given is already transformed from what it was, further to be transformed by that circumstance, passed on as given to the next circumstance, and so on, until the entire system stops. The process of epigenesis is continual, if uneven. As it applies to self and identity, the suggestion is that the initial gift of self combines with the initial givens of circumstantial identity, and that self and identity are from that moment complexly intertwined, interpenetrating, bound up with each other, inseparable, except by death, which is when the system stops as far as a particular individual is concerned.

The two kinds of gifts described above—initial endowment and accretions—produce a formed and presentable individual, changing, of course, throughout lived time. Roughly speaking, a self (the vertical) is given, about which identity characteristics (the horizontal) are continuously acquired, some of which are transient (e.g., high school student), some of which are quite permanent (e.g., female).

Much can and should be said about the giving of gifts, for arranged about this issue are the most powerful and telling questions of human justice and injustice. Cain slew Abel because he was jealous of Abel's gift having been more pleasing to their father than his own offering. Jacob cheated Esau out of the gift of his father's blessing. Abraham and all of Abraham's people were chosen to receive the gift of God's blessing. Christ makes the gift of God's blessing available to gentiles. Tragically, Jews were chosen for extermination by the Nazis not because of anything they had done, but because of what they were given-to-be, because of who they were and are.

Paul Monette was given-to-be gay, but as we have seen, wanted for a time to be identified as straight. Selves given-to-be female are sometimes born in bodies identified as male, and selves given-to-be male are sometimes born in bodies identified to be female.[14] Temple Grandin's autism is a given set of limitations on her capacity to achieve intuitive connections with other human beings, even though many other paths of achievement are open to her. Katherine Anne Power was born into a time and circumstance which made her into a revolutionary, and the complex interweavings of the epigenetic process have landed her in jail for a protracted sentence, for deeds which she perceived to be fully just at the time.

In *Stigma: Notes on the management of spoiled identity*, Goffman (1963), talks of cripples, misfits, criminals, deviants, the deformed, the misshapen, the disgraced. However a stigma is acquired—one thinks of the former wrestler who is now a paraplegic—it is carried into any social situation as a given, as something unalterable. A sense of the unfairness in the distribution of benefit in the world is palpably present in such situations, even though, as Goffman points out, interactions are often contrived in such a way as to avoid the pain of encountering or confronting the great underlying question of injustice. Accident victims, individuals near death, and parents of children with birth defects can cry out "Why me?", wait forever for an answer, and receiving none, simply conclude that what is, is—simply given to be.

Ted Williams is said to have been a natural baseball player, the same is said about Wayne Gretzky in hockey, Joe Louis in boxing, Pelé in soccer, Michael Jordan in basketball. Thousands of kids practice just as much, but special gifts are given to a few, the discovery of which depends upon the adventitious presence of special circumstances of nurturing. How many thousands of potentially great ballplayers have never thrown a ball? No one knows.

Gifts are given which potentially could become manifest in all fields of human endeavor—in music, in art, in science, in drama, in poetry, in political leadership. Mozart might be the most fully realized musical genius who ever lived, and it is easy to think of him exercising his vertical, spiritual self as a way of tapping into the vast resources of the music of the spheres, dwelling in the collective memory of the species. Similarly, Isaac Asimov, who wrote over 500 books in his lifetime, claimed that he was dealt a good genetic hand. Put another way, the genetic stuff he was given amounted to the realization of his giftedness as he proceeded through the epigenetic and interactive process of development.

Nothing is fair or just in this visitation of special power and privilege upon one individual, and devastating disability and limitation upon another. The attitude demanded is one of acceptance, but one cannot help envying on the one hand and pitying on the other. From the standpoint of the ideals of social justice it is troubling that human beings are not created equal but are singular selves wrapped in particular identities. Struggles for justice are most commonly warranted by the inequality of distribution of gifts of self and identity. No understanding of human conflict is adequate or complete without basing that understanding on the issues of self and identity that are at stake.

A FINAL IMAGE

The human paradox of the self arises because we are conscious of the world around us and ourselves in it. Someone has said that consciousness is a disease; at the least, consciousness tremendously complicates but is essential to the task of coming to understand our selves and our identities. We can reflect. But as we do, we know that the image received back is by some finite amount distant from that which we are at present. As all who have thought deeply about the problem of self have observed, we are not quick enough to turn around and catch ourselves in the act of observation.

So the self is invisible to itself, but is immersed in the manifold tracings it has left; and these comprise the material from which it constructs its identity and has its identity, more passively, constructed by others. Being is obscure; being-in-place is observable, but it is not permanent. The question of permanence of the self is not answerable on the basis of transient evidence, but transient evidence is all there is. This has not stopped such thinkers as Jung and James from speculating on the future of the self beyond the time of life, based, let us imagine, on such hunches as they derive from the taproot of their vertical selves as it extends out of time.

Emerson was known as a transcendentalist, and for this he is ridiculed by philosophers of a more positivistic persuasion. But he had a sense of something beyond and above mere mortality, and he could at least describe it metaphorically:

In groups where debate is earnest, and especially on high questions, the company become aware that the thought arises to an equal level in all bosoms. . . . They all become wiser than they were. It arches over them like a temple, this unity of thought in which every heart beats with nobler sense of power and duty, and thinks and acts with unusual solemnity. All are conscious of attaining to a higher self-possession. . . . We know better than we do. We do not yet possess ourselves, and we know at the same time that we are much more. I feel the same truth now often in my trivial conversations with my neighbors, that someone higher in each of us overlooks this by-play, and Jove nods to Jove from behind each of us. (Emerson 1883, pp. 260–261)

A gift of this kind of vision is, like other gifts, not equally distributed to all people. Some seem to have a sense of immortality; to others it is inconceivable and nonsensical. But because of the possibility of genuine conversation, human beings are not trapped in their solitude, but can share the visions and thus appreciate the gifts of others. Words can make foreign and remote perspectives come to life. The psychologist must heed the poet as well as the scientist for insights about our being and the circumstance within which we dwell. In the words of John Ciardi, "It is something—and more than something, much—to know that we do not matter except to each other; for then we can matter mightily, if only for awhile."

NOTES

1. Ortega used this expression in *Meditations on Quixote*, his first book, published in 1914. Later, he asserted that this expression "sums up my philosophical thought" (1961, p. 13).

2. To recognize correctly the identity of another requires the availability of a set of identity coordinates which are appropriate to that other person. This poses major difficulties for encounters between individuals of completely alien cultures. Octavio Paz has this commentary on what must have been among the most dramatic and baffling intercultural encounters in the history of the world—those between native inhabitants of the New World and the European invaders:

(A) torpor . . . immobilized Mesoamerican societies when they confronted the Spaniards. Their confusion was the terrible consequence of their inability to IMAGINE them. They could not imagine them because they lacked the intellectual and historical categories in which to place these beings who had come from no one knew where. To classify the stranger, they had to use the only category available to them for dealing with the unknown: the sacred. The Spaniards were gods and supernatural beings because the Mesoamericans had only two categories for people: the sedentary civilized and barbarians. As the Nahuas would say: Toltecs and Chichimecs. The Spaniards were neither one nor the other: therefore they must be gods, beings who came from beyond. For two thousand years the Mesoamerican cultures grew and lived alone; their encounter with the Other came too late and under conditions of terrible inequality. For that they were destroyed. (Paz 1987, p. 7)

3. In his autobiographical memoir of his experiences in Vietnam, Tim O'Brien has this observation about the experience of self-continuity:

It's now 1990. I'm forty-three years old, which would've seemed impossible to a fourth grader, and yet when I look at the photographs of myself as I was in 1956, I realize that in the important ways I haven't changed at all. I was Timmy then; now I'm Tim. But the essence remains the same. I'm not fooled by the baggy pants or the crewcut or the happy smile—I know my own eyes—and there is no doubt that the Timmy smiling at the camera is the Tim I am now. Inside the body, or beyond the body, there is something absolute and unchanging. The human life is all one thing, like a blade tracing loops on ice, a twenty-three-year-old infantry sergeant, a middle-aged writer knowing guilt and sorrow. (O'Brien 1990, pp. 264–265)

4. Milton Rokeach (1964) describes in *The three Christs of Ypsilanti* the curious case of three mental patients who all claimed to be Jesus Christ. This apparent disjunction between self and identity was tolerable to the patients, but not to the surrounding socius, which identified them as mental cases, not divine prophets. In the same book, Rokeach illustrates the more normal demand that most of us have for a consonance between ourselves and our identities by noting that his daughters were easily moved to tearful protests when he playfully but insistently traded their names and called them wrongly.

5. In *Varieties of religious experience* (1902/1984), James states that all religions share in a promise of deliverance from this disunity. He suggests that all religions are based on a premise of uneasiness and a promise of deliverance: "The uneasiness, reduced to its simplest terms, is a sense that there is *something wrong with us* as we naturally stand. . . . The solution is a sense that *we are saved from the wrongness* by making proper connection with the higher powers" (p. 254).

6. See James' (1889/1984) essay, "The will to believe," wherein he asserts, "Although in one sense we are passive portions of the universe, in another we show a curious autonomy, as if we were small active centres on our own account" (p. 324).

7. It is quite understandable that scientific psychology had no use for selves, for selves, in the sense implied here, are not replicable events or entities and hence not proper objects of scientific inquiry. Milan Kundera (1984) conveys this understanding of self in *The unbearable lightness of being*:

What is unique about the "I" hides itself exactly in what is unimaginable about a person. All we are able to imagine is what makes everyone like everyone else, what people have in common. The individual "I" is what differs from the common stock, that is, what cannot be guessed at or calculated, what must be unveiled, uncovered, conquered. (p. 199)

8. See Turing (1963) for the original exposition of this problem.

9. Clifford Geertz (1980) characterizes Goffman's view of society as,

an unbroken stream of gambits, ploys, artifices, bluffs, disguises, conspiracies, and outright impostures as individuals and coalitions of individuals struggle—sometimes cleverly, more often comically—to play enigmatical games whose structure is clear but whose point is not. Goffman's is a radically unromantic vision of things, acrid and bleakly knowing, and one which sits rather poorly with traditional humanistic pieties. But it is no less powerful for that. Nor, with its uncomplaining play-it-as-lays ethic, is it all that inhumane. (p. 170)

10. I am indebted to Theodore Sarbin for calling my attention to the following stanza from Thomas Gray's "Elegy Written in a Country Churchyard." This provides a metaphor for the condition of having a self without an identity.

> Full many a gem of purest ray serene,
> The dark unfathom'd caves of ocean bear:
> Full many a flower is born to blush unseen,
> And waste its sweetness on the desert air.

From Starr, H. W., & Hendrickson, J. R., (Eds.). *The Complete Poems of Thomas Gray*. London: Oxford University Press, 1966.

11. This from Jung (1958) on the quaternity thus provided by orthogonal coordinates:

The quaternity is an archetype of almost universal occurrence. It forms the logical basis for any whole judgement. If one wishes to pass such a judgement, it must have this fourfold aspect. For instance, if you want to describe the horizon as a whole, you name the four quarters of heaven. . . . There are always four elements, four prime qualities, four colors, four castes, four ways of spiritual development, etc. So, too, there are four aspects of psychological orientation. [Jung refers here to sensation, thinking, feeling, and intuition.] When this has been done, there is nothing more to say. . . . The ideal of completeness is the circle or sphere, but its natural minimal division is a quaternity. (p. 167)

12. I am aware of the parallel between these conceptions and those presented in Heidegger's work, particularly *Being and time* (1962), but also his *Discourse on thinking* (1966). To my surprise, I rediscovered that Heidegger also features the acts of meditation and conversation in his analysis, and that the concept of Dasein is not far removed from being-in-place.

13. This has not stopped many psychologists from asserting that they somehow know the experience of the infant. James (1890) guessed it was a "booming and buzzing confusion." Freud (1930/1962) endowed the infant with extraordinary powers of observation, sense of internal desire, and frustration from the outside. To Baldwin (1897) and to Piaget (1952) belong the credit for first making prolonged and systematic observations of infants as a way of informing their speculations. More recently, Michael Lewis (1992) and Jerome Kagan (1984) have combined careful empirical studies with informed speculation to give us the best current guesses as to how the ideas of self and one's identity-in-the-world emerge in the development of very young human beings.

14. See Amy Bloom's (1994) treatment of the subject of individuals who endure the protracted pain and expense of sex-change surgery in order to be transformed from female to male identity. Bloom effectively makes the argument that the gendered-given self remains consistent and is the central power; identity is rearranged around it by the surgical creation of a penis, the ingestion of testosterone, and other cosmetic manipulations.

Chapter 2

Historical Perspectives on the Presented Self

> For if anything in the world is worth wishing for . . . it is that a ray of
> light should fall on the obscurity of our being.
> —Arthur Schopenhauer

This chapter is a willfully partial slice through the history of theory and
research on the self in psychology. The design is to describe such rays of
light as have fallen along the way and to retrieve them from the obscurity
of temporal remoteness. This implies immediately what this chapter is not;
namely, it is not a complete or even fair history of theory and research on
the self in modern psychology. Such an order would be too large for a
chapter. The reader may find facets of such a general history in works by
Gergen (1984); Lynch, Norem-Hebeisen, and Gergen (1981); Schlenker
(1980); Mischel (1977); and Sarbin and Scheibe (1983). However, no comprehensive history of the self within psychology has been written. Perhaps
the recent surge of interest in the topic will encourage the preparation of
just such a work. For the present, we shall have to be content with partial,
incomplete, and highly selective historical reviews, of which the present
chapter is simply another example.

The selectivity of the present treatment is determined by several problematic issues. The first concerns the obvious shift in the dominant method
and content of writings about the self over the last hundred years in
American psychology. Are the questions William James found to be central
different from those that attract the attention of current researchers on the
self? And how are we to understand the tremendous change in preferred
methodology over this 100-year span? The second issue is related to the
first, for it is the question of the historical conditionality of the self. Is it
possible that the self as an object of inquiry has undergone a historical
transformation over the last hundred years? One extension of contempo-

rary narrative theories of the self suggests the possibility that selves are not
constant but are evolving products of history (Mancuso and Sarbin 1983;
Gergen & Gergen 1983; Boswell 1983).

It is difficult either to comment on the massive changes that have
occurred in the way psychologists have gone about their study of the self
or to consider the question of the historical conditionality of self without
encountering strongly charged questions of value. This suggests a third
issue for this chapter. Something in the modern spate of work on impression
management seems to cause offense, even moral outrage. Modern research
on the self touches upon issues of deceit, of hypocrisy, of manipulation, of
a cynical denucleation of human material. These issues deserve attention
in historical context. In the present chapter these questions are not discussed
in serial order; rather, they pervade and inform the entire discussion.

An additional caveat must be mentioned before tracing a particular line
of theory and research on the self in psychology. This book is about the self
in social context. Thus, little attention will be given in this history to theories
which concentrate on the psychology of the individual in isolation from
social context. One such tradition is psychoanalysis, which Freud developed
as a psychological theory out of his practice of treating individuals with
neurotic problems. Another is the Dasein tradition, again a preeminently
individual theory of self of continental European origin. This work is a
veritable lake of writing about self, from which only a minor tributary has
found its way into the main currents of contemporary theory and research
in North America (Heidegger 1962). In addition, Jung's analytic psychology,
as distinguished from traditional Freudian theory, is preeminently about the
self, and is concerned with the development and integration of self throughout the life span. Yet Jung's is also an individual psychology and it is not
prominent in major current writings on the self in psychology.

We may say, with just arbitration, that the line of development within the
psychology of the self begins with William James. This line includes also
James Mark Baldwin, whose exile from the United States for the latter part
of his career seems to have cost him the high regard which is his due. It
leads through Charles Horton Cooley and George Herbert Mead, seminal
figures in American sociology. As this line is absorbed into sociology, it
becomes lost to behavioral psychology, which had no use for it in any event.
Symbolic interactionism is the culmination of this line in contemporary
sociology (Manis and Meltzer 1978), but here again we encounter a body of
writings on the self which is largely isolated from corresponding treatments
within psychology. The contact between the sociological and psychological
lines of theory and research on the self has been achieved principally
through the work of Erving Goffman, whose brilliance and whose productivity have commanded the attention of social psychologists, even though
he has been the maverick of mavericks in sociology. Another major contribution to the reconnection of the James, Cooley, and Mead line to the

mainstream of social psychology is provided by the introduction of role theory into psychology, mainly through the writings of Theodore Sarbin (1954; Sarbin and Allen 1968; Allen and Scheibe 1982).

CURRENT RESEARCH ON THE SELF AND A CONSTRUCTION OF HOW IT AROSE

The self is a hot topic in contemporary psychology. Current journals and newly published books, of which this work is an example, manifest a new centrality for self and social identity in theory and research. For example, Schlenker's (1980) monograph on *Impression management* has over 500 references in its bibliography, 58 percent of which were published in the preceding decade. Within the previous two decades, 93 percent of the references are included. The 600–plus references in Sarbin and Scheibe's (1983) edited collection, *Studies in social identity*, show a similar profile for date of publication. Additional evidence of this new centrality of interest in self and identity is provided by a quantity of current research on self-aware-ness theory, as inspired by the original work of Duval and Wicklund (1972; Buss 1980). Bandura (1977) has turned his attention to self-efficacy, which he considers to be a "unifying theory of behavioral change." Similarly, Greenwald (1980), in writing of "the totalitarian ego," urges consideration of a "self-centered" theory as the best means of integrating the cognitive and behavioral perspectives of current psychology.

As suggested previously, it was not always thus. A generation ago in psychology, references to self were relatively rare. Wylie's (1974) book surveying research on *The self concept* was a landmark. In this book Wylie notes the hiatus of research and theory on the self during the period of major domination of American behaviorism, for most of the twentieth century. Prescott Lecky's (1945) *Self-consistency: A theory of personality* is a genuine exception to the norm. Lecky argued that the key to psychological devel-opment is provided by "self-consistency," both in terms of the person's self perception and in terms of perception by others. This book proved to be an anticipation, if not the direct antecedent, of the later development of balance theories within social psychology (Heider 1958), and, later, of attribution theory, which has been an especially fertile ground for empirical studies on self-perception (Kelley 1967). Similarly, Erikson's (1950) *Childhood and soci-ety*, while deriving from the psychoanalytic tradition, provided at least one current reference in the 1950s and 1960s for anyone seeking to understand the psychological significance of human identity.

One must return to the very beginnings of American psychology to encounter another period of strong interest in self and identity. The prag-matist-functionalist school, of which William James was the foremost rep-resentative, gave central importance to self. In this, as in much else, James must be regarded as a pivotal figure in the history of American psychology.

He devoted a single chapter in his famous *Principles of psychology* (1890) to "The consciousness of self." Thereafter, he never wrote with direct focus on this topic again. With this remarkable chapter, James not only provided a critical synthesis of previous philosophical writings on the self, but he also endowed succeeding generations of scholars with a fixed point of reference for their inquiries. James' chapter is the single most common reference in modern writings on the self. The next section of this chapter examines the method and content of James' chapter in some detail, for it is almost of monograph length (111 pages), and its contents merit more than the customary passing bow.

It is the generative importance of James' chapter that deserves emphasis at this point. Within psychology, it provided a recapitulation of the philosophically based views of self that proceeded it. It stands as intellectual parent to the work of Baldwin, Cooley, and Mead. But the death of James in 1910 was preceded by a general waning of his influential position in American psychology. His student, G. Stanley Hall, wrote an obituary notice for *The American Journal of Psychology* which praised James for his style, his humanity, his generosity of spirit, but also predicted that his substantive contributions to psychology would soon be eclipsed and forgotten with the gathering momentum of a more specialized and scientific, altogether less philosophical, psychology. Hall proved in the short run to be prescient, for within three years of James' death, behaviorism was to be launched. At the same time, the Gestalt school was founded by Kohler, Koffka, and Wertheimer in Germany, and psychoanalysis emerged as a major intellectual force.

The decade surrounding the death of James must be regarded as the period of the most profound creativity and change in the history of psychology. The general direction of these changes was very much in keeping with Hall's prediction. However, if one looks at psychology since 1965, it appears that there is a return to a more Jamesian pattern. With the emergence of modern cognitive psychology and with the growing recognition of the artificiality of the separation of psychological and philosophical questions, James is very much in the ascendancy (Sarason 1975; Adelson 1982). In 1981 Harvard University Press published a new three-volume edition of *Principles of psychology*, complete with scholarly commentary, a description of the 12–year period of composition, and facsimiles of manuscript pages. Many contemporary psychologists would claim that *Principles* is still the single most important psychology book ever published, not only for its vivid style and generous spirit but, also, *pace* Hall, for its substantive contribution to current problems in psychology, including the problem of self.

This is not a historical regression. In fact, if the reader has patience to heed James and Baldwin, Cooley, and Mead, the thought will occur that we have lost something. Mountains of accumulated empirical studies are in some ways not as instructive as were the frankly more meditative reflections of these earlier writers, whose main materials by way of data seem to have consisted of literature, drama, poetry, and philosophical writings. We now have data on the self in God's plenty, and most of it is recent. But it is an open question as to whether our understanding of this topic is significantly advanced. It is worth examining what that earlier understanding was.

WILLIAM JAMES' CHAPTER ON "THE CONSCIOUSNESS OF SELF"

Perhaps because James' chapter on the self is so frequently cited in modern writings on the self, it is a surprise to return to the actual source. Its contents are not what one would expect from the customary brief reference, and the context within which that content appears is further occasion for refreshing the understanding.

The passage that is most often quoted from James' chapter is this one:

Properly speaking, a man has as many social selves as there are individuals who recognize him and carry an image of him in their head. But as the individuals who carry the images fall naturally into classes, we may practically say that he has as many different social selves as there are distinct *groups* of persons about whose opinion he cares. (James 1890, p. 294)

This passage is certainly consistent with James' general view of the self. It is also a clear anticipation of the entire domain of work in social psychology known as reference group theory, wherein the individual is considered to derive an identity by association, affiliation, and identification with a particular set of social reference groups (Hyman and Singer 1968; Miller 1963). But taken by itself, as it usually is, the passage is entirely misleading as to the most general significance James attaches to the self. The preference of modern writers for this passage as a way of typing James' position on the self is both unfair to James and revealing of a preference to have a conception of self that is consistent with division, fragmentation, and pluralism. Perhaps the "me generation" of the late twentieth century wants just such a psychological condition.

The full title of James' chapter is "The Consciousness of Self." It directly follows the famous chapter on "The Stream of Thought," itself sixty-five pages long. It is evident that for James these two chapters are connected by a common concept. The consciousness of self is taken to be a particular but most significant portion of the stream of thought. James notes at the beginning of the stream of thought chapter that, "The universal conscious fact is not 'feelings and thoughts exist,' but 'I think' and 'I feel'" (1890, p. 226). The difference in these two ways of conceiving of consciousness is twofold. Thoughts and feelings are not passive occurrences, but active processes—processes directed by the individual to perceive and remember events selectively, in accord with what is meaningful and useful. Moreover, they are not just disembodied processes, but are appropriated or owned by the I, the self. Skipping now to the conclusion of the same chapter, we find an elaboration of the connection between consciousness and self:

One great splitting of the whole universe into two halves is made by each of us: and for each of us almost all of the interest attaches to one of the halves; but we all draw the line of division between them in a different place. When I say that we all call the two halves by the same names, and that those names are "me" and "not-me" respectively, it will at once be seen what I mean. (1890, p. 289)

Here James makes an observation not about his own consciousness but about "our" consciousness. The use of the first person plural pronoun is significant, for it presumes communality. It was only later (say around 1912) that the psychologist would rise above the subject matter—studying objects that are called Ss (subjects) by means of an intelligence called E (experimenter)—thus gaining "the psychologist's advantage" (Scheibe 1978). James' method of achieving assent to a claim could be called phenomenological, although there is no systematic observation of phenomena. It is certainly not introspective, for the entire effect of the stream-of-thought metaphor is to show that thought cannot be systematically analyzed by the methods of introspection, for thought is a complex and continuous flow which cannot in principle be exteriorized by the crude and slow representational means available to the observer. The assertion also provides us with a major contextual feature for James' discussion of the self, for he is saying that the self is a goodly portion of the stream of thought. The word *consciousness* in the title deserves as much emphasis as the word *self*, for self is seen as a specially significant portion of that consciousness. Interest in the self is simply taken as a commonsense given. "The altogether unique kind of interest which each human mind feels in these parts of creation which it can call *me* or *mine* may be a moral riddle, but it is a fundamental psychological fact" (James 1890, p. 289).

Proceeding to an examination of that special domain of thought for which the referent is *me* or *mine*, James presents a protracted and systematic exploration of the territory. He recognizes at the outset a major distinction between the empirical self (the "me")—that which can be observed—and the pure ego (the "I")—that which by implication provides a sort of nucleus of the self and performs the observations of various constituents of the empirical self. James' discussion of the constituents of the empirical self is based on a tripartite division—the material self, the social self, and the spiritual self. Each of these receives discussion in turn, and it is from a segment of the discussion of the second of these constituents that the famous statement about the multiplicity of social selves is taken. In his discussion of all these constituents, the emphasis on the self as thought content is constant. While the spiritual self represents a different sort of thought than the material self, this distinction is really not so great as it might appear. The material self concerns thoughts about possessions, gains and losses, economic affairs, investments, places, objects, and tangible things, which are in some sense *me* or *mine*. The spiritual self concerns thoughts and feelings about God, the cosmos, the mystery of one's inner life, curiosity about origins and destinies. It is only the referents for these thoughts which differ in their tangible qualities. As types of thoughts, they are equally thoughts. So, too, with the social selves, by which James means only that we have specific kinds of self-thoughts in relation to distinct social groups.

While in this empirical sense the selves are discontinuous, James does not intend to say that the self as a whole is discontinuous. His discussion of pure ego makes this plain. Pure ego is a concept defined only by functional implication, not by empirical necessity. James makes no claim for a substantial pure ego. His claim is for the functional interpretation of pure ego as providing the sense and conviction of continuity over time for the entire stream of self. The me is an empirical aggregate which is objectively knowable.

The I which knows them cannot itself be an aggregate. Neither for psychological purposes need it be considered to be an unchanging metaphysical entity like the Soul, or a principle like the pure Ego, viewed "out of time." It is a *Thought* at each moment different from that of the last moment, but appropriative of the latter, together with all that the latter called its own. (James 1890, p. 401)

Perhaps the second most famous quotation from James' chapter on self is one that describes the function of maintaining continuity of self, which James attributes not to any entity or empirical constituent of self, but to Thought itself:

Peter, awakening in the same bed with Paul, and recalling what both had in mind before they went to sleep, reidentifies and appropriates the "warm" ideas as his, and is never tempted to confuse them with those cold and pale-appearing ones which he ascribes to Paul. As well might he confound Paul's body, which he only sees, with his own body, which he sees but also feels. Each of us when he awakens says, Here's the same old self again, just as he says, Here's the same old bed, the same old room, the same old world. (James 1890, p. 334)

It is possible to regard James as contradicting himself when he argues first for a plurality of selves and then argues with equal conviction for the continuity and unity of self. This might seem a personological version of the mystery of the Trinity. But the real point about James' view of the self is that he does insist on having it both ways.

If from the one point of view they are one self, from others they are truly not one but many selves. And similarly of the attribute of continuity; it gives its own kind of unity to the self—that of mere connectedness, or unbrokenness, a perfectly definite phenomenal thing—but it gives not a jot or tittle more. And this unbrokenness in the stream of selves, like the unbrokenness in an exhibition of 'dissolving views,' in no wise implies any farther unity or contradicts any amount of plurality in other respects. (James 1890, p. 335)

The metaphor of "dissolving views" is significant, for it seems that James is referring to the "flip-picture" predecessors of the motion picture. In motion pictures we have phenomenal continuity laid over what is a series of discreet images, if viewed at a slower rate. It is consistent with James' conception of the unity and plurality of selves to employ a cinema metaphor which he could not have known—that of the montage. In making a motion picture scene, the camera or cameras operate in ways that are unrepresentative of the process of ordinary visual perception and would be totally impossible for an actual human observer. The camera moves back and forth, up and around its subject, or cuts are made from one perspective to a totally different perspective, and yet the viewer knows when the montage remains within the same scene and knows when the scene shifts to another scene, near or distant in space and time. All of this is accomplished with a minimum of strain. The view of a modern football game on television, with perhaps six different perspectives on the same play repeated in sequence, is visually unrepresentative and humanly impossible. And yet this disjointed experience is easily assimilated and accepted as a unified event. The visual sequence represented on film or television is normally experienced as having unity, despite the jerkings about, the discontinuities, the lack of realistic presentation.

The self is similar. James makes the claim that despite our many social roles and the masks they require, despite our combining dreaming with planning and hoping, and loafing, and loving, and feeling both secure and afraid at the same time—despite all of these discontinuities in the empirical constituents of our selves, we retain an overall conviction of unity and continuity. Just as shifting one's attention from the montage to the *making* of the montage somewhat spoils the illusion, so the focusing of attention on that which creates the montage "me" tends to threaten that unity which once seemed natural. Thus, it seems reasonable to expect behavioral and emotional consequences of enforced self-awareness. The stream of thought is never in the same condition twice, but even so, it is the same continuous stream. If this assertion is true when literally applied to an actual stream, then it is at least not a logical absurdity for it also to be true for the stream of thought.

I have noted above that James does not view this continuous and knowing I as some sort of metaphysical entity. Of course, James is insinuating, as a fundamental premise for this argument about the constituents and continuity of self, something that he has not demonstrated and something that is in principle not empirically demonstrable. The premise is that no thinker would deny the reality of his own thought. The premise is revealed again in an emphasized sentence at the conclusion of James' chapter: "*If the passing thought be the directly verifiable existent which no school has hitherto doubted it to be, then that thought is itself the thinker*" (1890, p. 401). But this was written before the advent of radical behaviorism in psychology or of radical empiricism in philosophy, and these schools make a point of showing their lack of sympathy for the premise which James considers unrefuted, for the simple reason that nobody had yet bothered to deny it. Today it cannot be said that no school has hitherto denied the existence of thought. The sequel to this denial, as shall be shown in later sections of this chapter, is the denial of that portion of the self which James considered to be unified and enduring.

Suppose for now that the denial of this nonempirical and functional "I" did, in fact, occur when a more rigorously scientific psychology took hold in the twentieth century. Suppose also that this denial of thought and of self is not just a trend for a set of academic psychologists, but in some way manifests a more pervasive historical transformation in cultural modes of self-regard. It is then possible to understand current assertions, which seem to insist upon a reintroduction of the conception of continuous self that James urged upon us over 100 years ago. Witness the following characterization of personality as a phenomenon akin to hypnotic trance. It is at once an assertion that subjective life can lose its sense of continuity and connection with reality, and at the same time it is a plea for the restoration of continuity and reality.

There are times when having a personality seems to me like a vastly elaborate defense erected against the mystery of living. It's as though the cultural, familial, and individual trances we are all in contribute to one large personal dream—a world view. It's as though we were all amnesiacs, having forgotten our truer identities; seeing, like the underside of a weaving, only a fraction of what's before us, unconscious to the ground of our own being, the unregarded river of our life. (Condon 1982, p. 26)

There is, of course, no stream of thought, no unregarded river of our life. But these metaphors are not merely sentimental or gratuitous, for they express something about the human condition which can be expressed in no other way. The positing of the knowing "I" seems a generous act of social grace, a grant to all of more than can be demonstrated in any. For James, who was later to write "The Will to Believe" as an apologia for the legitimacy of all sorts of beliefs on nonscientific but humanly significant questions, such a position is entirely in character. But a later and more skeptical age of psychologists would come to regard such wispy claims as an embarrassment to scientific integrity.

What is the motivational significance of the self for James? It is implicit in the preceding discussion that the care and grooming of the various components of the self constitute a major focus of human activity. James considered the impulse to enhance, expand, and integrate the self to be fundamental—a motivational given. In the language of his time, James considered social self-seeking to be instinctual. But while the self is at the center of human purposes and actions, the motives to which James refers are not hedonistic in the sense of either gratifying bodily needs or maximizing some rational expectation of gain. Several of James' own comments on this subject will help clarify his sense of the importance of the impulse to social self-seeking.

The noteworthy thing about the desire to be "recognized" by others is that its strength has so little to do with the worth of the recognition computed in sensational or rational terms. (1890, p. 308)

Not only the people but the places and things I know enlarge my Self in a sort of metaphoric social way. (1890, p. 308)

In the more positive and refined view of heaven many of its goods, the fellowship of the saints and of our dead ones, and the presence of God, are but social goods of the most exalted kind. It is only the search of the redeemed inward nature, the spotlessness from sin, whether here or hereafter, that can count as spiritual self-seeking pure and undefiled. (1890, p. 309)

Thus, for James, the evaluative significance of others, of places and things, and of heaven itself must be understood in terms of strivings of the self.

DEVELOPING CONCEPTIONS OF THE SOCIAL SELF: BALDWIN, COOLEY, AND MEAD

James Mark Baldwin (1861–1934), like many nineteenth-century American psychologists, was drawn to psychology from an earlier interest in religion. As a student at Princeton in the 1880s, Baldwin studied with President James McCosh, a philosopher who was newly converted to the empirical psychology of Wilhelm Wundt. Upon graduation, Baldwin departed for a year's study abroad, including a period with Wundt in Leipzig. On his return to the United States, Baldwin accepted a teaching post at Princeton Theological Seminary, and then a position in psychology at Lake Forest College in Illinois. In his peregrinations, he founded psychological laboratories at Toronto and at Princeton, was President of the American Psychological Association in 1897, and with James McKeen Cattell founded *The Psychological Review*. His last academic appointment in the United States was at Johns Hopkins University. He was dismissed from this position after an alleged incident of unprofessional conduct, for which he proclaimed his innocence (Evans and Scott 1978). After 1908, the year he left Johns Hopkins, Baldwin spent his career abroad, first in Mexico and later in Paris. It is important to know that Baldwin left the stage of American psychology, for his prodigious writing has had very little direct impact on the subsequent development of psychology, save in two respects, both of which are in their way remarkable.

Although Baldwin admired Wundt and himself did a number of experiments, his contributions are not chiefly experimental, nor were his beliefs about psychology consistent with the hard materialism that came to dominate American psychology. He was easily dismissed by Boring (1950) in his magisterial *History of experimental psychology* as being of essentially no importance to psychology—for Boring noted that his real interests and strengths were "philosophical," a telling reproach.

But Baldwin's importance to the history of psychology must necessarily be revised because of two of his contributions, one of which is somewhat tangential for this essay, the other of prime importance. The tangential issue has to do with Jean Piaget, whose impact upon developmental psychology and on psychological theory in general has been enormous. Baldwin was in Paris at the beginnings of Piaget's career, knew him, and must be regarded as a clear influence upon Piaget, both in method of research and in theoretical content. When his first child was born, Baldwin began to study "genetic psychology," that is, the psychology of mental development, based on close observations of the development of his own children. He described stages of mental development—prelogical thinking, logical thinking, hyperlogical thinking—and described the movement of the child through these stages of development as a function of a dialectical exchange of assimilation and accommodation. In his autobiographical assessment of his career, Baldwin makes some predictions about important future developments in psychology. He chooses for special emphasis "the child study movement in Switzerland centered in the J. J. Rousseau Institute and in the work of the group led by Piaget" (Baldwin 1930, p. 28). After saying this, he went on to excoriate the movements of psychoanalysis ("unreal" and "extravagant") and American behaviorism ("an intellectual fad"). Small wonder that Baldwin was written off by Boring and until recently has been quite out of favor.

Baldwin's importance for our present purpose lies in his elaboration and reworking of James' notion of the social self. This reworking is presented in the second of Baldwin's studies of mental development, *Social and ethical interpretations* (1897), which was meant as a general text in social psychology. In this book, Baldwin describes the process of development of the self out of social interaction. While such a process is implicit in James' conception of the empirical selves, it remained for Baldwin to work out and illustrate how the social genesis of self might occur. The general drift of his thesis is captured in the following statement:

The "ego" and the "alter" are thus born together. Both are crude and unreflective, largely organic. And the two get purified and clarified together by this twofold reaction.... My sense of myself grows by imitation of you, and my sense of yourself grows in terms of my sense of myself. Both *ego* and *alter* are thus essentially social, each is a *socius* and each is an imitative creation. (p. 9)

The self develops, according to Baldwin, as a function of the dialectic between the child and the socius; Baldwin relies heavily on the conception of imitation proposed by the French sociologist M. Tarde.

The development of the child's personality could not go on at all without the constant modification of his sense of himself by suggestions from others. So he himself, at every stage, is really in part someone else, even in his own thought of himself as the other's socius: and the only thing that remains more or less stable, throughout the whole growth, is the fact that there is a growing sense of self which includes both terms, the ego and the alter. (p. 24)

Baldwin sees both a habitual self and an accommodating self. The habitual self is a product of imitative assimilation—the self that is established and is resistant to change. The accommodating self, on the other hand, is an active agent of change, constantly seeking modifications in response to new experiences. Throughout the developmental span, the dialectic continues; the challenges to the habitual self are posed by continued interaction with the socius. Much of Baldwin's discussion concerns the way in which the child acquires a moral and ethical sense through the unfolding of this interactive process. This is the same problem and very similar terminology to Kohlberg's (1963) research on moral development. That Baldwin's conceptions and very language should resemble Kohlberg's is not a surprise if we remember that Piaget stands as the mediating link between them.

Just as Baldwin elaborated certain ideas of James about the self, so he influenced in turn the thinking of Charles Horton Cooley (1864–1929). Like Baldwin, Cooley found it impossible to consider the self as existing in isolation.

Persons are not separable and mutually exclusive . . . they interpenetrate one another, the same element pertaining to different persons at different times, or even at the same time. (Cooley 1902, p. 90)

To this assertion Cooley appends a footnote acknowledging his indebtedness to Baldwin's conception of the social self in the *Social and ethical interpretations,* and as well to James.

Cooley's life seems to have been one of smooth academic tranquility. Son of a law professor at the University of Michigan, his academic work was done at that institution; moreover, he served on Michigan's faculty for his entire academic career. His writing is meditative, contemplative—laced with references to Goethe, the Bible, Darwin, and to James and Baldwin. His empirical work is very limited—really unimportant in relation to the corpus of his writings. But he did, like Baldwin before him and Piaget after him, take advantage of his own children as a source of observations about social and personal development.

Cooley is widely identified in modern secondary sources as the author of the conception of the "looking glass self"—the idea that the raw empirical material for the formation of self consists of reflections provided by others. That Cooley is so closely identified with this conception is testimony to the power of metaphor as the vehicle of memory. While this identification is certainly correct, it seems a particular injustice to Cooley's life work to be so summarily captured in a snippet of a phrase. Philip Rieff states the matter well:

Cooley is best taken slowly; the student should linger long enough in his presence to appreciate some of his nobility of mind and rare gift for analyzing society as a whole, yet without over simplification. . . . Cooley is not the only sociologist whose works communicate a nobility, a magnanimity of mind. But there are not so many that students can be permitted, without cost to their development as sociologists, to spare themselves the experience of confronting him. (Rieff 1968, p. 33)

Cooley's solution to the problem of the relation between the individual and society is radical for all its gentility. For he considered self and society to be coterminous. Society is in the mind of each of us and everyone has a self that is product of the particular others with whom he has had contact in the course of development. Cooley considered human life to have two aspects—the individual and the social.

But [it] is always, as a matter of fact, both individual and general. In other words, "society" and "individual" do not denote separable phenomena, but are simply collective and distributive aspects of the same thing, the relation between them being like that between other expressions, one of which denotes a group as a whole and the other the members of the group, such as the army and the soldiers, the class and the students, and so on. (Cooley 1902, pp. 1–2)

Samples of Cooley's writing will have to suffice for this presentation, for they can convey the flavor of his work if not its texture and substance. "It is worth noting here that there is no separation between real and imaginary persons: indeed, to be imagined is to become real, in a social sense" (p. 60); and, "The life of the mind is essentially the life of intercourse" (p. 62). Like James, his psychological mentor, Cooley rejects the notion of a substantive or metaphysical discussion of pure ego, "whatever that may be." But he considers analysis of the empirical self to be no more difficult a matter than the analysis of any object of thought at all. His analysis of the empirical self begins along lines that we should now find similar to "ordinary language analysis" in philosophy. He inquires into what is meant in common speech by first-person singular pronouns. From this he concludes that the empirical self is essentially social, for the major portion of uses of first person pronouns have a social sense. Cooley does not follow James in including separate discussions of material and spiritual constituents of the empirical self. He prefers to think of the empirical self as social, "not as implying the existence of a self that is not social—for I think that 'I' of common language always has more or less distinct reference to other people as well as to the speaker, but because I wish to dwell upon the social aspect of it" (pp. 36–37).

The reader senses in Cooley a quality of moral loftiness, of gentle humanism, of tolerance and catholicity of mind. Perhaps the frequent quotations from Emerson, Shakespeare, and other classical sources have their effect in this way. But Cooley is overtly and decidedly a political moralist. He advocated democracy as the form of social organization that is most compatible with human nature. Like Mead after him, he proclaims himself to be an internationalist and lays claim to a vision of universalism.

George Herbert Mead (1863–1931) was educated at Oberlin and at Harvard, where he studied for a time with William James. He served briefly on the faculty at the University of Michigan, where he was contemporary with Cooley. In 1894, Mead joined John Dewey at the University of Chicago, where he remained and taught until his death. While the dates of Mead's works are practically identical to Cooley's, he seems logically to come after him. This is due, in part, to the peculiar pattern of the publication of Mead's scholarly work. He wrote no book during his lifetime, and published very few articles. His major work was pulled together by students after his death and published in several volumes, the most important of which is *Mind, self and society from the standpoint of a social behaviorist* (Mead 1934). For this reason, Mead's major publication dates succeed those of his more prolific contemporary, Cooley.

In other ways as well, Mead's work is successor to the line extending from James to Baldwin to Cooley. While all of these figures were defenders and advocates of Darwinian thinking in science, it was Mead who worked out a new way to conceptualize the social nature of man in Darwinian terms. As product of this conceptualization, he articulated a radically new set of relationships for mind, self, and society. This conceptual work was conducted under the disciplinary aegis of sociology and the philosophy of pragmatism. As such, it comprised a seminal achievement that had very little or no immediate impact upon psychology. Anselm Strauss (1956) notes in his introduction to *The social psychology of George Herbert Mead* that the individualistic psychology of Mead's day had little use for a social psychology based on the primacy of the socius. Strauss states that:

> The recently awakened interest of psychologists in problems of self and ego has not been affected greatly by Mead's discussion of these problems, perhaps because his assumptions differ from theirs. His I and Me . . . represent quite a different formulation of the relations of man to society and man to biological natures; and there is in Mead no trace of speculation about basic human drives toward self-consistency or self-realization. (Strauss 1956, p. xvi)

The particular evolutionary understanding that Mead developed of the social origins of self is succinctly described in a note in his chapter on the self:

> Man's behavior is such in his social group that he is able to become an object to himself, a fact which constitutes him a more advanced product of evolutionary development than are the lower animals. Fundamentally it is this social fact—and not his alleged possession of a soul or mind with which he, as an individual, has been mysteriously and supernaturally endowed and with which the lower animals have not been endowed—that differentiates him from them. (Strauss 1956, p. 214)

This position differs from that of James in that James' psychology of self was fundamentally an individual psychology, where part of the constituents of the self is considered to be social in nature. It differs from Baldwin in that it proposes the terms of the dialectic between self and alter to be initially asymmetrical, and in favor of the socius. In Mead's view, the self simply does not exist at birth, but arises as a result of social commerce. Mead's affinity to Cooley is obvious, but there is an important difference there, too.[1] Cooley defends a kind of social mentalism, where the socius essentially exists in the minds of individuals. Mead styles himself a social behaviorist and places emphasis on social actions, particularly the symbolic social actions mediated by language. These actions are the essential means by which selves and societies are both created and sustained. Fundamental to Mead's view is the concept of "taking the role of the other," and this again is a distinctive contribution to the line of theory to which he was heir:

> The individual experiences himself as such, not directly, but only indirectly, from the particular standpoints of other individual members of the same social group, or from the generalized standpoint of the social group as a whole to which he belongs. . . . He becomes an object to himself only by taking the attitudes of other individuals toward himself within a social environment or context of experience and behavior in which both they and he are involved. (Mead 1934, p. 140)

Mead's self is not of the "looking glass" variety proposed by Cooley. Cooley's metaphor implies a self looking at its own reflection in the passive mirror provided by alter. Mead suggests that we can take the position of alter and see ourselves, as it were, nonreversed and three-dimensional. By taking the role of the other, we can see ourselves "objectively." Moreover, the very development of an inward self is dependent first on gaining the outward perspective provided by the socius.

The form of behavior in which Mead is interested is certainly not bodily movement or physicalistic change. He is interested in the communicative acts among individuals, conducted by means of significant symbols. He further posits that social communication leads to the capacity of the individual to be a companion to oneself, to think of one as a self—indeed, to think. Mead insists that one cannot converse with oneself without first conversing with others. Thought is itself social in origin and interactive in its nature, with the thinker taking alternatively the role of actor and audience.

As social and self-development proceed, the child is considered by Mead to be morally fragmented in a way that reflects the differing interests or values of the social entities to which the child has been exposed. But gradually, the child learns to take toward him- or herself the attitude of the generalized other. "The organized community or social group which gives the individual his unity of self may be called 'the generalized other'" (Strauss 1956, p. 231). This generalized other can consist of abstractions or nonexistent groups. In a functional sense, it provides the individual both with a consistent way of thinking about oneself and with a generally useful perspective from which to decide the rightness of any contemplated course of action. The play of the child is the serious business of internalizing the other and at the same time developing skill in role-playing.

Mead is as much a pragmatist as any of the thinkers in his line, and he applies his pragmatism to the recurrent problem of the self as knower (the I) and the self as known (the me) in a way that is reminiscent of James, but with a special Meadian touch:

The simplest way of handling the problem would be in terms of memory. I talk to myself, and I remember what I said and perhaps the emotional content that went with it. The "I" of this moment is present in the "me" of the next moment. There again I cannot turn around quick enough to catch myself. (Strauss 1956, p. 242)

So as the "I" moves along, it leaves "me" in its wake and provides for the self a way of thinking about the self. Like James, Baldwin, and Cooley, Mead has no use for a metaphysical or essential "I" but uses the term to describe the activity that takes place in the specious present, including the contemplation of memories and the acts of past "I's". This point is extended by Mead to an implication about the limitations of self-knowledge. Since the I cannot know itself in the present, it never knows exactly what it is going to do in advance. The I is in this sense free and imparts a sense of initiative. "Exactly how we will act never gets into experience until after the action takes place" (Strauss 1956, p. 246). The adverb *exactly* deserves emphasis here, for Mead is not asserting that actions are unaffected by prior intentions and anticipations.

Mead also takes pains to account for originality and uniqueness in at least two other senses. Even though individual selves are of common social origin, still each self is unique in that the actual character of the social interactions experienced by any one person is unique. Also, society itself is not constant, for continual changes are introduced through the accretion throughout history of the consequences of gestures made by social actors. Of course, there are great gestures and small, great changes and small. "Profound changes which take place through the action of individual minds are only the extreme expression of the sort of changes that take place steadily through reactions which are not simply those of a 'me' but of an 'I'" (Strauss 1956, p. 249). Historical changes are due to the reactions of individuals to the social situations in which they find themselves. For Mead history is undetermined in the same way that the active "I's" are undetermined. The future is always to a degree unpredictable. In this, Mead would agree with Ortega y Gassett, who said:

[A]ll life, and consequently the life of history, is made up of simple moments, each of them relatively undetermined in respect of the previous one, so that in it reality hesitates, walks up and down, and is uncertain whether to decide for one or another of various possibilities. (Ortega y Gassett 1930/1932, p. 78)

It is, therefore, a mistake to think of Mead as the same sort of behaviorist as those who dominated psychology in his time, for they would admit no reflections either about self-consciousness nor about the indeterminacy of movement from the present to the future. In another sense as well, Mead is more similar to James than to his psychological contemporaries. Mead's discourse is full of the incorporative "we," as in, "We know that as we pass from one historical period to another. . . ." And, of course, Mead did not do experiments, did not rely upon empirical evidence to document his assertions. He may have styled himself a behaviorist to distinguish himself from what he considered to be the mentalism of Cooley, but he never thought of "self" or "mind" as predictive variables in a behavioral equation.

FREUD AND SULLIVAN: ANTITHESIS AND SYNTHESIS WITH THE PRAGMATIST'S LINE

With Mead, the line of theory which originated with James becomes completely submerged within sociology. There it would prove to be the germinal material for the development of symbolic interactionism and of role theory. Within behavioral psychology at the time of Mead's active influence in the 1920s and 1930s the self had just about disappeared as an object of concern. To be sure, behavioral psychology included many empirical studies on the description of self and the use of those descriptions for behavioral prediction. We shall examine some of this work in the next section of this chapter. But it is instructive to look first at the general conception of self that was emerging within the psychoanalytic tradition— particularly in the later work of Freud and in that of one of the deviationist American analysts, Harry Stack Sullivan.

Charles Morris notes in his introduction to *Mind, self and society* that at the headwaters of social psychology are to be found Darwinism and democracy. Indeed, the question of the fit between human nature and the optimal form of human governance is never far in the background for any of the four thinkers we have considered. It is more than a matter of coincidence that all considered democracy to be that ideal form. Their participation in the American form of democracy was at a time and in a condition that allowed patriotism, optimism, and internationalism to coexist without painful contradiction.

While Darwinism is also at the headwaters of psychoanalysis, democracy most assuredly is not. This is not the place to labor an explanation of the major directions taken by psychoanalytic thinking in terms of the political and social ambiance of authoritarian rule characteristic of late nineteenth-century Europe (Ellenberger 1970). However, it is descriptively correct to note a similarity between the brash optimism of the young American republic between 1880 and 1930 and the sorts of theories of self produced by James, Baldwin, Cooley, and Mead. On the other hand, the relation between the person and the socius conceived by Freud in the same period would seem to correspond to a political environment characterized by the traditional rule of authority, the acceptance of class divisions as given, and—by the time of Freud's later writings—a profound political pessimism engendered by World War I.

Psychoanalysis is preeminently a psychology of the individual. The individual psyche is the prime entity for analysis; its nature, genetic laws, mechanisms, disorders, and restorative properties are the chief features of psychoanalytic theory. The socius is not ignored, for it is by means of the conflict resulting from the contact of the developing psyche with the agents of society, usually the parents, that the ego begins to deploy its defenses, producing the development of personality. The id is supposed to be the repository of instinctual impulses and the superego is supposed to represent the tyrannical demands of society; the ego is sandwiched between them. Defense mechanisms are aptly named in psychoanalysis theory, for the ego is considered to be under a more or less constant state of siege.

In this brief discussion of a major and highly elaborate theoretical and interpretive structure, I must risk vast oversimplification. I am willing to do so for reasons of didactic clarity, in the belief that the fundamental contrast being proposed here is sound. Briefly, it is this: In *Civilization and its discontents*, Freud (1930/1962) suggested that the basic and most fundamental relation between the individual and civilization is one of enmity. As a consequence of the basic incompatibility of the interests of the individual and the pressures of society, the individual is literally forced to adapt by sublimating basic instinctual energies. The cost of this forced adaptation is repression, anxiety, and neurosis. Civilization demands a renunciation of individual sexual and aggressive impulses. As a consequence the person is made everlastingly guilty. Through the working off of this guilt the individual paradoxically makes a contribution to the development of civilization, with the result that the distance between the protean psyche and civilization becomes ever greater. "The two processes of individual and of cultural development must stand in hostile opposition to each other and mutually dispute the ground" (Freud 1930/1962, p. 88).

The contrast of this view of the relation of the self to society to that described in the last section for Mead's psychology is great and pointed. If one position is understood, then both are, for they are diametrically opposed. For Freud, the individual is primary; for Mead, the socius is primary. For Freud, the relation between the individual and the society is one of enmity; for Mead, it is one of mutual dependence (Pfeutze 1954). For Freud, the consequence of identification with the culture is self-renunciation; for Mead, the achievement of the perspective of the generalized other is coincident with the highest level of self-development and integration. Freud's is a psychology of mental pathology, in which normality is regarded as a special case. The opposite is true for Mead, where the dissociation of personality is viewed as an ordinary and nonneurotic phenomenon, resulting from role conflicts. For example, the role of "son" and the role of "fraternity brother" might be behaviorally incompatible for a college student—a garden-variety role conflict. Only in the most extreme cases is such dissociation to be regarded as pathological, and then the pathology is not absolute but is socially relative and contextual.

If it is correct to say that Freud and Mead represent antithetical views on the relation between self and society, then we might identify the interpersonal psychiatry of Sullivan as a synthesis, or at least a middle ground. Sullivan became the guide for a generation of dynamic psychiatrists in the 1940s and 1950s, but was subsequently replaced by guides who looked to Freud for their inspiration.

Harry Stack Sullivan (1892–1949) was the son of Irish-American parents in rural New York state. He earned a M.D. degree at the Chicago College of Medicine and Surgery in 1917, entering the specialty of psychiatry after completing his military service during World War I. His early career was spent in service to the Federal Government, in several government-run mental hospitals in Washington, D.C. From 1931 to 1938, he had a private practice in New York, returning to Washington and government service just before World War II. Like Mead, Sullivan never published a book in his lifetime, though he did publish many papers in psychiatric journals and helped to found *Psychiatry* (Mullahy 1970). Several volumes of Sullivan's work were published after his death.

Sullivan's theoretical orientation was initially that of classical Freudian psychoanalysis. However, his early professional responsibilities required attention to therapy with schizophrenics, and Freudian psychoanalysis was intended principally for neurotics, not psychotics. Through a combination of his early experience in devising therapeutic programs for schizophrenics and through his reading in the social sciences, Sullivan developed a variant of psychoanalytic theory which came to be called interpersonal psychiatry. The major differentiating feature of Sullivan's theory is the central importance it gives to interpersonal processes rather than intrapsychic processes. Mental disorders for Sullivan are seen to be social in origin and nature. As a consequence, therapy demands attention to the total social surroundings of the patient, not merely a talking out of intrapsychic tensions.

Sullivan's affinity to the line we have described from James to Mead is very clear. "For all I know every human being has as many personalities as he has clear interpersonal relations" (Perry 1982, p. 108). Further, "Mead demonstrated very clearly that the individual person was a complex derivative of many others" (Sullivan 1953, p. 17). Sullivan considered the self to be essentially social in origin. The relations established between the person and others enable the self to achieve some definition. Because the others with whom the self relates are many and diverse, the self will have many and diverse facets, and its precariousness or fragility derives from the precariousness or fragility of the communicative links established with others.

Two developments in popular psychology in the last twenty years are properly seen as products of the Sullivanian view on the nature of personal adjustment. One is represented by the book, *I'm OK, you're OK* by Harris (1973). Therapy is seen as a process of providing for the person a secure and unconditional recognition of the basic validity of one's being. This reassurance takes place "on the level," with the therapist first asserting his own self-acceptance and then the acceptance of the other. Sullivan has a view of human fulfillment and happiness that is represented not by the mutual orgasm, as the Reichian variant of the psychoanalytic line might have it, but by mutual intimacy, consisting of an entire and unqualified acceptance of ego and alter by each other.

Sullivan's psychology also is a direct antecedent to the book popularized by Berne (1978), *Games people play*. Games, for Berne, are not trivial or superficial exercises whereby one individual tries to gain mastery over another. Rather, Berne used the metaphor in a general way to characterize the ritualized or improvised series of moves and counter-moves that take place in all social interactions—interactions which comprise not only the very stuff of social life, but also the unique means by which individuals can come to have self-knowledge.

In order to understand the significance of Sullivan's thought in the tradition of research and theory on the social aspects of self, it is worth quoting his views on the social nature of anxiety at some length:

Anxiety is what keeps us from noticing things which would lead us to correct our faults. Anxiety is the thing that makes us hesitate before we spoil our standing with the stranger. Anxiety when it does not work so suavely becomes a psychiatric problem, because then it hashes our most polite utterances to the prospective boss, and causes us to tremble at the most inopportune times. So you see it is only reasonable and very much in keeping with an enormously capable organization, such as the human being, that anxiety becomes a problem only when it doesn't work smoothly, and that the anxiety which has had to be grasped as a fundamental factor in understanding interpersonal relations is by no means an anxiety attack, a hollow feeling in the stomach, and so on. Much more frequently it manifests as what I have called selective inattention, by which I mean you must miss all sorts of things which would cause you embarrassment, or in many cases, great profit to notice. It is the means by which you stay as you are, in spite of the efforts of worthy psychiatrists, clergymen, and others to help you mend your ways. You don't hear, you don't see, you don't feel, you don't observe, you don't think, all by the very suave manipulation of the contents of consciousness by anxiety—or, if you must . . . by the threat of anxiety, which still is anxiety. This very great extent of the effects of disapproval and the disturbance of euphoria by the significant people in early life—the people who are tremendously interested in getting you socialized—is what makes the concept of anxiety so crucially important in understanding all sorts of things. (Sullivan 1950, pp. 216–217)

This quotation is taken from an article published in *Psychiatry* shortly after Sullivan's death, called "The Illusion of Personal Individuality." The title is worth pondering, for it provides some warrant for thinking of Sullivan as a pivotal figure in a progression from Mead to Goffman. With anxiety making us deaf and blind to much of what is going on around us, the self survives only as an illusion—a more secure illusion when anxiety is functioning well. On this view, James' well-trained social anxiety allowed him to maintain confidence in the continuity of thought and of that self which is the thinker. But with Mead and now with Sullivan, the self is moved out of the body and into social space, where its vulnerability is measured by the potential inconstancies of our associates. It is all very well for the psychiatrist to say, "I'm OK, you're OK," but will he continue so to regard me after I have broken off my temporary game with him by no longer paying him? Sullivan envisages a terror of the person's entire self-system— an immanent collapse. Therapy in such a case consists not in explaining that fears are groundless or that conditions are really neutral. Therapy consists in the careful provision of social reassurance to the patient, which allows the reassertion of the illusion of personal individuality. Sullivan does not try to eliminate anxiety; he tries to get the patient to use his anxiety well, in a way that is socially and personally functional.

Sullivan's writings contain a disordered and dangerous kind of richness. They are disordered because he never systematized his ideas of personality in a coherent or complete fashion, and also because he attempted a synthesis of views about the self—the Freudian and the Meadian—which are essentially contradictory. They are dangerous because he seems ever ready to risk giving away the psychologist's advantage—his or her maintenance of a superior and invulnerable role vis-à-vis his or her patient or subject. The Sullivanian therapist, indeed Sullivan himself, must admit to the same sorts of anxieties and vulnerabilities which characterize the patient; the risk of the evaporation or fragmentation of self is fully shared. At least one biographer of Sullivan has suggested that he succumbed to a schizophrenic breakdown for two years, thus manifesting in this most direct way his shared vulnerability and lack of consistent advantage in relation to his patients (Perry 1982).

Sullivan is a borderline character for the mainstream of personality theory and research. He does merit brief inclusion in Hall and Lindzey's (1957) influential textbook. I will presently argue that social psychology has moved to appreciate Sullivan, or better, has become Sullivanian because of the prominence and importance of Erving Goffman, who wrote the book for us on impression management. But first we must pause for a brief interlude featuring research and theory on the self within psychology proper at mid-century, as represented by Ruth Wylie.

THE SURPRISING GUISE IN WHICH SELF REEMERGED IN PSYCHOLOGY

All of the approaches to self mentioned thus far have been responsive to the problem of understanding, as represented in the plaintive note from Schopenhauer, the epigraph for this chapter. From James through Sullivan, all writers on the problem of the self have taken it as their task to aid in casting a ray of light on the "obscurity of our being." All in the set we have surveyed have also been in some ways pragmatists and functionalists; they have been interested in what the self does, where it comes from, how it works, and not in what it *is*. None has been interested in the task of providing an operational definition of self, for none has found it possible to believe that the self is an entity, an existent. The empirical self does, of course, lend itself to description, but the description is always circumstantial, relational, contextual. None of the writers we have surveyed has made a claim that the empirical self could be described in a way that is fixed and general across all kinds of social conditions and contexts of action.

The view of self that emerges in Ruth Wylie's (1974) survey, *The self-concept*, is something entirely different. This book is a survey of research on the self within psychology proper—most of it not initially titled as research on the self, but rather on personality or personality assessment. *The self-concept* was revised in 1974 to include material published through 1972. I shall rely on this later edition for the characterizations which follow.[2]

Wylie's book contains a three-page introduction given to the historical background of interest in the self in psychology. James and Mead are mentioned, but only in passing. Cooley is not included, and Sullivan registers only in a single reference. Wylie correctly notes that, "During the second, third, and fourth decades of the twentieth century, constructs concerning the self did not receive much attention from the behaviorist and functionalist psychologies which were dominating the American scene" (Wylie 1974, p. 2). It is also obvious from examining the contents of Wylie's book that the dominant concerns of American psychology during this period fed into the way in which the self problem was conceptualized when it did reemerge. The major theme to be found in Wylie's book is a concern over the methodology of self-assessment and the extent to which those assessments could be used as a means of generating predictions of behavior. Chapter 2 is a survey of "self-concept theories and problems of research methodology." It is followed by chapters on description, on measurement, on operational definitions, and on actual attempts to use self-concept studies in a predictive fashion. The conclusion of all this is as laconic as it is sober, for Wylie suggests the even possibility that the entire area ought to be abandoned. She suggests that the reasons for this state of affairs are two: that self-concept theories are at present vague and incomplete; and that research methodology in this area has been very loose, imprecise, and generally not up to the level of control required for science.

Much of the argument that leads to these conclusions stems from a critical examination of methodological and substantive problems encountered in the tasks of self-assessment and the prediction of behavior from personality studies. Projective tests are notoriously unreliable. Response sets are vexing. Predictive indices are weak and do not replicate. Mischel's (1968) challenge to personality theories is strongly featured. The notion that assessed personality traits (components of the self-described self-concept) can be used as general predictors of behavior received a severe blow from Mischel's empirical and theoretical argument that situations determine much more behavioral variance than do fixed dispositions. There is no point in reviewing here the vast controversy produced by this challenge. (See Mischel & Peake [1982] for a critical statement on the problem.) In this present perspective, the argument about whether personality has predictive utility is tantamount to an argument about whether personality exists, or whether there exists a stable self. In the theoretical tradition we have been surveying, the answer is, "Of course not." It is curious that the enormous emphasis placed on methodological rigor and theoretical definition in American psychology during the twentieth century should have produced such simplistic thinking as to have loaded the import of Mischel's book, or a somewhat different challenge presented in the work of Crowne and

Marlowe (1964) on "social desirability" as a contaminant in the process of self-assessment.

The subtitle of Wylie's book is, "A review of methodological considerations and measuring instruments." The suggestion is that the legacy of psychology's visitation to the problem of self over the past seventy years has been a plethora of paper-and-pencil tools for self-assessment, plus an intricate set of arguments, pro and con, as to why such instruments should or should not work in the prediction of behavior. An outside observer would have to agree that paper-and-pencil self-assessments have a limited range of predictive utility. An outside observer would also be forced to conclude that the very quantity of trait names that have been suggested for enduring psychological dispositions is strong evidence that the contents of self are not unequivocally describable.[3]

The hegemony of behaviorism has evidently come to an end in psychology. Cognition has emerged again as the psychological counterpart of the philosophical problem of epistemology and the preeminent topic for experimental research. Mind is beginning to reappear in our discourse; as it becomes evident that in a functional sense machines can think, so it is no longer considered to be absurd to allow people the same functional capacity. And the self has emerged again. If it emerges in the Wylie volume and in succeeding literature on the "self-concept" as a reified grotesque, more recent thinking has been less guilty of ontological error. The methodological strictures accompanying behaviorism succeeded in producing just the sort of homunculus they were meant to exorcise—the elusive "self" of Wylie's books. Now that the arbitrariness of those strictures is more evident, inquiry into the problem of self can enjoy liberation.

This suggests one additional feature of contrast between the self-concept research presented by Wylie and the earlier theory of self we have reviewed: It is the contrast of literacy. Psychologists coming upon the problem of the self have acted as if they were discovering the problem for the first time— that nothing any poet, dramatist, historian, philosopher, or social critic might have said could have value or interest. Gone are the references to Shakespeare, to Carlyle, to Goethe, to John Donne, to Kant or Mill or Nietzsche. As Philip Rieff has said in an essay on Cooley, "Ours is a discipline suffering from a widespread belief in its own radical contemporaneity" (1968, p. 33). If one finds references to literature on self from outside of psychology in modern writings, they usually have the character and depth of the cartoon illustrations that seem to have become a permanent and ubiquitous feature of our undergraduate textbooks. One might quote a segment of description from *The double* by Dostoyevsky in order to illustrate some principle of impression management, but one really doesn't rely upon Dostoyevsky to provide any real light of his own upon the problem of self. These observations might easily be taken as a mark of sentimentality or nostalgia for a more picturesque literature in psychology.

But I think it is seriously worth considering that psychology might look to explore the fields of literature, theater, and philosophy for such insights as might there be found. If our topic is the self, we should be ready to welcome insights from any quarter.

ERVING GOFFMAN: A COLD NEW LIGHT ON THE SELF IN INTERACTION

Goffman's importance to contemporary thinking about the self can scarcely be overestimated. While he, like Mead and Cooley, was a sociologist, his productivity and genius were such as to make him a conspicuous—even unavoidable—presence in the social sciences generally; indeed, he influenced the world of ideas generally.

He was one of the very few sociologists whose work was known beyond the field—and his influence on the world, as well as within the disciplines of social science, has already been so great that he stands as a giant among the social thinkers of his day. (Daniels 1983, p. 1)

Goffman's principle writings are contained in 11 books written over a period of 25 years. The first is *The presentation of self in everyday life* (first published in 1956 in Scotland; American edition published in 1959), and the last is *Forms of talk* (Goffman 1981). While the specific topical reference in his work covers a wide range (mental hospitals, stigmatized individuals, gambling casinos, uses of gender in advertising, etc.), his work employs a singular methodology, has consistency of tone, and possesses thematic unity.

Goffman's special talent is that of the observer and commentator. If our earlier contributors to the study of self have been long on theory and short on empiricism, Goffman is quintessentially the empiricist. His first book is based on observational work with a village of crofters in the Shetland Islands of Scotland. His last work is based in large part on recordings and texts of "talk," including lectures, radio shows, public speeches, and informal discourse. Because of Goffman's observational power, it has been hard for critics to trace his origins in the history of social thought. Indeed, he never engages in extended discussion of somebody else's ideas, but refers to them as side supports to his own conceptions, which grow right out of his own observations (or "microanalysis") of the social life around him. Goffman performed no experiments, and never, to my knowledge, devised a paper-and-pencil assessment of anything. He swam, in fact, in the same social sea as the rest of us, with the difference that he had the capacity to make the most familiar observation a source of strange and fascinating insight. He identified himself quite insistently as a sociologist, allowed himself to be affiliated with anthropology, but was more wary of psychology. Psychology seems to want to carry its empiricism into the depths of the person, and this is territory Goffman was content to ignore. It is revealing to note the epigraph Goffman chose for his first work, from George Santayana. In part:

Living things in contact with the air must acquire a cuticle, and it is not urged against cuticles that they are not hearts; yet some philosophers seem to be angry with images for not being things, and with words for not being feelings. Words and images are like shells, no less integral parts of nature than are the substances they cover, but better addressed to the eye and more open to observation. (Goffman 1959)

It has often been urged against Goffman that his concern with cuticles and shells make him a mere chronicler of human superficiality. One finds little that is spiritually warm or morally uplifting in Goffman's writings. His obituary in the *New York Times* noted that he argued, "People are essentially performers whose main business is fabricating an identity." In fabricating his own identity, Goffman did little to dispel this impression. His regard for self is that of its presentation, its management, its outward interactions. Some would say that he denied inwardness. I would say that as a sociologist he considered that he could and should ignore it, for the methodological reason suggested by the Santayana aphorism.

Goffman's tone of commentary, as well as the content of what he said, conveys the impression of waspishness, or a certain lack of sympathy for the material of his microanalysis. Goffman, as an observer, seems to be "on the level" with the people he observed. But, unlike James, he concentrates only on the surface. He chooses not to wake people up, but to note "how they snore;" not to interfere with or perturb his material, but to note carefully how it acts. Goffman observes that actors expect others to take their performance seriously, to credit them with being sincere and genuine. "When his audience is also convinced in this way about the show he puts on—and this seems to be the typical case—then for the moment at least, only the sociologist or the socially disgruntled will have any doubts about the 'realness' of what is presented" (Goffman 1959, p. 17). It follows that one must be concerned with the fronts and faces that people manage to show to their audiences, in ways that are more or less ingenuous. Goffman's methodological ignoring of the inward self appears in his writing to be also a refusal to grant that inward self any sort of moral legitimacy; so that one's honesty becomes a matter of appearing to be honest or generating the impression of honesty, integrity becomes a matter of not being caught out. Thus the sociologist in Goffman is perpetually disgruntled; this puts him in a position to doubt the legitimacy of all puttings on and givings off.

No one should have wished Goffman to be more charitable; for his very coolness enables his perspicacity. Examples of the power of his posture are to be found throughout his writings. I chose an example from *Relations in public*:

This analysis began on the most magisterial note I can attempt: moral rules and their function as the link between self and society. This led, with little loss of abstractness, to a consideration of deviations from the rules and the ritual dialogue that provides a remedy. But now it has been argued that moral claims are made with respect to a multitude of minor territories of the self, and that correctives for infraction are to be found in body gloss—the indignities of overacted gesticulation. This brings the study of remedial activity into the street, into the little interactions that are forgotten about as soon as they occur, into what serious students of society never collect, into the slop of social life. (Goffman 1971, p. 138)

Of course, when Goffman analyzes the slop of social life, it becomes highly meaningful material—essential to our understanding of the intricacies of the interactions of persons. Just as the analysis of coprolites yields essential information to the archeologist about the diets and living habits of prehistoric peoples, so Goffman is able to show how the waste material in social life can lead us to a fuller understanding of the functioning of selves in society. Now we see body gloss, "withs," tucks, cants, filler gestures, and eye play in a way that fits analytic needs.

Goffman's vision is often taken to be cynical, but it is better seen as wry. As a final example of his tone, I cite a passage from *Forms of talk*, wherein he discusses the use of little jokes and wisecracks interpolated into discourse:

Thus the same little plum can be inserted at the beginning or end of quite different speakers' quite different talks with easy aptness. Stage plays provide similar opportunities in allowing for the performance of 'memorable' exchanges, that is, sprightly bits of dialogue that bear repeating and can be repeated apart from the play in which they occurred. (Goffman 1981, pp. 31–32)

The thematic unity in Goffman's work is obvious. He remained consistently interested in the topic that formed the theme of his first book—the management of impressions. His interest in the self is only in its empirical manifestations, and in this he is consistent with James, Baldwin, Cooley, Mead, and Sullivan. However, he eschewed an interest in thoughts about the self—that sort of empiricism—in favor of a meticulous cataloging and analysis of the self's cuticle—the air-hardened, outward surface of the self in interaction. Given his stubborn aloofness, it is perhaps inevitable that Goffman himself should have become a mystery, an enigma. And that he was.

Goffman appears not to have capitalized on his knowledge of the intricacies of impression management, for the impression he managed to convey of himself, particularly to reference groups that would seem to matter greatly—sociologists and other social scientists—was not entirely favorable. While all show a grudging respect for his style and his care for the quotidian detail, he has been charged with being preoccupied with the trivial, with dehumanizing and degrading human material, and with political and social amorality (Gouldner 1970; Young 1971; Hall 1977). His sociology does not start with recognition of the primacy of class stratification: While he does acknowledge and comment on dominance orderings in society, he often does not seem to take sides—with the weak against the powerful—and this appears to be a fault from the standpoint of conventional sociological morality.

Sociology has accorded Goffman its admiration principally for *The presentation of self in everyday life* and *Asylums*. As his later works received more favorable notice in the world of academic and intellectual life, they received from within sociology proportionally less praise. The view within sociology is that Goffman's later work is increasingly self-indulgent, increasingly careless or perhaps heedless of the impression he was conveying. Indeed, his later works show very brief bibliographies and refer mostly to his own work and that of his seminar students. His methodology seemed increasingly haphazard, his observations an odd collection of whatever came to hand.

In all of this we are led to examine again the difficult question of the relationship between the social scientist and his material. The traditional role of the experimental psychologist is one of temporary dominance and control over subject matter (Scheibe 1979). The psychoanalyst is in a position of unique advantage in relation to the patient—controlling, regulating, advising, seeing, but not being seen. What of Goffman? Published photographs are hard to find. Interviews are rarer still. And yet Goffman has somehow managed to place himself on the same level as that of his material. We end up concluding that he is no better than the rest of us in any moral sense, while we might conclude that he is decidedly more clever than any of us.

The thought occurs that Goffman's great moral triumph was precisely his refusal to contrive an image of moral superiority for himself. Certainly no one knew better than Goffman how to do this. And yet surely no one was more aware than Goffman of the pervasiveness of falseness—of contrived images, converting the self-love of the clever into a magnified adulation by the crowd. It may easily be supposed that Goffman simply found it morally preferable to walk away from such a prize—and in this he is like Kierkegaard. He seemed content to convey the impression that he was himself all cuticle, all the way down to his heart. I expect he allowed only a very close circle to know that this was not true.

THE CURRENT PLEA FOR SELF AS INWARD AND ACTIVE AGENT

Perhaps the spirit of an age selects for special prominence the voice which happens to respond most directly to the particular needs of that age. Ours is an era in which change seems more powerful than stability, when identities seem hollow, commitments tentative and fragile—an age of skepticism, a cosmetic age, an age of press agentry and the manufacturing of public image, an age in which a former Hollywood actor was groomed to become president of the United States, where appearance seems to matter for all, substance and essence for very little. I am not here characterizing our era, but merely referring to a rather common—even hackneyed—way in which it has been characterized. Goffman happens to be the voice within the social sciences that resonates most closely with these features of description. For this reason, a consummate student of the management of impression is taken to be some sort of advocate or apologist for human hollowness. It is a moot point whether Goffman changed the history of the self or was merely someone who wrote about changes in the history of the self that had already taken place. The involvement of moral and ethical issues with one's conception of the nature of self cannot be avoided. In a philosophical treatise on ethics, Alisdair MacIntyre makes this challenging assertion:

I am not merely contending that morality is not what it once was, but also and more importantly that what once was morality has to some large degree disappeared—and that this marks a degeneration, a grave cultural loss. (MacIntyre 1981, p. 31)

MacIntyre takes Goffman to be almost an architect of this cultural decay: "Erving Goffman . . . has liquidated the self into its role-playing, arguing that the self is no more than 'a peg' on which the clothes of the role are hung" (MacIntyre 1981). Jean-Paul Sartre is seen as performing the complementary task of characterizing the self in a way that is completely removed from transitory social roles. MacIntyre sees these moves as amounting to fundamentally the same thing:

Both see the self as entirely set over against the social world. For Goffman, for whom the social world is everything, the self is therefore nothing at all, it occupies no social space. For Sartre, whatever social space it occupies it does so only accidentally, and therefore he too sees the self as in no way an actuality. (MacIntyre 1981, p. 31)

This argument supposes that selves are products of historical manufacture and that the mode of their manufacture depends in some profound way on the ideas which philosophers and social scientists manage to make prevail by whatever special powers they may command. Since our ideas about the self are products of specific historical and ideological conditions, great power is attributed to those who shape those conditions and thus modify our sense of self, as well as our moral sense.

MacIntyre suggests that the Aristotelian conception of life, with its concern for the *telos* of a person's being, provided ground for morality and at the same time a morally constraining definition of selfhood. When the hold of the Aristotelian view was broken by the Enlightenment, it was no longer possible to align the virtue of the self with reason, for the overarching *telos* of human life is now rejected. In its place we have the elevation of reason—as a way of finding out truth, as a means of settling questions of fact. But this led immediately to "emotivist" doctrines on the origin and nature of values, morals, and goodness. Since questions of value are not resolvable by the enlightened methods of applied reason, their origins are not considered to have either consistency or coherence. Values and morals thus divorced from reason are quite ungrounded. MacIntyre argues that both Kant and Kierkegaard tried desperately to restore some ground for morality—the first through positing the criterion of "universalizability" as a means for determining the moral legitimacy of any action. If for Kant moral choices are product of a categorical imperative, for Kierkegaard the emphasis is on the agency of choice itself. Faced with the competing values of aesthetic self-indulgence and ethical self-restraint, the individual for Kierkegaard is compelled to choose—but it is not a choice compelled by reason. In different ways, then, Kant and Kierkegaard attempt to rescue morality for the self—the self which as product of the Enlightenment was found stripped of its *a priori* purpose for being, and thus immersed in anomie and liberty at the same time. But these attempts, says MacIntyre, were failures. It was Nietzsche who most powerfully and cogently showed these attempts to ground morality to be a sham. In *The genealogy of morals*, he characterized *all* previous attempts at human moralizing to be based on a profound immorality. It was Nietzsche, MacIntyre argues, who showed the abject moral nakedness of post-Enlightenment philosophy. Nietzsche mocks our ethical pretensions—and he mocks truly and with great effect— for there is nothing in the emotivist soul to make any serious claim to a grounded virtue. The psychological sequel to this moral surrender, which Nietzsche seems to demand, is cynicism, lack of will (what James referred to as *abulia*), a sense of lack of meaning or purpose in life. Thus the way is prepared for the existential anarchy of Jean-Paul Sartre as well as the hollow-selved impression managers of Erving Goffman.

MacIntyre argues that this new emptiness was made inevitable by the determination of those who survived the brutal human extermination of the spirit in the trenches of World War I that "nothing was ever going to matter to them again" (MacIntyre 1981, p. 40). There may be a similar sequence of psycho-logic between the massive genocidal horrors of World War II and a self-indulgent, self-complacent, consumer-oriented, narcissistic "me generation" of the 1970s, 1980s, and 1990s. Nietzsche had shown that all moralistic responses to answer seriously the pervasive question, "Why not?" were false pieties. And it is Erving Goffman, says MacIntyre, who is the modern apostle of Nietzsche's brilliant but caustic criticism of conventional morality.

Since MacIntyre claims that the distinctively modern self was a product of social and historical invention, he considers it to be possible, at least in principle, to invent a postmodern self to which some *telos* is restored. His book is intended as a move in this direction.

This is not the place to decide how much of this sort of argument is intellectual pretension and how much is worthy of claiming our belief and assent. I note only that many voices are now claiming that our view of self should in fact be rescued from the sociologists, and thereby be made to have a place for inwardness and perhaps even for purpose. Many examples of this sort of plea can be cited. Gergen (1982) suggests that the new view of the self is that of the active agent, to be contrasted with the traditional conception of passivity or reactivity. The self, for Gergen, is a moment-to-moment improvisation, with an independence of and even mastery over the impinging stimuli of the environment. Tyler concludes a review of modern theories of the self by suggesting, "Each individual represents a different sequence of selective acts by means of which only some of the developmental possibilities are chosen and organized" (Tyler 1978, p. 233). Sarbin (1976; 1993) has developed an extensive contextualist view of human conduct, in which both self and role combine in the context of meaning—a view which departs radically from the dominant, mechanistic worldview of traditional psychology. Juhasz (1983) has provided a brilliant sketch of how our conceptions of identity are at once personal, social, and human, participating necessarily in timeless requirements of our nature. Juhasz argues that no matter what history does to our social identity, the requirements for human identity are the same as they were for Aristotle and will always be the same. Thus, there may be no need for the restoration of a *telos*, only a recognition of it.

Psychologists are becoming literate again—in the sense in which I have earlier used that term. Some of the more challenging and fresh views of self to have emerged in the recent literature suggest that the self is author of its own story—an active, participating agent in the process of prospective construction (Gergen and Gergen 1983; Breakwell 1992). This line of thinking is in some ways an extension of Goffman's perspective, though it certainly is more upbeat. The narrative view of self also makes extensive use, perforce, of human stories as they are found and displayed in novel, drama, and poem. The literary critic and drama theorist, Kenneth Burke, was an influence in Goffman's thinking, and his influence is increasingly evident in recent writings on the self.

To return full circle, I note a conspicuous resurgence of interest in William James, not just as a historical point of reference, but for the substance of his ideas about self. The metaphor of the stream and the notion of self as active agent are elements enjoying renewed favor. In this sense, psychology has rediscovered its self. In the period of its disappearance from psychology, the self was somehow preserved within sociology, leading to the work of Erving Goffman. Upon its return to psychology, the self seemed to want some restoration of balance—between the social selves that comprised only a part of the Jamesian stream and the thinker's active core.

NOTES

1. Mead's assessment of Cooley's social psychology is carried in a footnote in the chapter on Self, and bears repeating here in part:

His psychological method carried with it the implication of complete solipsism; society really has no existence except in the individual's mind, and the concept of the self as in any sense intrinsically social is a product of imagination. Even for Cooley the self presupposes experience, and experience is a process within which selves arise; but since that process is for him primarily internal and individual rather than external and social, he is committed in his psychology to a subjectivistic and idealistic, rather than objectivistic and naturalistic metaphysical position. (Strauss 1956, p. 258)

2. In 1979, Wylie published a second volume on the self-concept, subtitled, "Theory and Research on Selected Topics." It consists of 825 pages, including over 4,500 citations. The tenor and conclusions of the second volume are entirely consistent with those presented in the first volume, though the survey of research is much more extensive and recent.

3. Personality psychologists do seem to be reaching some consensus on the universals of human personality. Hogan (1982; see also Hogan and Cheek, 1983) has identified a core group of traits as consistently emerging within the literature on personality assessment. Also, much attention is currently given to the "big five" personality traits, which represent something of a consensus on how human personality is to be described (John 1990).

Chapter 3

Socialization: The Formation of Identity

Children need people in order to become human.
                                        —Urie Bronfenbrenner

INTRODUCTION: WHAT IS SOCIALIZATION?

Texts and handbooks on human development offer their most assured generalizations about neonates and very young children. As behavior patterns and problems are discussed for each succeeding age level, generalizations become more and more highly qualified. The relative frequency of words like "if," "may," and "perhaps" increases markedly as puberty is discussed, and most texts give up the task of offering generalizations by age levels somewhere in the middle of adolescence. Parents are often amazed at the accuracy of description provided by Dr. Spock (1957). Young psychologists are equally amazed at how well Piaget's (1952) generalizations about cognitive development seem to fit what is occurring in their own children. But no book on adolescence has the surety of Dr. Spock's book on baby care, and at adolescent stages of cognitive development—particularly the stage of "formal operations"—psychologists begin to bicker with Piaget about possible cultural or idiosyncratic restrictions in his generalizations about mental functioning. Age-bound generalizations about psychological functioning make a tentative appearance again at senescence. Geriatric psychology, properly a part of developmental psychology, begins to recapture some of the descriptive assurance of neonatal psychology, one end of life being as certain and simple as the other.

But in the mid-range of life the possibilities for variation are enormous. No single volume—indeed, no library—could provide a comprehensive description of the psychological possibilities associated with the thirtieth year of human life. A large part of the task of psychology is to render an account of how developmental differentiation occurs. Used most abstractly, socialization refers to the developmental differentiation occurring in the individual as a result of the way that person is treated by the representatives of the surrounding society. In common usage, the term is more limited, referring primarily to the evaluative dispositions which the individual develops as a result of interactions in society. Thus, becoming a Yankee fan is a result of socialization, while learning who the Yankees are, although clearly a socially mediated process, is not ordinarily considered to be an example of socialization.

The intent of this chapter is to discuss the mechanisms, process, and content of socialization. Particular reference will be made to the development of valued loyalties to institutions such as the nation. Passions and politics are evidently closely connected, especially in times of national crisis. A major component of a person's identity is formed by the development of values about political institutions.

What socialization is defined to be can be made clearer by referring to the common distinction between beliefs and values (Scheibe 1970). Beliefs refer to questions of fact, questions about that which exists, what happened in history, or what might happen in the future. The term belief is the broadest generic label for a whole class of cognitive dispositions—expectations, hypotheses, or subjective probabilities. In the aggregate, a person's beliefs amount to one's functional knowledge about the way the world is put together and one's own place in that world. Future-oriented beliefs (expectations) act as guides to behavior, as operative behavior maps which tell the person what leads to what and what is likely to be the consequence of a contemplated course of action.

If beliefs answer to questions of fact or possibility, values answer to questions of preference or desirability. What is good? What do I want or like? What is right (in a moral rather than a factual sense)? The term value is the broadest generic label for human motivational dispositions—wants, desires, needs, preferences, loves, and hates. Functionally, values also operate in the direction of behavior, not as maps but rather as forces which attract and repel an individual with respect to the regions in the mapped portion of the world. To have a goal is to have a positive evaluative disposition toward some particular identifiable object or state of being.

A moment's reflection is sufficient to note that a number of values might be connected with a simple act, such as eating an apple. These values might include the positive value of acquiring nourishment, providing beneficial gum stimulation, "keeping the doctor away," providing employment to fruit pickers, or demonstrating solidarity with a new back-to-nature political movement whose chosen symbol is the apple. As a further complication, we note that values do not exist in a vacuum but refer to the content of knowledge or beliefs.

In a general way, a person's decisions may be considered to be consequences of beliefs and values, of what is considered to be true or likely and what is considered to be best or preferable. This paradigm is common to a wide variety of behavioral theories and is not a flagrant departure from common sense. People do what they want to do if they think they can. Of course, finding out what people want and what they think are formidable problems.

A good deal of psychological theory has been written and research done on the mechanisms by which the cognitive and emotional dispositions of the person combine with the configuration of influences presented in a particular behavior setting in such a way as to produce behavior. In fact, this may be considered to be one of the two major problems in psychology. The other problem, by no means secondary, is the developmental one to which reference has been made: How does the person come to have the particular cognitive and motivational dispositions which influence behavior? How are beliefs and values acquired? The problem of the development of beliefs is the problem of cognitive learning. The problem of the acquisition of values is that of socialization. Socialization is also a form of learning, but one in which the product is not knowledge but changed evaluations of persons, things, or events. Socialization refers to moral development in the broadest sense.

Surely there is a hidden supposition in this particular use of socialization. The supposition is that most behaviorally operative values have social origins, that they are acquired in some way from the social milieu of the developing person. This is why one rarely sees discussions of the so-called primary drives—hunger, thirst, and other tissue needs—in discussions of socialization, for it does not seem plausible that these operative values are social in origin. As we shall see later in this chapter, the sorts of values generally discussed under the heading of socialization are of a "higher" sort—moral values, or values having reference to human interaction.

Socialization is responsible for dramatic differences in moral standards over cultures. In a comparison of socialization in the old Soviet Union and the United States, Bronfenbrenner (1972) describes an example of a kind of moral socialization which would seem very peculiar by American standards.

The schoolroom poster shown in Figure 3.1 depicts a youthful Pioneer (a Soviet version of a Boy Scout) publicly exposing a bit of misbehavior of an unfortunate colleague:

As the drawing indicates, being truthful includes, as one Soviet educator preferred to put it, "expressing one's opinion publicly about a comrade's misconduct." (Note that the shamed seatmate had carved his name on the desk.) But there is a poster within the poster. It depicts a serious-faced Pioneer named Pavlik Morozov. Although the name is unfamiliar to most Westerners, it is a house-hold word in the U.S.S.R. A young Pioneer during the period of collectivization, Pavlik denounced

Figure 3.1
A Pioneer Tells the Truth and Treasures the Honor of His Unit

his own father as a collaborator with the Kulaks and testified against him in court. Pavlik was killed by people of the village for revenge, and is now regarded as a martyr in the cause of communism. A statue of him in Moscow is constantly visited by children, who keep it bedecked with fresh flowers, and many collective farms, Pioneer palaces, and libraries bear his name. (Bronfenbrenner 1972, p.47)

If one is socialized to one set of value standards and is judged by another set, then the consequence is sharp moral conflict—a profound disagreement about what course of action is right or makes sense. Another example, this one drawn from G. B. Shaw's fictionalized account of Christian martyrdom, illustrates this point from a slightly different perspective. In the play *Androcles and the Lion*, the following conversation occurs between Lavinia, one of the Christian martyrs, and a Roman Captain, who is speaking to a group of Roman legionnaires and their Christian prisoners:

Lavinia: Captain, is there no hope that this cruel persecution . . .

Captain: [*unmoved and somewhat sardonic*] Persecution is not a term applicable to the act of the Emperor. The Emperor is the Defender of the Faith. In throwing you to the lions he will be upholding the interests of the religion in Rome. If you were to throw him to the lions, that would no doubt be persecution. . . . I call the attention of the female prisoner Lavinia to the fact that as the Emperor is a divine personage, her imputation of cruelty is not only treason, but sacrilege. I point out further that there is no foundation for the charge, as the Emperor does not desire that any prisoner should suffer; nor can any Christian be harmed save through her own obstinacy. All that is necessary is to sacrifice to the gods, a simple and convenient ceremony effected by dropping a pinch of incense on the altar, after which the prisoner is at once set free. Under such circumstances you have only your own perverse folly to blame if you suffer. I suggest to you that if you cannot burn a morsel of incense as a matter of conviction, you might at least do so as a matter of good taste, to avoid shocking the religious convictions of your fellow citizens. I am aware that these considerations do not weigh with Christians; but it is my duty to call your attention to them in order that you may have no ground for complaining of your treatment or of accusing the Emperor of cruelty when he is showing you the most signal clemency. Looked at from this point of view, every Christian who has perished in the arena, has really committed suicide. (1962, pp. 437–38)

This is an unfortunate sort of conflict, for everyone involved seems to be acting from the best of motives, according to the kinds of values to which they have been socialized. The example is particularly useful because it illustrates the generalizability of values within a particular social role. Becoming a Christian is a transformation in identity, a taking on of a new role, with an accompanying shift in regulative norms. Similarly, becoming a

Roman captain or a Roman emperor is a transformation of identity entailing the acceptance by those who take these roles of the kinds of values that are considered to be appropriate. Also, this example illustrates the effect of certain cosmological beliefs on the evaluation of behavioral options. The decision of the martyrs not to forsake Christianity is a rational one if they believe the teaching of Christianity about the way this world is related to the next. As the Romans do not share this belief, they are continually astounded at the courage and almost jovial mood of the Christians. The behavior of the Romans also seems silly to the Christians, who do not believe there is anything divine about the emperor and hence feel that there is no value in being loyal to him or his officially sanctioned religion.

Much of the human conflict we see about us can be understood as the direct consequence of contact between individuals or sets of individuals who have been socialized to differing versions of what is truly valuable in the world. From a partisan point of view, wars are almost always seen as conflicts between good and evil. From a more detached perspective, the same wars can be seen as conflicts between two different versions of good. But there is no perspective, however detached, which does not carry with it norms or values which may be applied to persons, events, and ideas. One may be socialized, for example, to the role of scientist, which is supposed by many to be a value-free sort of identity. It may be value-free in the sense that the ideal scientist may have a greater respect for the quest of scientific truth than the scientist has for any political ideology or religious creed. However, the scientist has a creed, and an ethic: that it is good to know things, that it is good to exchange information freely, that human beings must continually strive to know more and more about nature, and that anything which competes with science for scarce resources is suspicious. It turns out that this is also a form of parochialism, increasingly recognized as such as the era of magical enamoration with science passes into history.

The root problem for socialization theory and research is to develop an understanding of how individuals come to adopt the values which guide their behavior. Necessarily, this involves a consideration of the person's social identity, the configuration of roles with which he has become associated in the process of development. Necessarily also, this entails a consideration of creeds and political ideologies, because these seem to form bases in beliefs about the real world from which important value judgments are drawn.

The content of the values to which human beings can be socialized is enormous. In some cultures, people can eat snails; in others, dogs and monkeys; and in others, people become sick at the idea of cooking beef to eat. In some cultures, infanticide is practiced without moral compunction (Neel 1970); in others, euthanasia is practiced for old people; and in others, aborting a one-month-old fetus is considered to be a mortal sin. But whatever their content, it is obvious that human societies are dependent upon the continual transmission from one generation to the next of value standards. Socialization occurs and, indeed, must occur in order for human societies to survive and prosper.

The anthropologist LeVine (1969) has argued that the norms transmitted through socialization practices have survival value for societies in the Darwinian sense, although the understanding of a particular norm within a culture may have no relation to the function it serves. LeVine cites as an example postpartum taboos on sexual intercourse, which were often considered—in underdeveloped societies such as parts of Kenya and Nigeria—to be based on the possibility that semen might contaminate the milk of the nursing mother or that evil spirits could enter the nursing infant as a result of intercourse with a lactating mother. From a modern scientific perspective, it makes more sense to view the postpartum taboo as a way of insuring a longer period of nursing, which enhances the child's chance of survival. Of course, it is perfectly possible that a social norm which has evolved in this functional way may lose its significance as conditions in the world change. For example, it may be that the strong veneration many societies have evolved for the nuclear family may no longer make the same sense in the modern technological world as it once did, when the means of production and distribution of goods and services on the face of the earth were in a more primitive condition.

It is clear that a significant portion of adult activity is devoted to attempts at influencing the course of development of their offspring. The continuity of human society seems dependent upon a constant effort of adult members to mold and shape new members of society. The object of socialization is to instill (or install) behavioral controls in each succeeding generation. This process begins at birth and probably continues throughout almost the entire lifetime of a person. As a person emerges from one stage of life into another, new values are assumed as appropriate to the new stage. Examples of such human developmental stages are childhood, puberty (menarche), adolescence, adulthood, old age (menopause), and senescence. To some extent, the enumeration and description of these stages is a matter of established cultural convention. Ariès (1962) suggested that children were once regarded as miniature adults rather than as a separate category of beings, as is currently the case. Keniston (1970) has suggested that in the post-World War II era a new phase of life has been created between adolescence and adulthood—a phase of life which he calls "youth." What makes a stage of life distinguishable are the particular kinds of social norms which are associated with it; whatever these are, they must comprise the evaluative content toward which succeeding generations of entrants are socialized.

Intriguing psychological problems can be identified for all these levels of consideration of socialization. The special focus of this chapter will be upon the kind of socialization represented in the examples of Pavlik Morozov and of the characters in Shaw's *Androcles and the lion*. More specifically, the interest will center upon the way in which a political or quasi political system determines the values to which individuals are socialized. But before embarking on a discussion of the mechanisms of socialization and the process of political socialization, it will be appropriate to make a few additional conceptual distinctions and to sketch in some of the history of socialization theory and research in psychology.

SOME CONCEPTUAL DISTINCTIONS

Socialization can be studied and described on the level of mechanisms, processes, contents, and—by way of contrast—compared with other kinds of psychological development.

Mechanisms

The mechanisms of socialization refer to the means by which changed evaluative dispositions occur in the individual. For example, the social psychologist Zajonc (1968) argues that familiarity with social stimuli increases the judged attractiveness of those stimuli. He has shown that frequency of exposure determines the judged attractiveness of human faces (Saegert, Swap, and Zajonc 1973; Heingartner and Hall, 1974). Generalizing from this principle, one might suggest that at least one of the mechanisms for socialization involves the frequency of exposure of stimulus materials to the developing person. Alternatively, the classic stimulus-response (S-R) position on mechanisms of socialization gives central importance to the principle of reinforcement, whereby stimuli come to acquire attractive properties by being paired in presentation with other stimuli such as food or water which have primary drive-reducing properties.

Still another mechanism is suggested by Harlow's (1971) work on the development of "love" in infant monkeys. Harlow finds that the provision of nutriment has little to do with the developing affectional bond between a mother monkey and her infant. Instead, such properties of the mother as softness and warmth are instrumental to the development of positive affective bonds. In Harlow's experiments, surrogate mothers made of terry cloth drew more affectionate regard than surrogate mothers made of wire, even though the latter devices were fitted with bottles for feeding and the former were not. Although Harlow does not name the mechanism responsible for the diversification of affectional responses in monkeys, he has demonstrated the presence of a natural maturational sequence for the species. Because development to the successive stages of this sequence is dependent upon the presence of specific conditions or stimulus configurations, the mechanism might be referred to as "conditional maturation," with the understanding that the conditions necessary for progressive affectional development are specific to a given species.

Yet another kind of socialization mechanism is described by Freud and those in the psychoanalytic tradition. Freud considers the basic relationship between the individual and host society to be one of enmity. Civilization prohibits the individual from directly satisfying instinctual urges. But in the course of development a person becomes "civilized" through the introjection of the standards of civilization. The basic mechanism for the acquisition of these standards is identification, whereby the child takes as its own such values as are presented to it by the agents of society, most notably, its parents. In *Civilization and its discontents*, Freud (1930/1962) speculates on the manner in which civilization is built up as a cumulative effect of the renunciation of individual instincts. The individual is forced to identify with society in order to maintain psychic economy. Through social learning the individual is transformed into an agent of society.

Modern social learning theorists consider one of the major mechanisms of socialization to be imitation, a concept which has much in common with identification (Mussen 1967). In the course of development, a child is exposed to a set of models who exhibit their values in their behaviors. Bandura, Ross, and Ross (1963) have shown that behaviorally operative values are acquired through direct observation of models, without the implication that the children have identified with the models, in the psychoanalytic sense of that term.

Finally, role-playing is widely regarded as a means by which socialization is accomplished. A child playing with imaginary playmates or enacting a make-believe role comes to recognize the legitimacy of particular kinds of social norms in the regulation of social behavior (Sarbin and Allen, 1968).

It is unlikely that any one mechanism of socialization is responsible for the acquisition of the entire range of social values. Also, it should be clear that the use of the term "mechanism" is metaphoric. No one has ever observed the details of the mechanical or chemical process, presumably on the neurological level, which is associated with a shift in values. One observes, instead, certain regular associations of antecedent conditions with subsequent shifts in behavior. A "mechanism" is described in a way that fits this observed association. Familiarization, reinforcement, conditional maturation, identification, imitation, and role playing are examples of such terms.

Socialization as Process

If several or many mechanisms are involved in the socialization of an individual and if innumerable events have socializing consequences for the person, then socialization may be described as a long-term process, the evolution or development of values in the person. The anthropologist views the process of socialization as enculturation. The sociologist sees it as the acquisition of social norms, and the psychologist as the learning of values or as moral development. Of course, all refer to different aspects of the same general process, which goes on no matter what it is called and regardless of how badly it is understood. A good sense of the process of socialization can be gained from extended case studies of individuals. Good psychological biography achieves a convincing description of how a person's values took their characteristic form. Some examples of this form are Erikson's *Young man Luther* (1958) and *Ghandi's truth* (1969). Additional examples are George and George's (1956) study of Woodrow Wilson or Freud's (1916/1964) study of Leonardo da Vinci. Collective case studies offer descriptions of the developmental history of classes of individuals. For example, MacKinnon offers the following composite picture of the background of creative architects:

An extraordinary respect by the parent for the child, and an early granting to him of an unusual freedom in exploring his universe and in making decisions for himself; an expectation that the child would act independently but reasonably and responsibly; a lack of intense closeness between parent and child so that neither overdependence was fostered nor a feeling of rejection experienced, in other words, the sort of interpersonal relationship between parent and child which has a liberating effect upon the child; a plentiful supply in the child's extended social environment of models for identification and the promotion of ego ideals; the presence within the family of clear standards of conduct and ideas as to what was right and wrong; but at the same time an expectation, if not requirement, of active exploration and internalization of a framework of personal conduct; an emphasis upon the development of one's own ethical code; the experience of frequent moving within a single community, or from community to community, or from country to country which provided an enrichment of experience, both cultural and personal, but which at the same time contributed to experiences of aloneness, shyness, isolation, and solitariness during childhood and adolescence; the possession of skills and abilities which, though encouraged and rewarded, were nevertheless allowed to develop at their own pace; and finally the absence of pressures to establish prematurely one's professional identity. (1965, p. 280)

Of course, more careful, controlled, and exhaustive observations can be made on other species of animals. As Harlow (1971) and Goodall (1971) have shown, primates are rewarding to watch, since they resemble man in many ways but have a relatively short developmental period.

Harlow's book, *Learning to love*, is a composite description of the process of socialization as it occurs for groups of rhesus monkeys raised in his laboratories at the University of Wisconsin. Harlow notes that the affectional responses of monkeys develop through four distinct periods, which he refers to as maternal love, age-mate or peer love, heterosexual love, and paternal love. Harlow emphasizes the dependency of this progression on specific social events and circumstances in the development of the young monkey. For example, if a young monkey does not have a fair amount of contact and interaction with a mothering monkey, its heterosexual affectional responses do not emerge properly later in development. The process of socialization for monkeys—and most assuredly for human beings—is well described as a progression of stages. The way in which one stage of development is realized determines the potential for socialization at the next stage.

The Content of Socialization

Socialization, then, is a process which occurs over the developmental history of the person and is accomplished by one or more of a set of mechanisms for transforming social influences into changed dispositions of the person. But what is the content of socialization? How might the range of evaluative dispositions which are the product of socialization be described?

According to anthropologists (Ford and Beach, 1951), the taboo against incest is universal. If we presume that individuals are not born with an automatic repulsion toward sexual relations with near relatives, then this norm must be the product of socialization. Through some mechanism—whether it be accounted for in terms of the Oedipus complex, conditioning theory, or role theory is of little importance for the present—a process occurs whereby individuals come to hold negative values toward incest. This does not mean, of course, that incest does not occur in human society; it most certainly does. But part of the universal content of socialization is the incest taboo.

Other universal contents of socialization could be enumerated—prohibitions against in-group aggression, nurturance and support for helpless infants, norms for protection from out-group aggression, and so on. But the known range of cultural diversity in social norms means that the process of socialization can produce fantastically diverse contents. Even within a given society, the content of socialization varies tremendously.

Consider a brief list of social types in our own society: the playboy, the ambitious executive, the middle-American, the yuppie, the artist, the dope addict, the revolutionary, the healer, the preacher, the wise old man, the prostitute, the politician, the professor, the groupie. Each of these labels evokes an idea of the content of socialization. The content of the rules by which people in these categories live varies enormously, but all of them live by rules of some kind, that is, by regular, recurrent evaluative standards which are invoked as ways of deciding upon possible courses of behavior.

A substantial contribution to research and theory on socialization was made by Kohlberg and his co-workers at Harvard University who attempted to develop a characterization of the process of socialization by describing, at a somewhat abstract level, the content of socialization at various stages of development. Kohlberg's characterization of moral de-

Table 3.1
Classification of Moral Judgment into Levels and Stages of Development

Levels	Basis of moral judgment	Stages of development
I	Moral value resides in external, quasi-physical happenings, in bad acts, or in quasi-physical needs rather than in persons and standards.	Stage 1: Obedience and punishment orientation. Egocentric deference to superior power or prestige, or a trouble-avoiding set. Objective responsibility.
		Stage 2: Naively egoistic orientation. Right action is that instrumentally satisfying the self's needs and occasionally others'. Awareness of relativism of value to each actor's needs and perspective. Naive egalitarianism and orientation to exchange and reciprocity.
II	Moral value resides in performing good or right roles, in maintaining the conventional order and the expectancies of others.	Stage 3: Good-boy orientation. Orientation to approval and to pleasing and helping others. Conformity to stereotypical images of majority or natural role behavior, and judgment by intention.
		Stage 4: Authority and social-order maintaining orientation. Orientation to "doing duty" and to showing respect for authority and maintaining the given social order for its own sake. Regard for earned expectations of others.
III	Moral value resides in conformity by the self to shared or shareable standards, rights, or duties.	Stage 5: Contractual legalistic orientation. Recognition of an arbitrary element or starting point in rules or expectations for the sake of agreement. Duty defined in terms of contract, general avoidance of violation of the will or rights of others, and majority will and welfare.
		Stage 6: Conscience or principle orientation. Orientation not only to actually ordained social rules but also to principles of choice involving appeal to logical universality and consistency. Orientation to conscience as a directing agent and to mutual respect and trust.

velopment is based largely on the logical features of Piaget's theory of cognitive development. Specifically, Kohlberg has proposed that "universal and regular age trends of development may be found in moral judgment, and these have a formal-cognitive base. Many aspects of moral judgment do not have such a cognitive base, but these aspects do not define universal and regular trends of moral development" (Kohlberg 1969, p. 375). The stages which Kohlberg believes are universal and general are listed in Table 3.1.

Kohlberg has gathered evidence from long-term studies in the United States which show that this sequence of moral development is, in fact, characteristic. A child at an early stage of development will apply moral standards that derive from immediate consequences, whether punishment or praise is likely to follow from a given action. At an intermediate stage of development, the child will obey rules which are general and attempt to "live up to standards." At the latter stages of moral development, the child questions arbitrary standards according to general principles of justice and morality which he has evolved. It is important to note two things about this progression: First, the content of morality becomes more and more abstract, general, and "decentered," as development occurs. Second, the general progression of development is considered by Kohlberg to be in a positive moral direction, that is, he approves of the higher stages of development. The implication is that procedures should be devised to encourage as much development of abstract morality as possible.

By no means is development to the highest stages of morality inevitable. Since development through stages is dependent on a complex series of social interaction within each stage, development may be retarded or arrested at any point. Kohlberg notes that development to the higher stages of moral development is faster and more frequent in the United States than in the other cultures he has studied, such as Taiwan, Turkey, and Mexico. Also, middle-class children show a faster rate of moral development than do lower-class children. But rate of moral development is no respecter of religious faith: Christians, Buddhists, Jews, Muslims, and atheists are not found to have different rates of progress through Kohlberg's stages.

In order to clarify the kind of moral content that is characteristic of Kohlberg's progression, it is instructive to consider an example from the early work of Piaget (1932), who is the acknowledged inspiration for the extensive research and theory accomplished by Kohlberg. Piaget undoubtedly spent many hours as a boy playing the game of marbles. Later, he was to make systematic observations of the way little children play marbles, and he noticed a fascinating progression in the way in which the children seemed to regard the rules of the game at different ages. The very youngest children had to be taught the rules, and their adherence to the rules of the game had to be constantly enforced. That is, they seemed to be operating on a moral system that depended upon constant external provision of rewards and punishments in order to keep their behavior within legal bounds. Somewhat older children did not have to be constantly sanctioned in order for them to play by the rules. They knew the rules and adhered to them strictly without threat of punishment for infractions and without special incentives for playing honestly. But for these children, the rules seemed absolutely given; they were presumed to be the only legitimate rules, permitting no modification or questioning. Still older children were able to realize that rules made by men can be changed by men and frequently made modifications of the rules to suit particular occasions or to increase the variation and interest in the game. All the while, the content of the moral rules used by children pertained, in this case, to the playing of the game of marbles. But the nature of that content was seen by Piaget to have exhibited a characteristic evolution or development in the direction of "decentration." For example, in the cognitive domain, Piaget showed that children become able, at a certain stage, to imagine what a landscape would look like from another geographic perspective. In the moral domain, he was able to show a similar progression. The higher stages of moral development, for both Piaget and Kohlberg, consist of an ability to shift perspectives and imagine consequences, to treat various concrete situations with great flexibility but with a consistency of application of general abstract principles of morality.

A major qualification to the generality of Kohlberg's posited stages of moral development is suggested by Gilligan (1982) in her book *A different voice*. Gilligan observed that Kohlberg's theoretical progression makes no allowance or differentiation by gender. Her own research shows that men and women in our culture differ in the way they make moral judgments, differ in their moral sensitivities, and that Kohlberg's progression is not an adequate descriptive account of the content of socialization for women. Gilligan's research shows, for example, that women place a higher value on affiliation than do men, while men are more interested in individual achievement.

Both Kohlberg and Gilligan point out that the content of socialization is much broader than consistently applied moral rules. Most of the value judgments which individuals make, even though they are at the highest level of moral development, are not systemically derived from some consistent set of principles, of whatever kind. In fact, one of the best documented facts about the contents of socialization is that such contents are not terribly consistent over time. Individuals who are honest in one situation, for example, simply may not be depended upon to be honest in a different situation. The conclusion of a classic series of studies by Hartshorne and May (1928–1930) was that honesty is not a general trait. In ordinary academic situations, for example, a large proportion of college students will cheat on an examination when given the opportunity to do so. Such an opportunity arises, for example, when students are allowed to grade their own exams; when the teacher has surreptitiously corrected them previously, but without making any marks on the paper, this cheating can be detected.

Referring again to the example cited at the beginning of this section, the taboo against incest may very well be universal. But the observance of this taboo is not universal, that is, behavior does not follow unequivocally from general social norms. Still earlier in this chapter, it was emphasized that many values are commonly involved in the execution of a very simple action. The same individuals who protest that they would not voluntarily hurt other people for no reason are willing accomplices in an experimental situation in which they are required to administer what appears to be severe punishment to another person (Milgram 1963). Persons who would not think of themselves as killers of other men can be made to kill other men by first being initiated and trained into the role of soldier. Soldiers who think of themselves as honest and uncorrupted can still be made to falsify documents in order to cover up some unsavory incident if it appears that the orders for falsification come from legitimate sources. Zimbardo has shown that college students recruited to be prison guards for a psychological experiment quickly become cruel and persecute their prisoners in a way that later surprises them (Haney, Banks, and Zimbardo 1988). Over 900 people died in the Jonestown massacre in 1978 and scores were killed in the Branch Davidian complex in Waco, Texas, in 1993. These events illustrate the power of the social situation in drastically modifying the operative values guiding individual choices and behaviors.

That Which Socialization Is Not

The point of these last examples is to demonstrate that no unequivocal relation exists between general socialization and behavior. It is a mistake, albeit an inviting mistake, to think of the process of socialization taking place in a cumulative and directed way, so that at any given time the person is consistent and defined and will act to give clear expression to evolved values. Such a conception overlooks the tremendous effect that variations in roles play in modifying the behavior potential of the person. Also, this conception greatly oversimplifies the relation between values and behavior. We must admit that socialization is not the only, or even the major antecedent to social behavior.

Other qualifications should be placed on the concept of socialization. Certainly socialization should be considered subsidiary to psychological development; the terms are not synonymous. The kind of unfolding or maturational development described by Gesell (1954), for example, is not appropriately called socialization. The neuromuscular maturational sequence which leads to head-lifting, rolling over, sitting up, crawling, standing, and walking is certainly influenced to some extent by the way in which the infant is handled. However, this sequence is relatively invariant over cultures and is in no clear way related to later evaluative dispositions of the person. It would also be strained usage to think of language acquisition as a product of socialization, even though the particular language learned is clearly a function of social stimuli and even though language, as an abstract symbol system, undoubtedly plays a large role in the mechanisms, process, and content of socialization. Of course, how a person speaks, to whom he addresses commands and requests, whether he speaks at all in certain circumstances, and the forms of speech and types of inflection used in social settings is a matter of socialization. That a child speaks is not a matter of socialization; that he does not speak in the company of certain elders or during certain ceremonies is definitely a result of socialization.

This way of talking about socialization presumes no specific position on the question of the genetic determination of behavior. It is not necessary to assume, as the early behaviorists did or as Skinner (1971) suggested, that any well-formed baby can be brought up to be just about anything its enlightened trainer wanted it to be. Indeed, strong presumptive evidence exists that the development of both cognitive and motivational dispositions in the person are conditional upon the form of the given genetic stuff.

To recapitulate this section, socialization refers to a part of psychological development. It is accomplished by mechanisms such as identification, conditioning, familiarization, or role learning. The mechanisms of socialization result in a process by which the individual comes to incorporate in some unique way a set of evaluative possibilities which are displayed or taught by the social host in which development occurs. The result is a set of constantly evolving evaluative standards, consisting partly of stable principles, partly of a medley of constantly fluctuating preferences and tastes. Socialization does not produce a sharply defined set of constant values in the individual, though the individual might evolve some consistent and enduring principles. Some theorists, such as Piaget and Kohlberg, have suggested that the general direction of development of such principles is away from egocentrism and toward general principles of evaluation such as justice, equity, and consistency.

The next two sections of this chapter are devoted to a consideration of examples of the mechanisms and process of socialization. First, attention will be directed to the best-developed series of empirical studies on socialization mechanisms, that of Albert Bandura and his colleagues at Stanford University. Then the process of political socialization, alluded to already several times in this chapter, will be discussed.

SOCIALIZATION THROUGH OBSERVATION

Yogi Berra is credited with the remark "You can learn a lot just by watching." This simple idea has the germ of common sense. But it would have been derided by most orthodox psychologists a generation ago, because the accepted position was that nothing is learned by mere observation. Indeed, it was thought that practice and reward were necessary conditions for the occurrence of learning. Any learning occurring without practice or reward was referred to as "incidental." Fortunately, modern psychologists are likely to give Mr. Berra due credit for his wisdom on how to learn.

While Freud certainly recognized the imitation by children of value standards of their parents, modern experimental confirmation of imitation learning was provided in the 1960s at Stanford University (Bandura, Ross, and Ross 1963). This research, initiated by Albert Bandura, is based on a simple experimental paradigm. The subject, usually a nursery school child, is allowed to observe the behavior of a model (the experimenter, in the role of "teacher") in some novel circumstances. The model displays a carefully prepared set of critical behaviors or expressions when engaged in some activity. A control group of children is given preliminary experience with the activity, but without the critical set of behaviors shown by the model. Later all subjects are given an opportunity to engage in the activity by themselves, not in the presence of the model. Performances are scored by observers for the number of critical behaviors exhibited by the model which are imitated by the children. For example, a model may hit an inflated doll with a bat, while uttering the appropriate expressions, "Biff!" "Take that," and so on. Bandura found that the observing children later exhibited these same behaviors when given an opportunity to do so. Clearly, the relationship of the child to the model is of some importance, since it is obvious that children don't go around imitating every bit of behavior they see when given the opportunity to do so. Also, characteristics of the model are important. Baron (1970) performed a replication of the Bandura experiment, but he varied the attractiveness and the competence of the model. His results showed that both of these variables were important in eliciting imitative responses from observing children.

Throughout his research, Bandura has maintained the distinction between acquisition by the child of the potential to behave in a particular way and the actual execution of that behavior. It seems plausible that the process of acquisition is silent and does not require motoric participation from the subject. Performance occurs only when the occasion arises and when other aspects of the situation are favorable to the evocation of the bit of observed behavior. The implication of this distinction should be clear: A child does not have to practice the social performances he is observing in order to come to recognize their appropriateness. Over time he sees a great deal of social behavior from teachers, parents, older children, television characters, and actors. Role-learning takes place in this way, and children acquire in this fashion a huge quantity of impressions about what kinds of behaviors are appropriate in what kinds of situations. Then, when similar situations arise for them, they draw upon this stock of understandings as a way of guiding their own behavior.

Figure 3.2
Percentage of Change in Approach Behavior, Fearfulness, and Attitudes
Displayed by Subjects Who Received Different Components of the
Modeling-Guided Participation Treatment

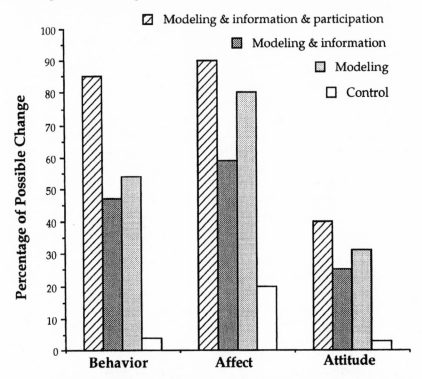

Figure from *Principles of behavior modification* by Albert Bandura, copyright © 1969 by Holt,
Rinehart and Winston, Inc., reproduced by permission of the publisher.

Bandura has extended his research to show that imitation learning takes
place when models are observed not directly but on television or film. In
one experiment, children were shown films of other children being introduced to an inflated Bobo doll by the aggressive model. In another condition, children were shown aggressive episodes of an animated cartoon
figure. The experimenters conclude, "Subjects who viewed the aggressive
human and cartoon models on film exhibited nearly twice as much aggression than did subjects in the control group who were not exposed to the
aggressive film content" (Bandura 1963, p. 370).

In addition to showing that aggressive responses can be imparted via
imitation, Bandura and his colleagues have demonstrated similar effects
with a number of other types of content. For example, children with strong
phobic reactions to dogs were allowed to observe other children interacting
successfully with dogs. In this case, the model was a child, who engaged in

a graduated series of more and more courageous interactions with a dog. Initially the model just looked at the dog and occasionally patted it. At the end of the series he had climbed in the pen with the dog, allowed it to eat out of his hand, and rested his head on it. Observation of the films of these events effectively reduced the displayed avoidance reactions of the children initially phobic to dogs. In an even more dramatic demonstration of the same kind of effect, Blanchard (1969) showed that observations of films in which models handled snakes were effective in reducing the strength of snake phobias in a group of adult subjects who had for many years been troubled by an irrational fear of snakes. Blanchard included four conditions in his experiment, as illustrated in Figure 3.2. In the three experimental conditions, visual modeling of snake handling was present. In one of these conditions, verbal information was added to the visual modeling, and in the third, the subject participated more directly in a graduated approach toward the snakes. It may be seen from the figure that by far the largest effect on changes in approach behavior, affective response, and measured attitude were attributable to the effects of visual modeling alone.

While caution should be exercised in the interpretation of these findings, they constitute at least a dramatic illustration of the way an individual's evaluative behavior may be modified by observation and imitation. In these experiments, the salience, attractiveness, and competence of the model is assuredly high; and because of the nature of the experimental contract, the subject's attention is necessarily directed in the proper way. Under such conditions, the subject is in a perfect situation for vicarious learning. It is as if the subject were engaged in the modeled behavior and may easily observe that no negative consequences are forthcoming. Gradually, as this kind of observation is repeated and extended, the subject acquires confidence in the ability to control fear reactions in the presence of the formerly dreaded object.

The significance of studies of the effects of mere observations on the shaping of aggression and approach-avoidance behaviors is potentially great in our society. We often assume implicitly that nothing children see has any effect on them. The average amount of time an American child, ages two to eleven, watches television is almost twenty-eight hours per week (Comstock 1991, p. 57). Certainly a fair amount of what the child sees, if translated into actual behavior in the appropriate circumstances, would not meet with the approval of parents, who spend far fewer hours per week with the child than do his televised companions and models. Bronfenbrenner has suggested that parents in the United States seem to have abdicated their role as the main socializing agent for children. In a cross-cultural survey involving several nations, only the English were found to spend less time with their children or to express less concern over the child's development and activity.

The controversy on the relation between televised violence and aggression in children should be something of an embarrassment to social psychology, for the results should have appeared far less controversial in terms of determining the factual character of the relationship. The study by Bandura, Ross, and Ross on the effect of filmed aggression has already been cited. Additional studies showing the instigating effects of vicarious aggression have been performed by Berkowitz (1964) and by Berkowitz, Corwin, and Heironimus (1963). While these are all laboratory studies which might be criticized because they do not reproduce natural viewing conditions, a nonexperimental study by Eron, Lefkowitz, Huesman, and Walder (1972) shows a strong relation between the amount of violence observed on television and later aggression. This study was based upon a longitudinal survey of over 400 teenagers, in which viewing habits were assessed over a ten-year period of time. The main dependent variable was peer-rated aggression. This variable was strongly related to the preference for watching violent television programs. As to the enduring quality of this effect, the authors conclude, "It was found that the violence of programs preferred by the male subjects in Grade 3 was even more strongly related to aggression ten years later" (Eron, Lefkowitz, Huesman, and Walder 1972, p. 263).

The relation between observed violence and aggressive behavior is not, however, a settled issue in psychological research. Feshbach and Singer (1971) have published a major experimental study which showed no such effect, except as reflected in the fantasies, not the behaviors, of the television-exposed subjects. A study by Geen and Stonner (1973) has shown that the aggression-instigating effect of observed violence is dependent on both the state of the subject (attacked or nonattacked) and the particular meaning of the depicted violence (vengeance, "professional" violence, or unexplained). The position taken here is that some relation exists between observed violence and aggressive behavior and that television is thus implicated in the causal chain for at least some aggressive acts. The details of this relationship are not well established. Yet a consensus exists in research reviews that the relation between observed violence and exhibited aggression does exist (Friedrich-Cofer and Huston 1986; Comstock and Strasburger 1990).

The implications of socialization through imitation are not all negative. Evidence is in hand that altruism as well as aggression is influenced by observational learning. Bryan and Test (1967) have provided a series of illustrations that behaviors such as contributing to beggars and Salvation Army pots are positively influenced by the priming behaviors of models. Probably auctioneers and hustlers of all varieties have known of this phenomenon for ages. The "shill" is someone who wins conspicuously at a gambling house, eagerly makes the first purchase of a worthless lot in Florida, or bids with happy abandon at an Atlantic City sidewalk auction parlor.

Experimental evidence also shows that subjects can be induced to dissent from participation in an apparently noxious procedure by observing models initiate the breaking of the experimental contract (Feldman and Scheibe 1972). When no models exhibited dissent behavior, no subjects dissented from participating in a procedure which was perceived as being unpleasant.

SOCIALIZATION AS ROLE LEARNING

These observations on the imitation mechanism of socialization can be readily accommodated in the language of social role theory. While the classical study of learning mechanisms and processes has had only the most distant potential application to the problem of social learning, the kind of research just described is clearly related to what is meant by role-learning. Sarbin and Allen assert,

In role-learning, the importance of persons enacting complementary roles, the importance of teachers, models, and coaches, and the importance of relevant audiences cannot be overemphasized. In fact, this role relationship itself deserves careful analysis. . . . Research on role-learning must deal with the particular kind of learning that occurs in interactional settings and must recognize the complexity of the content of the learning, the pervasiveness of the influence of other persons, and the crucial importance of the role relationship itself. (1968, p. 545)

The metaphor of the drama employed by role theory encourages us to think of the child as a fledgling actor, someone who is actively trying to learn the parts required of an adult in society. A conventional distinction is made within role theory between roles which are granted or ascribed to a child immediately, through no exercise of option on the child's part, and roles which are attained or achieved. Occupational roles and professional attainments are not ascribed but are achieved as a result of choice and of confirming, validating actions. Sex, kinship, race, and sometimes religion are ascribed to the child. But even though these are granted components of the child's identity, he or she must learn the kinds of behaviors appropriate for that which the child already is. Sex-role training begins at an early age, perhaps as soon as the child is born (Kagan 1964). Similarly, the child must learn all the rules of behavior that go with being a member of a particular family, church, race, or social class. Socialization accomplishes an accommodation of the child to the requirements of each of these ascribed roles. In this process, the function of individuals in complementary role positions—parents, teachers, nurses, coaches, and trainers—is of critical importance. While the acquisition of labels for ascribed components of identity is automatic, learning the behaviors proper to those components of identity requires considerable time and involvement. Moreover, strong negative sanctions are administered for failing adequately to discharge one's duty or responsibility as a son, a member of the family, or a citizen in the community.

Some authors prefer to use the word "enculturation" to describe the learning of achieved or attained roles and to reserve the term socialization for the acquisition of granted roles. While this usage will not be maintained here, it is of interest to consider the distinction which prompted it. Once the skills associated with granted roles are learned, one may behave in society in such a way as to avoid embarrassment or trouble. However, in order to gain special recognition, power, and responsibility in society, it is necessary for special instruction to be given in preparation for the assumption of achieved roles. This latter kind of instruction is much more likely to be considered formal education—primarily verbal presentation of information which is necessary for the assumption of achieved roles. Handbooks, manuals, courses, and degree programs are offered in a pre-packaged way so that a person might gain access to achieved positions such as doctor, lawyer, politician, or truck driver. At the same time, it is considered necessary to impart to the person all sorts of information which will be of no use whatever in the discharge of achieved responsibilities. One must learn about wars, kings, composers, artists, architectural styles, grammatical conventions in various languages, styles of dress in ages gone by, customs of remote tribes, styles of ancient and contemporary authors, and details of the careers of remote culture heroes. All this "enculturation" may be seen as a forced effort to make one's identity seem to be a great achievement. While the process of socialization to granted components of identity takes place naturally and without great difficulty on the part of the sharply observant child, the process of formal education for achieved components of identity is often onerous and labored.

In the composite, a person's social identity is a combination of that which was granted and that which is attained. A birthright—a life charter—is implicitly granted to a person upon the event of birth. The most powerful lessons to be learned about identity consist in a discovery by the developing child of the terms of his birthright: Who am I? What is my name? What am I given? What are my rights and obligations as a person? Most of the early part of socialization is a matter of the child's becoming that which was called for in the birthright. The evolution of identity continues as the child is taught the requisite skills for entry into achieved roles. For both kinds of role learning, social mediators in complementary role positions are of critical importance.

This conception of socialization as role learning and the earlier description of socialization as moral development (viz. Kohlberg) may be brought together by considering some aspects of the thought of George Herbert Mead, who is critically important to the history of both of these traditions. The title of Mead's (1934) major work is *Mind, self, and society*. Mead's radical thesis is that mind, self, and society come into existence only in relation to each other. Human individuals come into self-consciousness only through social interaction. Mind is social both in origin and effect. Mind and self emerge from the interaction of the protean individual with society. Mead considers socialization to be the essential process by which human beings become human beings. A few quotations from Mead will provide a clearer sense of these ideas:

The individual enters as such into his own experience only as an object, not as a subject; and he can enter as an object only on the basis of social relation and interaction, only by means of his experiential transactions with other individuals in an organized social environment. (Quoted in Pfeutze 1954, p. 92.) The individual is there only through cooperative interaction with others in the community. (Quoted in Pfeutze 1954, p. 57.)

Socialization is identity formation as a consequence of social interaction. The acquisition of roles results in the development of self conceptions. In time, the person is able to view the self, as it were, from outside the self—as mirrored reflections of an objective being. Similarly, the person becomes able to take a broad social perspective when regarding other people or social events. Like Piaget, Mead considers the person to become increasingly capable of attaining a decentered perspective as development proceeds through stages of interaction with others. Social training and moral training are seen as having similar roots.

That which creates the duties, rights, the customs, the laws and the various institutions in human society, as distinguished from the physiological relationships of an ant hill or a beehive, is the capacity of the human individual to assume the organized attitude of the community toward himself as well as toward others. (Mead 1938, p. 625)

The process of role taking is considered to be essential to psychological development and also essential to the development of a mature moral perspective, the kind of perspective represented in the highest stages of Kohlberg's schematization. Playing with other children, playing at imaginary games, and continued involvement with games is moral training, for the individual learns the meaning of social control both as operator and subject and comes to appreciate the norms of justice. "[The self] is constituted by an organization of the social attitudes of the generalized other or the social group as a whole to which he belongs" (Pfeutze 1954, p. 87).

Mead's social psychology is one of the few systems of thought within psychology in which acts of altruism seem sensible and nonparadoxical. The broad social collectivity not only contributes individuality to the person, but it also becomes incorporated into the person. Mature moral judgments are made from the perspective of the "generalized other." This is not an alien perspective to the person, but rather one which has been incorporated and owned. Of course, the extent to which the person has internalized this perspective depends very much on the way in which social interactions take place at the various stages of development. Programs for moral education can be devised in such a way as to maximize the likelihood of a swift attainment of the highest stages of moral development. But now a fundamental problem has been touched: A system of moral education is based on certain premises about human rights and responsibility, indeed, on a particular conception of the idealized nature of human beings. The practice of socialization by each distinct human collectivity is dictated by two kinds of premises: first, by what sorts of techniques are most effective in forming children into the kinds of beings we idealize and, second, by what kinds of beings we idealize. Disagreements on the first score can presumably be settled by the appropriate research on developmental psychology. Disagreements about what people should become, however, are not resolvable by research of any kind, but are ground-level disputations over values.

It is for this reason that political ideologies become conditions of fundamental importance in understanding the process of human socialization. Aside from such technical ideas about child-rearing as may spring from a political ideology, it is sure that the ideology will define the limits of the moral dimensions of socialization. Since political regimes usually control the educational process for children, it is reasonable to suppose that the explicit or implicit ideology of the political regime will be translated into practice through the schools. The modern nation state, as a definer of the law for its people, is also the most potent moral force in society, either implicitly or explicitly. But the importance of the body politic as an institution of socialization is so fundamental that it is often overlooked.[1] The next section addresses this issue.

SOCIALIZATION TO NATIONAL IDENTITY

We hold these truths to be self-evident, that all men are created equal, that they are endowed by their Creator with certain inalienable rights, that among these are Life, Liberty, and the pursuit of Happiness. That to secure these rights, Governments are instituted among Men, deriving their just powers from the consent of the governed. . . .

If the history of the human race were compressed to a day, the time elapsed since 1776 would amount to no more than an eye blink. Although the truths in the first sentence quoted from the Declaration of Independence are laid down as self-evident, it is a good bet that it was not always thus. These truths are the product of a rather highly evolved line of European philosophical thought, the Enlightenment. Two centuries ago they may have seemed arbitrary or debatable assertions, but they are more nearly self-evident now, for their statement has constituted a moral ideal to which succeeding generations in the United States, as well as in other parts of the world, have been socialized.

The second sentence in the excerpt is less frequently quoted than the first, but it is much to the point of this section. Truths once stated do not prevail by themselves. Governments must be established in such a way as to make them prevail. The Declaration of Independence is, after all, a document for the justification of a fraternal war. The justification is drawn from what are set up to be universal moral principles. If those principles are accepted, the justification is successful. Of course, after the war was won the principles were sanctified by blood and remain as a proud expression of the highest ideals of the nation, and the government remains an entity dedicated to the continual securing of these rights. If its initial job was to gain political independence from England in order to implement its ideals, its continuing job is to maintain that independence from all foreign powers and at the same time to socialize succeeding generations of its own people to these ideals, so that the nation is not subverted from within.

Clearly, socialization has failed to achieve its objectives if individuals come to challenge the principle of human equality and the right to life, liberty, and the pursuit of happiness. Subject to their history of socialization, it is difficult for Americans to realize that these ideals do not stand at the moral foundations of all nations and that a different set of self-evident truths may be made to prevail by a different government.

Because international comparisons are likely to impinge upon high passions, it is best to begin with an easier case as an illustration of what socialization to collective ideals entails. A good example is provided by a legal case (*State of Wisconsin vs. Yoder* [1972]) regarding the right of a religious sect, the Amish, to maintain complete control over the education of their children. While the Amish are hardly a nation, their insistence on religious and cultural autonomy makes them a kind of self-contained and unique enclave within the United States.

The Supreme Court case centered on the conviction of three Amish parents by a state court for failing to send their children to school beyond the eighth grade, as is required by law in Wisconsin. The Amish provide their own schools for their children, but they do not continue formal school beyond the eighth grade, when the child is from thirteen to fifteen years old. After this, the young adolescent continues to learn the skills which are considered necessary within the community, but these are imparted in the informal setting of barnyard, house, or shop. The State of Wisconsin considered that it had an obligation, in the words of its chief prosecutor, "to liberate the children from oppression . . . to expose them to the good things in life which the outside world has to offer."

For over two hundred years the Amish have been a self-sufficient segment of society in the United States. Their fundamentalist religious beliefs lead them to avoid contact with the modern world; electricity, automobiles, telephones, and the like are looked upon as unnecessary and corrupting. In the same way, science is not regarded as an activity worthy of human effort, and learning of a non-Biblical variety is looked upon with suspicion. "The social unit is small, communal, and enforced by strict shunning of those who violate community values. Their life-style and daily lives are the expression of their religious worship" (Arons 1972, p. 52). Their educational system is efficient for their purposes. No problems of unemployment, poverty, juvenile delinquency, or crime plague them. Evidently, the socialization techniques they have evolved, completely without the aid and advice of child psychologists, are quite effective.

But without question, the children in the Amish society are denied a certain access to "Life, Liberty, and the pursuit of Happiness." In the *Brown* decision of 1954, the Supreme Court held that separate education of minority groups is inherently unequal. Not only are the Amish children completely segregated from other minorities and the dominant majority in Wisconsin, they are also subject to an unusually strict and well-controlled regime in all phases of their life—at home, at school, or in the community.

A strong argument in favor of the Amish was their long success as an independent community. If certain rights were denied their children, the Court effectively decided on balance that the greater virtue lay in the preservation of their distinctness and affirmed their right to be different. But the Court pointed out that this exclusion would not apply to all. "Chief Justice Burger took pains to exclude from the ruling, 'a group (presumably non-religious) claiming to have recently discovered some progressive or more enlightened process for rearing children for modern life'" (*New York Times*, May 14, 1972).

It is an open question as to whether the Amish could survive as a distinct subculture in the United States without jealous protection of their right to maintain complete control over the socializing regime to which their children are exposed. But survival is surely facilitated by the maintenance of control. Compulsory education was established in the middle of the nineteenth century in the United States, in part as a way of assuring the continued loyalty of the populace. The Amish see the same kind of advantage in the control of their educational system.

The school functions as the primary mechanism by which political socialization is accomplished. Extensive studies on political socialization in the United States (Hess and Torney 1968) yield this general conclusion. The school, here and elsewhere, has the double function of developing the cognitive skills of children and at the same time inculcating in them a veneration for the moral ideals which are held to be fundamental to the nation. What are the techniques by which the child acquires an identification with the nation? And why does this process sometimes not work?

Doubtless most of the readers of this chapter are familiar with the means by which schools in the United States attempt to accomplish an identification of the child with the nation and with the "principles for which it stands." No point would be served by a recitation of the familiar here. It is likely that the process of political socialization can be seen more clearly at a distance. However, for comparative purposes it would be useful to consider one's own experience of political socialization in relation to the account presented in the next section of this process in another culture.

THE GREAT EXPERIMENT IN POLITICAL
SOCIALIZATION: THE U.S.S.R.

In 1991, the Soviet Union effectively came to an end. The Soviet communist regime had attempted, over a period of more than seventy years, a new experiment in political socialization. Now that experiment is over. No longer is the vast area of the former Soviet Union dominated by a single political ideology. It is impossible to say what will emerge from the host of competing national, religious, and ideological interests now striving for influence. But it is instructive to examine how socialization was directed by political creeds in the former Soviet Union.

"In the collective, by the collective, for the collective" is the slogan coined by Makarenko, who was the most widely read and highly regarded authority on the upbringing of children in the Soviet Union. As an ideal for the socialization of children, this slogan represented a bridge between the theoretical ideals of the Soviet state and the actual techniques used to rear children. This slogan also epitomized a difference in cultural ideals between the Soviet Union and the United States, where the emphasis on individual freedom and liberty conflicts sharply with the ideal of collectivization. A study by Bronfenbrenner (1972) of childhood socialization in the former Soviet Union and the United States describes how socialization to these diverse ideals was implemented.

According to Bronfenbrenner, the primary objective of early socialization in the Russian family was to teach the child obedience and self-discipline. The idea was to get the child to obey parents willingly, "fulfilling the wishes of adults not as commands from without but as internally motivated desires" (p. 12). Bronfenbrenner quotes a leading authority on child development on the question of independence training: "What about developing independence in children? We shall answer: if a child does not obey and does not consider others, then his independence invariably takes ugly forms. Ordinarily this gives rise to anarchistic behavior, which can in no way be reconciled with laws of living in Soviet society" (p. 13). Obviously, socialization toward the norm of self-discipline required effective techniques. Those most frequently employed by Soviet parents were withdrawal of love, encouragement and praise, and for older children, verbal persuasion and explanation. Physical punishment was viewed as potentially harmful and was generally avoided. While the technique of withdrawal of love was given great importance, it took place in context of very close and affectionate contact between parent and child. Bronfenbrenner reports that the amount of physical contact of children with their parents and with other adults was far greater in the Soviet Union than it is in the United States. Also, Soviet parents spent more of their nonworking hours with their children. Solicitousness towards children was general in the Soviet Union, not only from parents but also from adolescents and other adults.

In the schools, the norm of collective responsibility was the constant theme, and a method analogous to withdrawal of love, public criticism or, in extreme cases, ostracism, was the primary mechanism for punishing deviations from the norm. Children who attended nursery schools began immediately to play in groups and were taught to perform socially useful acts, such as feeding pets, watering plants, or cleaning floors. Many collective games and activities were organized. All children in the Soviet Union began primary school at age seven. The opening of school was the occasion for happy celebrations, and the teachers were regarded with admiration and respect. In primary school, great emphasis was given to cooperation and group competition. The objective was to teach children to rely on each other and, reciprocally, to assume responsibility for the behavior of others in the group.

The relationship between cooperation and competition as norms of socialization are illustrated in a quotation from a Soviet school manual:

It is not difficult to see that a direct approach to the class with the command, "All sit straight," often doesn't bring the desired effect since a demand in this form does not reach the sensibilities of the pupils and does not activate them. . . . [instead the teacher should say], "Let's see which row can sit the straightest." The children not only try to do everything as well as possible themselves, but also take an evaluative attitude toward those who are undermining the achievement of the row. If similar measures arousing the spirit of competition in the children are systematically applied by experienced teachers in the primary classes, then gradually the children themselves begin to monitor the behavior of their comrades and remind those of them who forget about the rules set by the teacher, not to forget what needs to be done and what should not be done. The teacher soon has helpers. (Bronfenbrenner 1972, pp. 54–55)

The competition for approval was continuous and the emphasis was always on self-monitoring. The example of Pavlik Morozov, the heroic boy who betrayed his father, set the high ideal for Soviet children of placing loyalty to the collectivity above all else, so that the collectivity will prosper. Teachers seem to be quite successful in delegating their authority to classroom monitors, who took seriously their responsibility for controlling infractions.

Bronfenbrenner and his colleagues performed a study in which various kinds of social misdemeanors were described to children. The children were asked what action they would take in relation to an infraction such as stealing something, cheating on an examination, and so on. The answers of children in the United States were found to depend greatly on who they thought would see their responses; they tended to show little or no concern with the infraction if they thought their responses would be seen by their peers. Soviet children, by contrast, showed no such differential. Their classmates were just as effective as parents or teachers in controlling misbehavior.

Apparently, the techniques for controlling misbehavior were quite effective. Incidents of antisocial behavior in the schools were rare by our standards. Of course, the techniques used to enforce good behavior also appear to be morally repugnant by standards in the United States.

For example, a fifth-grade boy who is having difficulty with his mathematics is made the subject of a class discussion. After considerable debate, a girl proposes that two students be assigned to the struggling student to help him. He protests:

"I don't need them. I can do it myself. I promise." But Lyolya is not impressed. Turning to Vova, she says quietly, "We have seen what you do by yourself. Now two of your classmates will work with you and when *they* say you are ready to work alone, we'll believe it." (Bronfenbrenner 1972, p. 65)

Another example is provided in a description of a third-grade classroom, drawn from a Soviet school manual:

Class 3–B is just an ordinary class; it's not especially well-disciplined nor is it outstandingly industrious. It has its lazy members and its responsible ones, quiet ones and active ones, daring, shy, and immodest ones.

The teacher has led this class now for three years and she has earned the affection, respect and acceptance as an authority from her pupils. Her word is law for them.

The bell has rung, but the teacher has not arrived. She has delayed deliberately in order to check on how the class will conduct itself.

In the class all is quiet. After the noisy class break, it isn't so easy to mobilize yourself and to quell the restlessness within you! Two monitors at the desk silently observe the class. On their faces is reflected the full importance and seriousness of the job they are performing. But there is no need for them to make any reprimands: the youngsters with pleasure and pride maintain scrupulous discipline; they are proud of the fact that their class conducts itself in a manner that merits the confidence of the teacher. And when the teacher enters and quietly says to be seated, all understand that she deliberately refrains from praising them for the quiet and order, since in their class it could not be otherwise. . . .

"What are you fooling around for? You're holding up the whole link," whispers Kolya to his neighbor during the preparation period for the lesson. And during the break he teaches her how to organize better the books and pads in her knapsack.

"Work more carefully," says Olya to her girl friend. "See, on account of you, our link got behind today. You come to me and we'll work together at home." (Bronfenbrenner 1972, pp. 59–60)

Kohlberg (1971) quotes a similar incident as an example of socialization to the norm of fundamental group loyalty. But Kohlberg is critical of the line of philosophic thinking, identified with Durkheim as well as Marx, which leads to the justification of these techniques.

We see . . . that when this line of thinking is carried to its logical conclusion, it leads to a definition of moral education as the promotion of collective national discipline which most of us feel is consistent neither with rational ethics nor with the American constitutional tradition. What I am arguing is that the trouble with [this approach] is not that [it] starts from a conception of moral development, but rather that [it] starts from an *erroneous* conception of moral development. (p. 28) (emphasis added)

To be sure, this kind of collective control does seem to be inconsistent with the norms of individual autonomy so prevalent in the United States. Also, Kohlberg's suggestion that these techniques are inconsistent with American constitutional liberties certainly seems plausible. But in what sense is this "an erroneous conception of moral development?" Certainly not in a technical or factual sense is the conception erroneous: It stands the pragmatic test of giving just about the kind of results its administrators intend to produce. But in a moral sense, it does deviate from the norms to which Americans have been socialized. The hottest place in the American version of Hell would be reserved for the likes of Pavlik Morozov. Anyone who has taken a realistic view of the way "honor systems" function in American institutions must conclude that students do not assume a great deal of responsibility for the success or honesty of their peers. "Do your own thing" is a modern American motto, and privatism a way of life.

In their introduction to a volume of essays on *Moral education*, Sizer and Sizer (1970) summarize American morality in this fashion:

The moralisms of the prairie have a strong hold on the large remnant of Middle America. Nixon's "forgotten American" learned much from simple sermonizing. For a class of people it worked; it took hold. *But was it moral? . . .*The answer is a qualified no; sermonizing denies individual autonomy, which, with justice, lies at the heart of a new morality. (p. 3)

Later these authors describe the new morality as follows:

Moral autonomy, the independent arrival at a conviction of one's accountability toward one's fellow men, the rational and emotional acceptance of justice as the most proper atmosphere in which all individuals can flourish, including even one's secret self—this is the "new morality" toward which we are to guide ourselves and other people. (p. 4)

Although this is not the place to enter a critique of the meaning of justice as an abstract moral principle, it is sufficient to recall the speech of the Roman Captain in response to Lavinia in Shaw's *Androcles and the lion*, wherein he makes it clear that the determination of what is just rests upon prior suppositions about who is divine.

The moral autonomy part of the "new morality" is given clearer expression in a quotation attributed to the late Fritz Perls, founder of the Gestalt therapy movement:

I do my thing and you do your thing. I am not in this world to live up to your expectations, and you are not in this world to live up to mine. You are you, and I am I; if by chance we find each other, it's beautiful. If not, it can't be helped. (Perls 1969, p. 4)

This is certainly a far cry from the Soviet slogan, "Mine is ours, ours is mine." Soviet children were socialized to the idea that they were responsible to the expectations of their peers. If they failed to live up to these expectations, the result was public criticism and perhaps rejection by the group. It is a good bet that children raised in the United States would have made poor citizens of the Soviet Union, and vice versa. The former would have been ostracized socially for their individualism, and the latter would have been pilloried for acting as finks for the system.

Speculations on the consequences of technological advance, migration to the city, and the decline of religious institutions have their place in discussions of the evolution of contemporary moral standards in Western society. Human institutions and the moral force carried by them are not fixed entities but are constantly in flux. However, our concern here is not with the cultural history of current moral standards but with the ways in which those standards come to influence the process of socialization for individuals. Those interested in the cultural history of current moral standards might consult the previously cited set of essays edited by Sizer and Sizer or the collection of essays by Lifton (1971). In the next section, attention is directed to some of the consequences for individuals of contemporary moral standards in the United States.

CONTEMPORARY PROBLEMS IN SOCIALIZATION IN THE UNITED STATES

If primary socialization is performed by those institutions which grant to the individual the ascribed components of identity, then concern is justified about how well the task of primary socialization is being performed in the United States. The United States is increasingly a secularized society; organized religions maintain little of the authority they once held. It is no secret that the nuclear family is breaking down: one out of every three marriages ends in divorce (Cooper 1970). Those families which do remain together do not set permanent roots in the community: One out of every five families in the United States may be expected to move each year. Book titles in the social sciences are clues to this condition: in *The temporary society* (Bennis and Slater 1968) Americans are engaged in a *Collective search for identity* (Klapp 1969). Americans are becoming a nation of existential nomads, restlessly trying on new life-styles and new identities with the aid of the therapeutic and the cosmetic industries.

One institution which might continue as the ultimate definer of individual birthrights is the United States. But during the Vietnam and Watergate eras, the nation seems somehow to have squandered its legitimacy in the eyes of many of its youth (Keniston 1968).

Studies of the psychological histories of men of draft age who chose to go to prison or to Sweden or Canada in preference to serving in the armed forces during the Vietnam war are paradigms of ambiguous political socialization (Gaylin 1970; Borgida 1972). Between 1965 and 1971, between 60,000 and 70,000 men immigrated to Canada alone, as a way of avoiding or escaping military service.

Borgida (1972) interviewed a number of draft dodgers and deserters in Toronto:

For the draft dodgers and deserters, the draft and military service created a role conflict between the national role demands for supreme loyalty to nation and the salience of other social roles, primary group ties, or moral and ethical principles.... For example, one twenty-five-year-old draft dodger from the Midwest did not define his obligation to the nation as a military obligation: "My obligations to society are that I be a productive member of it in some respect. But to fight a battle for the government—no!—especially if I don't agree with the end or aims." Similarly, a draft dodger who had completed one year of graduate study before he left the United States and came to the Toronto area, felt that his only "supreme loyalty" was to himself: "I didn't feel that I had to serve in the Army to fulfill the obligation to my country. I didn't feel it was a necessary obligation to do something like that for my country." . . . Most of the dodgers and deserters interviewed strongly believe that "The government has no right to impose the draft on a man's life and, in effect, demand that he fight in a war which he regards as particularly illegitimate and immoral," said a dodger whose father is a Southern Baptist deacon. (pp. 8–9)

Of course, these individuals and those like them who found other solutions to the problem of avoiding military service were still a small minority of their age group. At the peak of youth protests against the war in Vietnam, a Survey Research Institute study of attitudes among high school students showed the overwhelming majority to be in support of their government's position and expressing a willingness to serve in the armed forces if called (Johnston and Bachman 1970). But it is quite clear that all the emphasis placed on the development of the morally autonomous individual in our society has had consequences. A large number of the young people in the United States simply refused to march to the nation's drums, when called upon to do so.

IN CONCLUSION

This chapter has construed the process of socialization basically as the evolution and development of values in the individual. From a slightly different perspective this amounts to the formation of a social identity. At this stage of our knowledge about the way in which developmental changes are encoded in the human organism, it is inappropriate to consider this process to be the result of a single, identifiable mechanism. Among the mechanisms by which socialization occurs are familiarization, identification, imitation, and the direct administration of social sanctions—punishments and rewards. At each stage of his development, the individual has an operative set of values which function both as a way of choosing among possible courses of action and as a way of defining the self in relation to other people and social institutions.

Most of the research and thinking within psychology in the past on the topic of socialization has been oriented around the question of mechanisms. While these are problems of fundamental significance, they are no more fundamental than the question of the relation of socializing institutions to the developing individual. While considerable concern has centered on the institution of the family as a socializing influence, little work has been done within psychology on the effect of broader social institutions such as political collectivities on socialization. Yet these institutions effectively set the ground conditions for the objectives of socialization within a society.

In the context of contemporary conditions within the United States, it makes sense to reaffirm the obvious proposition that experiences and examples to which developing individuals are exposed will have consequences on their moral development. It makes sense to say this, because implicitly we have believed the contrafactual proposition that the influences to which children are exposed don't much matter. The null hypothesis has been that the observation of violence on television will have no consequences, that the shift of the custody of the child from the parent to the television set will have no consequences, that the breakup of marriages and the disruption of community stability encouraged by modern corporate emphasis on mobility will have no consequences, that allowing cities to become overpopulated and decrepit will have no consequences, that the destruction of venerable landmarks and places of quiet beauty in the interest of progress will have no consequences, that avoiding our children will have no consequences. In all of these cases the null hypothesis is most certainly false. However, the alternative hypothesis, which describes the true relation between each of these manipulations or events on the process of human socialization, is in most cases not known. But it is perilous to assume, because the precise effects are unknown, that no negative effects are likely to occur. Just as the changes wrought by humans in the physical environment produce readjustments in the ecology which extend over hundreds of years, so will changes in the social developmental milieu for human beings produce unanticipated consequences which will continue to be realized for a considerable period of time.

Bronfenbrenner has suggested as one measure of the moral development of a civilization the amount of concern one generation has for the next generation. Even given the enormous cultural differences in the content of social norms, the constant factor of directed concern of parents for the upbringing of their young continues to produce a modicum of humanization for each generation of our species. Perhaps the specific direction of socialization is less important than the fact that it is directed. The care devoted to children will determine the extent to which those children, as adults, will be capable of caring.

NOTE

1. An exception to this neglect is provided in the work of Adelson and his co-workers, which is descriptive of the significance of political ideas in the process of moral development. (Gallatin and Adelson 1971; Adelson, Green and O'Neil 1966.)

Chapter 4

The Transvaluation of Social Identity

The purpose of this chapter is to present a model of social identity that will clarify the processes of social degradation and the processes of social enhancement—upgrading.[1] Degradation and upgrading are forms of transvaluation—a reorganizing of the valuations declared on a person. As such, they are relevant to theories of individual and social change.

The model is an organizational heuristic. It organizes the social upgrading and degradation processes into three dimensions which can be represented as a geometric figure. The theoretical model is a convenient way of organizing generalizations about the process of social transvaluation. These generalizations have to do with the mechanisms of actual transvaluation. Of course, certain values must be presupposed in order for any conception of social transvaluation even to be advanced. Slavery is wrong, basic human rights should not be abridged, society should offer everyone the means of social advancement, people should not gratuitously harm others, and so on. It might be said that these sorts of value judgments are absorbed from the social and cultural context of our times. No author can stand outside of the structure of these values when offering a way of organizing observations about how the process of social transvaluation occurs. This is a major caveat, for the values of this time and place might seem unquestionable, but are certainly context specific. The political correctness of one generation is the outmoded dogma of the next.

As a further qualification, because a person may have many evaluating audiences, no one valuation of that person is uniquely appropriate. Valuations involve both subjects and objects. The same person may be quite differently valued by the several social judges for whom the person is an object. If there were such a thing as an organized and extensive dominant society or "establishment," it would seem that a person could acquire only one valuation. Indeed, the settings of many total institutions allow only one established authority to make declarations of value on individuals. For example, only prison officials have the authority to value prisoners. Similarly, individuals' valuations of themselves—their self-respect and self-esteem—will depend upon the particular reference group or groups that are important to them. One of the prime contributions of reference group theory and research has been to demonstrate that individual self-valuations vary over time as a function of variation in reference groups (Hyman and Singer 1968). Reference group theory has also illuminated the paradoxical independence of individual discontent and apparent well-being (Stouffer 1949; Pettigrew 1964). People may not be able to think well of themselves unless they know that they are accepted by their peers. The modulating effect of reference groups on individual valuation is a basic premise for all our arguments. The systematic propositions to be developed concerning the process of social transvaluation will clarify modulating functions of reference groups.

Basic observations for the process of social transvaluation are many. Degradation is illustrated in the treatment meted out to convicts, patients in mental hospitals, prisoners of war, political rivals, members of minority groups, traitors, and the disreputable poor. Advancement is illustrated in the ceremonies of job and school promotion, election to office, wedding celebrations, prison pardons, and the honoring of heroes.

By application of these social procedures of degradation and promotion, human beings acquire differential valuation. This differential valuation, as we shall demonstrate, has powerful implications for the conduct of individuals and groups. The consequences of degradation are the loss of freedom, loss of respect, loss of esteem, and limitations on power and privilege. The consequences of promotion are increased esteem, increased freedom of movement, and an expanded set of powers and perquisites.

SOCIAL ROLE THEORY

The theoretical idiom of choice for these issues is provided by modern social role theory (Sarbin and Allen 1968). In order to avoid a common misunderstanding that derives from the use of the dramaturgical idiom, it is important to assert that role enactments are not, and need not be, considered trivial, superficial, or artificial performances. The candidates competing for the office of president of the United States are in equivalent social positions. But when one is elected, inaugurated, and assumes the functions of the office, and the other is defeated and relegated to some secondary professional activity, great social and psychological distance comes between them. Such psychological effects are demonstrable, and the use of role theoretical language to describe these events should create no impression of artificiality.

In the arguments to be set forth, the underlying premise is that a person's social identity at any time is a function of his or her validated social positions. These positions are validated through appropriate, proper, and convincing role enactments. The model provides a means of comparing different patterns of roles that are specific to different individuals or to the same individual at different times.

The beginning postulate is that people's survival depends on their ability to locate themselves accurately in their various ecologies. Efficient behavior choices depend on the correct placements of self in the world of occurrences. Among the various ecologies into which the world may be differentiated is the social ecology or role system. People are constantly faced with the necessity of locating themselves in relation to others. Misplacement of self in the role system may have embarrassing, perilous, or even fatal consequences.

The self is located in the role system through an inferential process. On the basis of available clues, individuals infer the role of others and concurrently of themselves. A homeward-bound pedestrian, late at night, may locate herself as a potential victim of assault at the same time as she locates another pedestrian as a potential assailant. This process of location in the role system may be described as the formulation of answers to the recurrent question *Who am I?* The answers to this question mean nothing without explicit or implicit answers to the questions *Who are you?* or *Who is he?*

H. A. Mulford and W. W. Salisbury (1964) provide an empirical illustration of the way self-conceptions emerge in response to this question. Subjects were asked to reply to the question, "Who are you?" Their answers were commonly constructed in role terms: "I am a physician," "I am a husband," "I am a citizen," "I am a prisoner," and so forth. It must be emphasized that such answers are footless if they are not ratified through actual or symbolic interaction with occupants of complementary positions. The declaration, "I am a physician" requires as a sequel that healing acts be directed to patients. The assertion, "I am a father" is valid only if the person has at least minimal interactions with his children. Thus one's social identity is defined as the multiple product of attempts to locate oneself in the role system—symbolically represented by asking and answering the question "Who am I?"

It follows that planned or unplanned changes in role relationships will modify inferences about social identity because they provide people with different information concerning who they are. That is, one's location in social space is different when one is interacting with an adult or with a child; with a police officer or with a victimizer. Such induced transitory modifications in social identity should not be confused with the substitution of one identity for another. How far social identity may be modified by changes in social reference individuals and groups is a question that should properly remain open.

Consider this example. A recent graduate from high school, perhaps alienated in his local version of the standard average American culture, applies to enter the Jesuit order and is accepted. He enters the novitiate, renounces all his worldly goods and goes into retreat. A month later, he emerges a "new man," a Jesuit novice.

A degraded denizen of skid row joins Alcoholics Anonymous. After achieving the "twelve steps," he emerges as a respectable, teetotaling citizen.

A United States Army officer is captured in combat. Despite the incontrovertible facts that characterized him as patriotic, loyal, and trustworthy, after six months of brainwashing, he tapes a series of broadcasts denouncing his country.

Given such well-formed shifts in identity, the proposed model makes it possible to determine their evaluative significance.

The necessary features of the model are expressed in terms of three dimensions. These jointly describe a solid of roughly specifiable shape. The shaped model is a device for illustrating the relationships among variables. While the metric significance of the dimensions is weak, the generally important relationships can be clearly represented in this manner. The three dimensions are (1) the status dimension, (2) the involvement dimension, and (3) the value dimension.

Status

A *status* is an abstraction defined by the expectations held by members of the relevant society. *Role* is a set of behaviors enacted by an individual in an effort to make good his or her occupancy of a particular status. Another way of considering the distinction between these related concepts is to regard status as a cognitive notion—a set of expectations. Role, on the other hand, may be regarded as a unit of conduct, characterized by overt actions.

R. Linton (1936) was the first to make the conventional distinction between ascribed and achieved statuses. Some statuses are given: they are ascribed to a person by virtue of sex, age, race, and kinship. Other statuses are achieved by following decisions made by the person or by other people. This distinction, which many authors have found convenient and acceptable, is not sufficiently clear, since the differentiating criteria for achieved and ascribed statuses have never been explicitly specified. However, even using the major implied criterion in Linton's distinction—the presence or absence of choice—it would seem that the classification of statuses should be more than two-valued.

The term *ascribed* implies granted or given. In the discussion that follows, the term *granted* will frequently be used as a synonym for the more opaque term *ascribed*. The term *achieved* has a surplus meaning in current usage that does not always contribute to the sense of this discussion. The terms *attained* or *selected* will generally be used in its place.

There are two difficulties with Linton's dichotomous conception. First, he specifies no criteria for deciding whether a given status is granted or attained. Second, in many instances, both factors contribute. Is the sex role of the successful transvestite granted or attained? How about the role of the father who deserts his family and establishes himself as a bachelor? Does the natural successor to a king win his position by ascription or by achievement? These and other difficult cases may be dealt with consistently if social statuses are regarded as falling along a continuum based upon the degree of choice prior to entering a given social position. Thus, occupying a given status may under some circumstances be a great attainment and under other circumstances be completely taken for granted.

The degree of choice for any status is determined by considering two factors—the number of alternatives available to the actor, and the degree to which these alternatives are optional. More choice is exercised entering the position of lawyer than before entering the position of factory worker. The potential lawyer may choose, at least theoretically, many positions below that of lawyer in the occupational status hierarchy. The potential factory worker has fewer occupations from which to choose. Similarly, less choice is involved in becoming a parent than in becoming a godparent. The social forces toward parenthood are more compelling than those toward godparenthood.

The term *choice* is used in a sense that is consistent with selectivity. It does not mean freedom or lack of determining constraints. Decisions may be made for or about a person who is placed on the path to great attainments. One may have little sense of choosing one's own destiny. Nonetheless, choice operates to a very high degree in the development of virtuoso attainment. For during the course of this virtuoso's life, many selective decisions must have been made that helped him or her to attain high status.

Social statuses and their corresponding roles can be ordered with respect to optionality. For any society, the position of "cultural participant" is placed at the granted end of the status continuum—so are sex roles, age roles, and kinship roles. Occupational and recreational roles, such as a member of the Book-of-the-Month Club, member of the Socialist Party, and physician, are placed at the other end.

Granted roles may be further characterized as less differentiated and as applying to many members of society. Thus every person is initially granted the role of cultural participant. As such, the person is expected to act according to certain basic rules of propriety that preempt the requirements of any particular attained position. This grant carries with it the legitimacy of claims for certain inalienable rights.

Each person is born with a birthright. This includes a set of political rights bestowed without regard for prior accomplishment or ability. In the United States, the Bill of Rights, together with other written and unwritten principles, constitutes a large part of each person's birthright. This initial endowment determines the minimal expectations that are consistent with status as a human being. It also determines the rights and privileges of being human within a particular granting structure—the dominant society. Of course, birthrights are not necessarily bestowed equally. The birthright of slaves in the United States did not include any "human" rights. Slaves were defined as chattels (cattle), and their status was that of a nonperson. The Emancipation Proclamation was an instrument that granted certain minimal human rights to former slaves. That is, it granted them the right to be treated as people. It is sadly instructive to note that legal provisions influence, but do not control, the granting of human rights.

The concept of fundamental human equality, the origin of which Cassirer (1946) attributes to the Stoics of ancient Greece, is a prescriptive injunction against the withholding of a human birthright from any person on *a priori* grounds. The kind of social progress represented or instigated by the Magna Carta, the Declaration of Independence, the Nineteenth Amendment to the Constitution, and the Civil Rights Act of 1964 is an approach to this ideal.

At the other extreme of the status dimension, highly attained roles are richly differentiated and apply to relatively few members of society. Examples are Supreme Court Justice, violin virtuoso, or Secretary General of the United Nations. Legitimate power and social esteem accrue to occupants of attained positions.

The placement of a role along the status dimension is a matter of the observers' collective judgment regarding the degree of choice the person exercised before entering a social position. Because shared values and experiences are readily apparent, individual portraits of the social structure may be blended into a common conceptualization.

Roles can be placed along the status dimension in another way—selectivity, a probability of attainment. A certain probability of attainment exists for every distinct social position. Probability, in this context, has the conventional relative frequency interpretation. The probability associated with a position is determined by the proportion of individuals who opt for a position and attain it. The odds of any American being drafted into the military forces during wartime are perhaps five in 100. The odds of becoming a general are perhaps two in 250,000. The higher the *a priori* odds against placement in a given social position, the more attained the role. Thus the degree of attainment is often reflected in the relative number of individuals in various positions. There are always more Indians than chiefs, privates than generals, tellers than bank presidents. More students make it into large state universities than are accepted by selective colleges.

Before an achieved position is occupied, choice is exercised by several means. A person attains a position by election, nomination, special training, responding to a revelation or "calling," volunteering, or demonstrating some special skill. In each case, the process of promotion to the achieved position is reciprocal. The person must choose (or at least accede), and at the same time the relevant social reference groups must recognize and certify the promotion. The initial choosing is done by the person or by the social reference groups, or by both. Achievements are a joint product of *choosing* and of *being chosen*. The selectivity involved in both of these choosing processes compounds to form the degree of choice prior to achievement. This degree of choice is the means of indexing the location of a given position on the status dimension.

To recapitulate, a person's social identity is composed of a number of roles located at different points on the status dimension. To approximate a full description of a given social identity, the person's validated social positions are listed. Such listings can be used to infer how much legitimate power the person has, or to predict his or her conduct. However, the significance of status for a theory of conduct must be understood in relation to involvement and valuation.

Involvement

The second major dimension to be considered is *opportunity for variation in involvement*, or simply *involvement*. Role enactments vary in the degree to which the actor is involved in the role. But statuses also vary in the extent to which they allow variations in role involvement.

Involvement is considered a dimension of the intensity with which a role is enacted. When involvement is low, role and self are clearly differentiated, few organismic systems are activated, and the actor expends little effort in enacting the role. When involvement is high, self and role are undifferentiated, the entire organism is activated, and the actor expends a great deal of effort. Sarbin and Allen (1968) identify eight levels of involvement. An example of zero involvement would be a lapsed membership in a club in which a person spent no time, by which one would never think to identify oneself, and which required absolutely no effort. An example of midrange involvement would be stage acting, "playing the part." Examples of level eight involvement would be ecstasy, possession, and mystical unions. Cases of voodoo death, bewitchment, and magic-induced illnesses are examples of extremely high involvement in the role of victim. In these cases, involvement is so total that normal social and physiological regulatory mechanisms are blocked.

Time is an index of role involvement. A role is highly self-involving if the person is "in the role" most of the time. Being "in the role" means engaging in activities that are role specific. Thus the role of adult female, for example, is highly self-involving because it means being "on" almost continuously. While the organismic involvement required of the Sunday sailor is temporarily high, this is not a very self-involving role because little time is spent actually sailing. On the other hand, sailor is an extremely self-involving role for a professional yachtsman, for he devotes a great deal of time to the role enactment.

Some roles (such as person, male, mother, and daughter) demand more or less constant involvement. Others, especially some occupational roles, call for cyclical involvement. Involvement is high when a worker is on the job. Involvement lapses temporarily with coffee breaks and work stoppages, and may disappear altogether at the end of the day to reappear only when the whistle sounds the following morning. Cycles are daily (worker), weekly (churchgoer), monthly (lodge or club member), annual (taxpayer), or even longer. Furthermore, cycles may be regular, as in the examples cited, or irregular, as wedding guests, hostesses, or airline passengers.

In short, role involvement varies situationally and temporally. It varies widely for some positions and little for others. The problem is to account systematically for these differences. Our observations suggest that variability in role involvement is a function of placement on the status dimension. The closer a status is to the granted end of the continuum, the less potential it has for *differential* involvement. Conversely, the closer a status is to the attainment end of the continuum, the more role involvement will vary.

For the ultimate ascribed role—that of person or human being—it is difficult to imagine less than continuous high involvement. Occasionally people lose involvement in the role of person through meditation, disease, or the use of drugs. But our language has almost no words to describe this condition. People are expected always to behave in a way that is consistent with their culture's definition of human nature. Role enactments deviating from the cultural definition of human nature cause the actor to be classified as the negative counterpart of a civilized human. This, however, does not relieve the actor of continuous high involvement. He or she is defined as a substandard or beastly being, and involvement remains virtually complete.

Attained roles, on the other hand, are put on and off like cloaks. Most attained roles are cyclical, and while intense organismic involvement may be demanded for certain periods, it rarely lasts very long. A professional baseball player is highly involved in his role when he is on the diamond, in spring training, or reviewing batting averages. He is relatively uninvolved in it when he is attending a funeral, writing letters, or visiting friends.

Involvement can be as high at the attained end of the status continuum as at the granted end. While a man is President of the United States, he is just as involved in that role as he is in the more granted roles of human being, man, and citizen. But any attained role includes the opportunity for complete disinvolvement—for escape. The resignation of Richard Nixon from the presidency is a case in point. Opportunities for disinvolvement are fewer for granted roles.

This posited relationship between potential for variability in involvement and the status dimension is roughly represented by a triangle. The triangle comes to a point at the granted end of the dimension. (See Figure 4.1.) In the

Figure 4.1
Opportunity for Variation in Involvement Related to Status

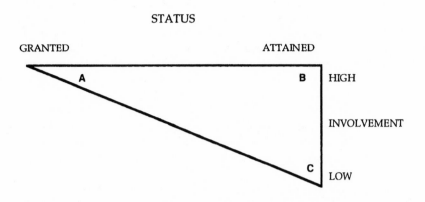

relatively totalistic setting of prisons, mental hospitals, and forced labor camps, opportunities for variation in involvement are restricted. In these settings the statuses are heavily weighted with ascriptive features, and involvement is typically high—not by choice, but by the demands of the situation. The social identity of a member of these classes does not include many attained roles, the enactment of which may be cyclical. When one's identity is composed exclusively of granted roles, one cannot obtain role distance (Goffman 1959). That is, when people are enacting a granted role, they are "on" all the time. They have little or no opportunity to gain distance to view their conduct from the perspective of another role.

Valuation

Positive and negative valuations bear an orderly relation to status and involvement. The valuation dimension is constructed at right angles to the status and involvement dimensions. Like them, it is a continuum. It is marked with a neutral point and positive and negative limiting extremes. The prime question is: What is the relation between potential gain and loss in the value of a social identity and various statuses and various levels of involvement?

This conception of valuation has some distinctive features. First, the valuation of social identity and corresponding psychological well-being is not unitary. It is a composite whose components have different significance and prominence at different times. On the level of observation, this varying composite corresponds to mood changes, or in extreme cases to manic-depressive swings.

Second, the mere identification of a person with a position has no necessary implications for the value the person gains from that position. Thus one may say, for example, "Jones is a philosopher." But the role of philosopher may be more or less attained and more or less involving. Moreover, the constellation of validated roles within which philosopher appears as one component of identity may impart to that component more or less weight. If a person is gaining no social value at all from his or her other statuses, the role of philosopher carries great weight.

Third, physical well-being and psychological well-being are not the same. Consider candidates for martyrdom who feel a lot better than they should according to their objective circumstances, and upper-middle-class neurotics, who feel much worse than their circumstances would seem to warrant. Both represent paradoxes that will be resolved by the working out of this conception.

Consider first the range of potential valuation applicable to the occupancy of attained statuses, which is the right portion of the straight line in Figure 4.2. Valuations declared on nonperformance or poor performance are near the neutral point. That is, strongly negative valuations are not applied for failures to validate highly attained statuses. The fact that one has been fired from a glee club, dropped from a team, or dismissed from college does not enrage or perturb the community. Such failures are considered to be due to lack of practice, underachievement, poor judgment, limited talent, or misfortune, and are met with verbal expressions of sadness, disappointment, sympathy, regret, and so on. On the other hand, the *proper* performance of attained roles earns tokens of high positive value. These include prizes, public recognition, monetary rewards, and other indicators of public esteem. For attained statuses, then, values range from neutral to positive—there is much to gain and little to lose.

Now consider the range of potential valuation applicable to granted statuses. (See Figure 4.2.) Here there is less to gain and more to lose. One is not praised for participating in a culture as a female, an adult, a mother, or a person. One is expected to enact these roles without positive public valuations. The *nonperformance* of these roles, however, earns strong negative valuations. Consider the valuations declared on a mother who is indifferent to her children's welfare. She is labeled "selfish," "unloving." Consider the valuations declared on people who fail to act according to age standards. They are called "immature," "childish," or "regressive." Consider the valuations declared on people who act in opposition to fundamental principles of law. They are called "punks," or "outlaws."

It follows that the most universal common expectations for behavior are associated with the extreme granted status of *person*. While there are cultural variations in conceptions of the nature of humans, all persons within a given culture are expected to conform to a basic definition. Especially strong negative sanctions are reserved for acts that are held to be nonhuman

Figure 4.2
Positive and Negative Valuation in Relation to Status

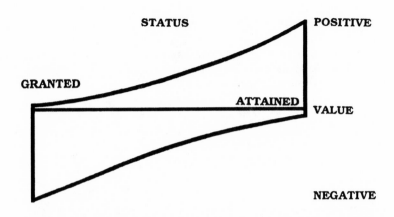

or unnatural. Expectations associated with the basic grant of personhood are usually concerned with communication, propriety, and in-group aggression. People who violate these norms are marked more or less permanently with a strongly pejorative label. Many forms of this label are used. All have the common function of denoting the social identity of a *nonperson*. Once the pejorative label is applied, society begins to treat the individual as something less than human.

The concept most widely used to represent nonperson status is that of "brute." This concept is sometimes rendered as beast, animal, or low-grade human being (Sarbin and Stein 1967; Platt and Diamond 1965). In the vernacular, these valuations emerge in such epithets as "pig," "dog," "worm," "jackass," and "son of a bitch."

The status of a nonperson is denoted by labels ordinarily used to describe nonliving matters. Examples are "dirt," "clod," and "stone." The vernacular also includes many terms derived from human and animal excrement (Kochman 1969). Even abstractions of quality are used to convey the notion of nonperson. Thus, "I am a zero," or "You're nothing but a nothing." It is noteworthy that such terms or their polite equivalents are not a part of the scientific and professional lexicon. In our efforts to be professional and humanistic, we have coined special euphemisms, which for a short time conceal the strong negative valuation. Examples of these euphemisms are "disadvantaged," "homeless," "underdeveloped," "culturally deprived," "mentally ill," "welfare recipients," "problem families," "patients," "inmates," and so on. These labels carry much of the meaning of a nonperson. The person so labeled is likely to be regarded as if he or she were at the lowest grade on the status dimension and at the negative end of the value dimension.

A further qualification must be added to the valuation dimension. This dimension is represented by a single line. However, the *quality* of the valuation below the neutral point differs from the quality of valuation above the neutral point. Positive valuations of attained roles appear to coincide with esteem, as this term is commonly understood. The public performance of the attained role is the basis for the according of esteem. By contract, positive valuations of granted roles are best denoted by the term *respect*. When people fail to perform ascribed roles, they lose the respect that inheres to the associated status. Motherhood is respected until a mother publicly fails to meet the group's minimal expectations concerning child care. The performance of granted roles, however, earns no special tokens of esteem. One is expected to perform granted roles without special incentives. Disrespect and associated negative sanctions follow nonperformance.

Role linkage

So far, components of social identity have been discussed as if they were independent of each other. At this point, this simplifying fiction can be eliminated. In any social structure certain validated statuses are prerequuisite for promotion to achieved positions. What are the social characteristics necessary to become a candidate for a particular achieved validated status? The concept of role linkage describes these and other functional connections between roles.

First, there are at least two criteria for deciding whether two roles are linked. Is one validated status prerequisite to another? For example, medical students must usually present a college degree among their qualifications for admission to medical schools. Other qualifications of status have in the past been effectively linked to admission to medical school and other selective professions—qualifications of race, religion, social class, and gender. The affirmative action policies and changing social values of the past generation have done much to modify these unwritten linkages.

The second criterion is based on the effect promotion or demotion of one status has on another. Ex-felons are forbidden to hold certain positions in government, for example. In fact, if a person in an attained position is convicted of a felony, he or she is very likely to lose that position. A boxing champion was stripped of his title because he had failed to discharge the military service obligations that were expected of young, male citizens. A former president and a vice-president were disbarred for violating laws and customs pertaining to honesty.

Normally, elaborate linkages are set up for entry into those attained statuses in which the actor wields some power or bears some responsibility for the welfare of others. Police officers, judges, physicians, senators, pharmacists, teachers, and diplomats arrive at their positions only by satisfying the licensing and certifying agencies that they have qualified on a number of prerequisites. For these positions of public trust, there is the uniform requirement that the individuals chosen be of "good basic character," loyal, upright, fair, and so forth.

The example of physicians is illuminating. If a patient dies because of "technical difficulties" in an operation, the surgeon is not charged with murder. However, a physician found to be practicing with a fraudulent license is treated severely and is subject to criminal proceedings, even though that doctor's patients are prospering. It is very difficult for society to view political leaders, magistrates, and surgeons as murderers, even though they might kill people in the same way as those who lack their attainments. But if a person in such an achieved position can be convicted of a fault on an ascribed and prerequisite status, then he or she is removed from that attained position and prosecuted.

This implies that the components of identity for promotions are required in a regular order. Promotion always requires prior validation of roles that are relatively more ascribed. The most selective positions are prerequisite to nothing. No job description would list president of the United States or Nobel Laureate as necessary qualifications. However, a great achievement does serve to exempt the person from the normal qualification rules for somewhat less attained positions. For example, former slave Frederick Douglass was honored by Abraham Lincoln for being a famous abolitionist and distinguished orator.

Attained roles differ greatly in the linkages they maintain with more ascribed components of identity. There are only weak linkages between the highly achieved status of great artist and the more granted status of family man. For some highly attained positions, there are no or only weak linkages to granted statuses. Michelangelo could lack granted status as a family man and still be granted status as an artist. But could Caesar?

Role linkages are governed by rules that can be changed. Through collective social processes, the qualification "male" has been removed from the right to vote, thus destroying a linkage. The linkage between "male" and professional jockey has been severed. The linkage between gender and combat soldier is being renegotiated, as is sexual orientation and military status. Similar social processes create linkages. For example, a university may declare that only Ph.D.s will be employed as professors. In this case the linkage is established between two statuses that are relatively attained. Some universities might create a linkage between granted racial status and the achievement of student status in their black studies programs.

Idiosyncratic Features of Role Linkage

The preceding sections suggest that the criteria for ascription or grant-edness of roles are, to a certain extent, arbitrary. The criteria for age, sex, and kinship roles are frequently under attack. The validity of such criteria is often questioned, and this questioning is often supported by reference to historical and cultural relativism.

Subcultures arise and the arbitrary criteria for ascribed roles are enlarged to include expectations associated with achievements. Thus a proper child will not only show the filial conduct that is traditionally expected, but will also enter an approved vocation. In this way, the child is maintaining *respect* at the same time as earning esteem from others. The esteem declarations of others (the public) may be the hidden dimension for the respect declarations by significant others (the parents).

The masculine ideal as a model for validity occupying the status male has been repeatedly challenged, most recently by social groups identified as gay or homosexual. The linking of gender to jobs is a cultural arrangement that has the stamp of historical tradition. A midwestern housewife on her first visit to an English pub was outraged that the "man behind the bar" was a woman. A controversy developed over the feminist claims that girls should be allowed to participate in Little League baseball. The following conundrum illustrates the traditional linkage between the job and gender:

A man and his teenage son were returning from a holiday. Road conditions were treacherous. Missing a turn in the road, their car ran into a concrete abutment. The father was killed instantly. The son sustained multiple injuries and was taken by ambulance to the emergency hospital. He was wheeled, unconscious, into the operating room. The surgeon, in the act of preparing to operate, glanced at the youth's face and in a state of excitement exclaimed, "I cannot operate on this boy. He is my son."
Query: Who is the surgeon?

To answer the query, of course, requires a readiness to entertain the possibility that a woman may be a surgeon.

Linkages between ascribed and achieved statuses are arbitrarily constructed by individuals. In this case, the connection reflects the person's own commitment to certain values. A boy was locked out of his house by his father for having fumbled the ball at a crucial point in a high school football game. Here the father arbitrarily linked the ascribed role son with the attained role football player.

The Protestant ethic has frequently been incorporated into the role linkages. This is particularly apparent in the time-honored expectation that the son will enter the family business. Consider the generations of artists and writers who were regarded as eccentric, indolent, even insane, for refusing such achieved roles as regional manager of sales, production engineer, or executive trainee in the family business. Negative evaluations up to and including disinheritance have been declared on the occupant of the status son for failure to enact such achieved roles. In such idiosyncratic cases, achieved roles take on the characteristics of ascribed statuses.

TRANSFORMATION OF SOCIAL IDENTITY

At any given time, a person's social identity is composed of a set of validated statuses. These might be indexed in terms of the extent to which they are granted or attained and in terms of the degree of involvement they entail. These validated statuses determine the social valuations that are applied to a person.

This concept of social validations is intended to illustrate how psychological change depends upon changing social interactions. For convenience, we shall consider the two aspects of social validation separately: the process of degradation and the process of enhancement.

Degradation

The model implies that there are two ways by which the values of a person's social identity may be lowered: *derogation* and *demotion*.

The root meaning of derogation is to rescind, annul, or reverse a previous privilege. *Derogation* is the process of transforming a role with potential for esteem to its negative counterpart. To derogate is to identify a person as a "bad actor," an ineffective incumbent of a status. The model accommodates the differential significance of derogation for roles at different points along the status dimension. A person's identity is damaged greatly by allegations of being a "bad person," a "bad daughter," or an "impotent male." Each allegation involves a considerable loss of respect. For a less significant role—like weekend gardener—the loss of status (implied by the allegation "he is a poor gardener") would not necessarily induce any loss of respect.

Demotion is the stripping away from a person of certain attained statuses. This process might also be called "disparagement"—a word whose root sense suggests a comparison between inferior and superior elements. To treat an adult as a child is degrading in this sense, as are actual demotions such as removing an officer from rank or assigning a varsity player to the junior varsity team. Demotions from achieved positions deprive the person of opportunities for enjoying esteem.

It follows that the most degrading processes are those which combine derogation and demotion. If a person is relieved of all achieved statuses—professional and avocational—and is derogated with respect to all ascribed roles—including sex, age, kinship, and citizenship roles—he or she is reduced to the lowest possible value. It is the extreme of degradation to treat a person as "nothing but a beast." ("Nothing but" implies demotion, and "beast" implies derogation.)

The following quotation from an 1885 edition of *The Catholic Dictionary* illustrates how the two degradation processes were applied to priests:

Degradation is of two kinds, verbal and real. By the first a criminous cleric is declared to be perpetually deposed from clerical orders, or from the execution thereof, so as to be deprived of all order and function...and of any benefice which he might have previously enjoyed. . . . Real or actual degradation is that which, besides deposing a cleric from the exercise of his ministry, actually strips him of his orders, according to a prescribed ceremonial, and delivers him to the secular arm to be punished. (p. 203)

The first kind of degradation is what we call derogation. The second, "real or actual degradation," is what we call demotion. The first is primarily verbal or symbolic; the second is primarily instrumental.

Enhancement

The model applies equally well to the enhancement of social identity. The development of heroes, champions, and successful and self-fulfilled people is typified by the logical opposites to the processes of derogations and demotions. These processes might be called, respectively, *commendation* and *promotion*.

Commendation is positive public recognition. It is given for proper performance in a given status. Commendation is provided in the form of verbal and symbolic acts that serve as social reinforcers. The varieties of commendation are many: the roar of the crowd in athletic contests, curtain calls in the theater, prizes and awards for achievement, honorific titles, and so on. Medals, grades in school, merit citations, and ordinary forms of praise and positive regard are other common kinds of commendation. Often when a speaker is introduced, the audience is informed of his or her validated statuses—"a mother, a citizen of the commonwealth, a senator"—and also of the commendations received—"oak leaf clusters, Man-of-the-Year Award, Guest Prize for Poetry."

A *promotion* is movement from one role to another, higher status role. A newly attained status opens up fresh possibilities for gaining esteem. In general, the greater the jump in rank, the greater the gain in esteem.

The most highly valued human beings, then, are those who have succeeded in doing two things. They have achieved rare social positions and have been commended highly for their performances in them. At the same time, they have also maintained their respectability.

These are the basic mechanisms of social transvaluation. The model has implications for various configurations of roles.

Extreme Granted Roles (Vertex A of Figure 4.1)

Involvement for the most granted role is consistently high. The social category employed at this point is that of human being, member of a society, participant in a culture, or person. It remains to consider the values that might be attached to effective validation of the most granted status—human being—as well as the valuation for insufficient or improper performance in this position.

The negative consequences of being classified as a nonperson or a "beast" are very great indeed. Platt and Diamond (1965) have traced the history of the "wild beast" theory of criminal insanity. Their findings support the view that no other categorical appellation has had such consistent negative potency. Eric Partridge provides evidence that derogatory slang is often a literal allegation that a person is not human (Partridge 1950). Nineteenth century California ranchers disported themselves by exterminating "varmints," the remnants of a tribe of Digger Indians. Until the modern era, death by drawing and quartering was reserved for those judged to be no better than animals. Hitler decreed that those responsible for the 1944 assassination plot be slaughtered like pigs and their carcasses hung on meat hooks, and so they were. While Mussolini was given an animal execution, the world was cheated of revenge on Hitler by his peremptory, and very human, suicide.

Compared to the great negative value of being classified as a nonperson, positive validation of human status carries a weak payoff. In absolute terms, the difference in value for social identity between person status is enormous. However, in itself, status as a person carries no positive value for social identity. Validation of this status is universally expected and is a minimum prerequisite for any form of promotion.

Highly Involving Achieved Roles (Vertex B of Figure 4.1)

The position of president of the United States is one of maximum achievement and involvement. So are the positions of violin virtuoso, Nobel Laureate, athletic champion, and Pope. Clearly, the maximum possible positive value for social identity is associated with proper performance in these positions. They provide access to power, prestige, and wealth.

What of the negative counterparts of these achieved roles? As examples we might cite an ineffective president, a losing coach, and an incomprehensible philosopher. If society agrees that the failure in each of these cases is *only* with respect to the requirements of the attained role, then the value it declares on the occupant of that position would not be negative. That is, it would not be expressed in terms of *disrespect*. A President's inability to halt inflation, for example, could result in declarations of disesteem, but not disrespect. The president might still be regarded as an accomplished raconteur, and the incomprehensible philosopher might be regarded as a patriot.

With respect to value, extremely achieved roles that are highly involving present just the opposite case from that of granted roles. (See Figure 4.3.)

Figure 4.3
The Three-Dimensional Model of Social Identity: Status, Value, and Involvement

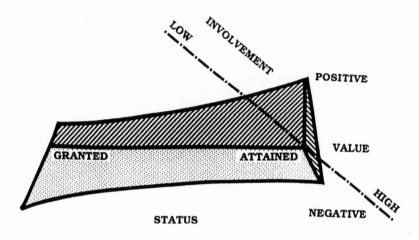

The absolute difference between maximum success and maximum failure for achieved roles is, again, enormous. But most of the potential is for positive value rather than for negative value. *There is much to gain and little to lose in trying for attained positions.* One does not invoke sanctions against a virtuoso for missing a note or playing badly. One does invoke sanctions for a temporary lapse from the requirements of being human.

The loss of attainments can have profoundly degrading consequences. One French pastry chef committed suicide upon learning that his restaurant had lost its four-star rating. Such cases are newsworthy, however, because they are rare. In fact, if we knew the whole story, we would probably discover real or imagined defects in some of the granted components of this man's social identity.

So the negative value attached to the derogatory counterpart of attained roles is not great. Of course difficulties are contained in this proposition. To strip away a virtuoso designation, championship status, or honorific title is very damaging to the individual so degraded. It is most degrading of all if the person is highly involved in his or her role. However, the amount of damage would depend on the density of validated statuses in the intervening space between highly attained and less attained, more granted roles. Marilyn Monroe, who believed she had failed as a mother, wife, actress, intellectual, and daughter, and who had given up her original name and family identity, must have suffered a profound identity crisis. Her status as sex queen could not be maintained as she grew older. Her suicide was probably a reaction to a loss of respect rather than to a loss of esteem. An appropriate term for this condition would be "undermined identity."

Minimally Involving Attained Roles (Vertex C of Figure 4.1)

Sometimes a person is no longer involved in an attained role. Examples would be retired generals and executives, members of honorary societies, and professors emeriti. When this happens, the status that pertains to that role is latent. Zero involvement in a role implies zero value for social identity. Zero involvement in an attained role means that a person is not active in that role, though he or she could become active again later.

Obviously, degree of involvement depends on social context. The Grand Plenipotentiary of the Secret Dragons might enjoy great esteem at his conventions and none at all at his place of work. Scholastic honors and publication records mean nothing when one is trying to board a subway. In such cases, the individual can derive satisfaction from implicit role involvement by thinking about personal achievements. However, it seems patent that self-esteem as well as public prestige depend upon valuations assigned by reference groups and individuals. Reference groups and individuals make their evaluations on the basis of the convincingness of the actor's performance. And this, in turn, is a function of involvement.

Linked Roles

Role linkages are important in the degrading and upgrading processes. For upgrading to occur, the person must have satisfied the formal and informal regulations regarding prerequisite validated positions. Once upgrading has occurred, one must not violate norms pertaining to prerequisite statuses. If a medical superintendent were to admit that she had forgotten her medical knowledge, she would probably be demoted. This demotion would occur, not because the forgotten knowledge had any direct function in the discharge of her daily duties, but because powerful medical societies have created and supported the linkage between qualified physician and medical superintendent. Similarly, the White House official in the Johnson administration who was revealed to be a homosexual was no longer allowed to function in his attained position. He was demoted from his job and derogated as a man. That President Clinton could make major administrative appointments of individuals who are openly gay illustrates the mutability of culturally sanctioned role linkages.

Many highly achieved positions are not closely linked with other, more ascribed statuses. Thus a person can attain esteem as a great actor without graduating from college, without working his way up through the corporation, without having a respectable marriage, and without adhering to conventional religious beliefs. However, if one wants to be a politician, one must take care to touch the requisite bases. That is, one must not violate granted role prescriptions before one attempts to gain promotion. Similarly, peccadillos are tolerated with amusement in movie stars that would outrage the public were they exhibited by a magistrate. If a well known musical conductor and a Hollywood actress live together and have a child without benefit of clergy, there is no public outcry. However, resignation from office was the only option for a high government official who maintained an intimate relation with a "secretary," and television evangelists are expected to be both honest and chaste.

Sometimes failure in an attained status is brought about not by incapacity to discharge the demands of that role, but by a defect in a granted category. When this happens, the degradation and disgrace are great. Oscar Wilde was not a failure as a playwright, pundit, or writer (attained statuses) but was seen as a failed man—and at a time in Victorian England when strong implicit linkages existed between masculinity and these attainments. From our point of view, Hitler was not so much a failure as a military leader as he was a failure as a human being. Because of the role linkage between granted and attained positions, failing to meet the requirements of a granted position may bring about derogation and demotion from achieved positions.

The Faust legend provides an excellent example of transvaluation in which the long-term effects of degradation differ markedly from the short-term effects. When Faust bargains his soul away to the Devil in return for earthly favors, he effectively degrades himself with respect to the most ascribed component of his identity—his claim to conventional humanity, to being a normal person. In return, he receives a set of "achievements"—conquests in love and other affairs. In the terms employed here, he has traded respect for esteem. In the modern idiom, he has "sold out"—he has accepted promotion without legitimizing his claims to the more ascribed component of his identity—his humanity.

The Faust legend illustrates the condition that we have called "undermined identity." The combination of achieved statuses and weak or undefined granted statuses produces a perilous psychological condition. Since there is no solid basis for self-respect deriving from granted statuses, the person is continually dependent on public recognition of personal attainments. As kinship ceases to be meaningful, as sexual adequacy is called into question, as the nation loses respectability as an object of patriotism, and as the established church ceases to provide believable answers to the question, "Who are you?" the only basic grant of respect that remains is that of *human being*. But even this grant of respect is challenged by participation in a society that seems to regard human beings as objects to be processed, or as specially adept animals, or as creatures without individual responsibility. Marx made clear that a significant effect of industrialization is the mechanizing of persons along with the personification of things. Modern humans receive much information that tell them, in effect, that there is nothing particularly special about being human. If one accepts this proposition, and if family, church, and nation do not completely contradict it, then one must depend completely upon transitory attainments. When involvement in attained roles lapses, one has no means of earning respect. The hollow man alone is no man at all.

O'Neil (1993) has described many case histories of men and women in the United States who have been tremendous successes in terms of power, position, and money, and yet who are suffering deep inner turmoil, manifest in substance abuse, depression, and stress-related symptoms. His book, *The paradox of success*, is replete with examples of individuals who have placed their achievements at greater importance than their ascribed identities as persons, sons and daughters, wives and husbands, fathers and mothers.

UTILITY OF THE MODEL

The utility of any model is demonstrated by the extent to which it illuminates a wide variety of observations and suggests consistent interpretations. The present model has already been employed to clarify a number of problems. These include the nature of deviance (Shaver and Scheibe 1967; Sarbin 1968), the process of conduct reorganization (Sarbin and Adler, 1971), terrorism (Scheibe 1974), the concept of danger (Sarbin 1967b), the effects of participation in the subculture of poverty (Sarbin 1968), effectiveness of cross-age tutoring (Sarbin 1975), national loyalty (Scheibe 1967), and the variable identities of incarcerated felons (Rotenburg and Sarbin 1971).

The conflict between the civil service and political employees of government agencies is easily conceptualized as a problem in role linkages. The relative prestige of varying governmental positions is a function of the mechanisms of selectivity—the greater the apparent selectivity, the greater the esteem. The problems that most members of law enforcement agencies have to deal with are really problems of deviance from the requirements of granted roles. Major problems in law enforcement arise when people with a great deal of accumulated social esteem and power commit crimes. The conception of social identity makes it easy to see why it is so difficult for lower-class people to serve as law enforcers for powerful upper-class people.

CONCLUSION

The valuation of persons can take the form of enhancement or of degradation in a social process. That is, its form and direction depend upon the nature of the social organization in which it occurs. The model of social identity presented in this chapter provides a social psychological language for analyzing valuation. The model itself is a heuristic device. Its utility is to be measured by its success in establishing the processes of enhancement and degradation as knowable events—events to be illuminated by social psychological research and analysis.

Using role theory as a conceptual starting point, it is proposed that a person's social identity be regarded as a composite of social positions or statuses—the occupancy of which he or she has made good by performing appropriate acts.

The extent to which each of the components of social identity contributes value to the composite depends on two things. The first is the extent to which the position was granted (ascribed) as opposed to attained (achieved). The second is the degree to which the person is involved in role enactment. A person's social identity is not an absolute. Obviously, differently composed reference groups will not assign the same valuations to any particular presentation of self. Valuation is a reciprocal social process. Values do not inhere in either the subject or the object of valuation but emerge from the interaction between them.

From this perspective, *respect* is seen as the maintenance of status grants—birthrights, political and religious orthodoxies, and other minimal expectations for personal conduct. Respect provides a person with a grant of social credit. The loss of this grant of social credit amounts to a loss of respectability. *Esteem*, on the other hand, is earned. It is acquired as the socially proffered wages for attainments. The more selective the attainment, the higher the wages, the greater the esteem.

Social identity is considered to be composed of a complex of references at various points along the status dimension. In contrast to the religious conception of humanity, which emphasizes one's ascribed attributes, and to the economic conception, which values only one's attainments, the nature of social organization demands that the effectively functioning person have grants of respect and opportunities to gain esteem. Observations of alienation, anomie, depersonalization, and so on, can be conceptualized according to this model, particularly in terms of the improper validation of granted statuses.

The proposed model of social identity has a very wide range of application. Additional topics that might be discussed include suicide, political revolution, race relations, feminism, antinomianism, generational conflicts, student movements, and power as a social commodity.

NOTE

1. This chapter was co-authored in its original version by Theodore Sarbin (see Sarbin and Scheibe 1980). It is based on work done originally by the two authors and Professor Rolf O. Kroger of the University of Toronto. A working manuscript was prepared in the summer of 1965, when these three were together at the

University of California. Sarbin and Scheibe were able to spend considerable time reworking and developing this material during the 1968–69 and 1973–74 academic years at Wesleyan University where Sarbin was a Fellow at the Center for Advanced Studies. Kroger's strong involvement in the initial phases of this work was of critical importance, but because he was not able to participate in the writing of the manuscript, he did not appear as an author in the original version. However, it is appropriate that he be credited with creative participation in the basic conceptual work from which this paper was developed.

Chapter 5

The Psychology of National Identity

Ernst Cassirer concludes *The myth of the state* with a Babylonian legend, according to which the god Marduk uses the limbs of a monster serpent he has slain as the material for the creation of mankind and the world. Cassirer suggests this myth as a simile for the development of human culture:

It could not arise until the darkness of myth was fought and overcome. But the mythical monsters were not entirely destroyed. They were used for the creation of a new universe, and they still survive in this universe. The powers of myth were checked and subdued by superior forces. As long as these forces, intellectual, ethical, and artistic, are in full strength, myth is tamed and subdued. But once they begin to lose their strength chaos is come again. (1946, p. 298)

The name of the Babylonian monster serpent was Tiamat. But there is no proper name for a force that may arise in many guises or modes of expression. In many of its forms, this mythic force will not appear so recognizably evil as a monster serpent. The main difficulty in discussing the psychology of national identity and of nationalism derives from a similar distinction between a general but unnamed human disposition and a historically particular form. Nationalism is a named form, but surely it is not an essential name for that which it manifests in human nature. Nazism has been seen by some as an exaggerated or extreme form of nationalism. Let us surmise that Nazism is the monster serpent that Cassirer had in mind, for his work was written just at the conclusion of World War II. But nationalism also appears in more favorable colors, for it has been the principle force at work in the massive postwar trend toward the decolonization of territories formerly dominated by European powers. Now with the breakup of the Soviet Union and the disintegration of monolithic domination over the states of Eastern Europe, nationalism is seen again in less favorable colors, as Georgians, Serbs, Croats, Bosnians, Lithuanians, and many other groups are free to vie for the privilege of providing a sustained and respected claim for national definition and sovereignty.

The basic premise of this chapter is that nationalism is linked to the psychology of the person because it comprises a functional response to the general problem of social identity. But it cannot be supposed that this connection is a necessary or timeless one. In fact, the importance of the nation in providing a partial solution to the problem of identity is completely dependent upon historical context. So a discussion of nationalism or national identity is secular psychology. I take it as given that the psychological dispositions that make nationalism in its many forms possible must be more general than any historically dated phenomena.

This is not to say that the behavior of a person as a member of a nation can be reduced to universal psychological traits or needs but rather that the psychological functioning of modern humanity must be understood, in part, in national terms. In the present dispensation, men and women are members of nations, and their lives are strongly influenced by the particular form taken by this relationship. Understandably, the leaders of the "superior forces" decided at the conclusion of World War II to pronounce an official condemnation of proud and expansive nationalism. The founding of the United Nations was an attempt to demonstrate the earnestness of this judgment. However, the postwar years have shown that the states comprising the United Nations really did not believe in universalism or in the death of nationalism. Indeed, there is increasing evidence that nations will remain *the* fundamental political reality for a long time to come.[1] It is my belief that the nation will long remain a fundamental psychological reality and that it is time for psychologists to recognize it as such.

WHAT IS THE PSYCHOLOGICAL INTEREST IN THE QUESTION OF NATIONALITY?

A dependent relationship between national identity and psychology takes two basic forms. Either political behavior is considered to result from psychological dispositions or else psychological functioning is considered to depend on the political or national ambience.

Certainly, attempts have been made to extend general psychological theory to cover or render an account of political behavior. The general stock for this borrowing consists mainly of psychoanalytic theory and some of its variants. The term psychohistory has been coined as a collective name for a set of efforts to render psychological accounts of major political figures or conspicuous political types (DeMause 1982; Erikson 1969; Freud and Bullitt 1966; George and George 1956; Keniston 1965; Pomper 1973). These efforts are ambitious, often stylistically elegant, and in some cases genuinely original, especially when the reductive pressure is temporarily dismissed and the writer presents a discussion of a particular form of political behavior or character in its own terms.

It is my view that the borrowing from psychological theory by political scientists and historians has been hampered by misconceptions about the current state of psychological theory and consequent unrealistic expectations about the power of traditional personality theories as means of accounting for the lives and careers of major historical figures. In the traditional style of nineteenth-century positivism, scholars have sought to ground their own disciplines in something more fundamental. Psychologists are looked to for the real (inner) reasons for a political assassination, for the intransigence of Wilson at Paris, for Hitler's destructive mania or for Saddam Hussein's despotism. If one accepts the Freudian premise that all important character traits are laid down prior to puberty and if one adopts the common belief that actions are expressions of inner dispositions, then it seems logical to expect psychology to provide some answers to major historical problems. But each of these beliefs—in preformation and in behavior as trait expression—is highly questionable, if not out of date, in contemporary psychological theory (Hunt 1965; Mischel 1977; Scheibe 1979).

Also, the several premises leading to the expectation that one discipline may be grounded in another is questionable. In particular, the notion that historical and political occurrences can be accounted for in the idiom of personality theory is perhaps the strongest reason for the failures of psychology and history, both as separate and conjoint disciplines (Gergen 1973; Gergen and Morawski 1980).

Within psychology a small subdiscipline has developed that is concerned with the obverse problem of studying the dependency between psychological functioning and the political ambience. It is possible for psychology to borrow from history and political science but without repeating the mistake of thinking of this borrowing as a grounding. Psychology might employ the idiom of political science or history in order to fulfill its own purpose—that of rendering a satisfactory account of contemporary human behavior.

Psychologists have for a long time considered the nuclear family to be the fundamental institutional reality in human life. Psychological theory has been built up largely on this premise. However, the premise is quite obviously time- and culture-bound, and a partial truth even within a given culture and epoch. For the last 200 years in Western society, the nation has been an institution of varying salience for human beings. Yet psychologists have treated this institution as if it did not exist, or as if it were one of a general class of "group identifications," or as if attachments of the person to the nation could only be viewed as a kind of mistake or aberration from the "normal" dependency of the person on the nuclear family. The most difficult whale for psychologists to swallow is that what is psychologically essential is often accidental. That is, while the nuclear family played an essential role for millennia, it is a role that could be played by another institution that is clearly not a nuclear family. As historical and cultural developments occur, the substantive content of psychology actually changes, if not the nature of basic processes.

The idea of a nation in a psychologically salient sense—that is, an idealized entity with which the person truly identifies—is not a historical constant but a recent human invention.

What now seems natural once was unfamiliar, needing argument, persuasion, evidences of many kinds; what seems simple and transparent is really obscure and contrived, the outcome of circumstances now forgotten and preoccupations now academic, the residue of metaphysical systems sometimes incompatible and even contradictory. (Kedourie 1961, p. 9)

This is not to say that the identification of the person with the nation was something that emerged suddenly and full blown at a given date in Europe. But whatever the date or mode of transition, the nation today is a psychologically fundamental reality for most human beings. Our actions as well as our self-conceptions are highly conditional upon our particular conception of the nature of our nation—its history and present reality.

Psychological theory can either be extended to account for political occurrences or else it can be expanded by the inclusion of historical and political factors as determinants of psychological functioning. The former enterprise is by now familiar and has earned a label if not broad recognition of success. This latter enterprise is more novel and has been given the provisional label of "historical psychology" (Morawski 1982). It is the aim of the next section to suggest what kind of success might be realized.

PSYCHOLOGICAL QUESTIONS REQUIRING AN EXPANSION OF PSYCHOLOGICAL VOCABULARY TO INCLUDE THE CONCEPT OF NATION

Men go to war and face the prospect of death for reasons that are obscure and impersonal. Some Buddhist monks destroyed themselves by fire as a political gesture and the gesture was imitated by a few throughout the world. An American Jew conducts a shootout in a mosque in Jerusalem for reasons he considers to be above reproach. From the Truman to the Bush presidencies in the United States, massive arms expenditures were justified against all instrumental reason, so that our nation would not appear to be in the relatively weak position *vis à vis* our adversaries. Civil wars rage now in El Salvador, now in Angola, now in Bosnia, now in Rwanda. Argentina claimed sovereignty over the Falkland/Malvinas Islands, and Great Britain went to war to defend her national honor. U.S. national interests have been defended by arms in most Caribbean and Central American nations, in the Persian Gulf, and in Libya—to consider only the nondeclared conflicts.

All of these events, all of these observations have a psychological aspect. The decision to revolt against one's country entails a complete psychological transformation, similar to a religious conversion. The nation functions as protection for the person—a source of power. Or it can be an object of fear or hatred. The state is a guardian, but as such it may either be protector or tyrant. What determines the manner in which personal destiny and national destiny are intertwined? How does the state extend or limit the life aspirations of a person?

At certain times and in certain places patriotism is strong and positive. What is the function of such displays for the individual? Why is it sometimes important to celebrate the nation? Why and under what circumstances does a manifest hatred of one's nation become psychologically functional?

What is the psychological significance of compatibility or incompatibility between church and nation? Between race and nation? What are the effects of foreign travel, acquaintance with foreigners at home, and information about other countries on self-conceptions? What are the psychological consequences of insults to the nation? What are the psychological consequences of national successes in wars, Olympics, the World Cup, Nobel prize competition, treaties, or the United Nations?

Does a person derive part of his self-conception from clauses contained in the national charter regarding "natural human rights?" To what extent does the nation ultimately define the rules of guilt or shame for the person? What are the psychological consequences of transformation of an individual into a citizen of a newly developing nation?

What are the psychological consequences of universalism—of the possibility of the disappearance of all national boundaries?

Obviously, it is not possible to consider more than a few of these questions in this essay. But the foregoing set should serve to illustrate the range of problems to which a psychology of national identity should be responsive. It is obvious that the nation plays a role in the psychological task of self-definition, and similarly it plays a role in critical, personal decisions, such as whether or not to go to war, leave home, engage in an act of sabotage, or drop out of college.

PAST PSYCHOLOGICAL PERSPECTIVES ON THE PROBLEM OF NATIONAL IDENTITY

Modern psychology has displayed a characteristic antipathy to strong national identification. Perhaps Freud (1930/1962) set the tradition within psychology of regarding with distrust all strong attachments between the person and external social institutions.

Floyd Allport (1927) presents the classic behavioristic view of the development and function of nationalism and patriotism. According to Allport, the young child is frequently exposed to symbols of the nation—the flag, photographs of leaders, anthems, and so forth—in connection with positive emotional stimuli that were established within the family setting; i.e., smiles, expressions of pleasure and approval. Thus, the young child is conditioned to react favorably to national symbols as he would to symbols having to do with his own family. Thereby the child is woven into a connection with the nation by repetition and variation of the conditioning mechanism. At a later time, the national symbols can be used to elicit loyalty and obedience. Allport applied the label "nationalist fallacy" to the view that nationalism consists of anything more than the result of conditioned obedience to authority. One may see a modern version of this same understanding of national identity in Skinners' (1948) *Walden two*, in which citizens are securely conditioned into the proper regard for their form of governance. In this scheme of things, people are not loyal out of choice but because they have to be loyal to that which they have been conditioned—there is no other possibility.

A variation on this view was presented by Ross Stagner (1946). Stagner similarly considered national loyalties to be a result of direct conditioning but suggested that a person can gain some insight into the mode of conditioning and thereby achieve some rational control over automatic impulses.

Self-insight is integrally related to the preservation of World peace because it is only with insight that reason achieves control of human behavior. A man who lacks understanding of his own emotions easily falls prey to propaganda . . . he may be induced to project aggression onto foreign peoples and . . . act in an irrational manner. (Stagner 1946, p. 895)

It is not far from this view to a psychoanalytic conception of national identity, in which the identification with the nation is viewed as a form of narcissism extended outwards from the self to the family, to the clan, to the tribe, and finally to the nation. The similarity is in the conception that national narcissism is inevitable, automatic, and, from the standpoint of the individual or the collectivity, disadvantageous in the long run. Appel (1945) called nationalism a form of neurosis. Nationalism is considered to be an irrational dependency between the person and the nation. On this view, psychological health is truly compatible only with universalism to which humankind must move in any case if peace is to be achieved and preserved.

The same kind of argument was presented by Alexander (1941) who suggested that world peace can be achieved only by a dilution and extension of narcissism to cover all of humanity. He favored the establishment of a world government empowered to enforce law and order over the entire globe. He saw the need for such a police force diminishing as nations become educated away from narrow self-interest and dedicate themselves voluntarily to world democracy.

More modern social psychological views of national identity may be found in Guetzkow (1955) and Kleinberg (1964), but the major features of the position remain unchanged. National identification is seen to result from a process of direct tuition, with a strong connection to the emotional needs of the person. Nationalism is considered to be consistent neither with maximal psychological health nor with the progress and well-being of world civilization. Again, education and accompanying self-insight are seen as mechanisms for replacing nationalism with a more extended loyalty to humanity.

The psychologist has tended to view national identity and nationalism in the same way that racism is regarded. Beliefs in the inherent superiority of racial or national groups are considered to be without scientific support. These myths of superiority are destructive—accounting in large measure for the antagonism that threatens the existence of humankind. So the psychologist's work has been a moral enterprise—the condemnation of the primitive and aberrant belief in racial or national superiority. But in the process the interesting question of the functional significance of beliefs in native superiority have been ignored.

Psychologists have had the view that if only human beings could be saved from certain primitive errors in thinking, then one world of universal brotherhood and mutual respect would more or less automatically follow. As professionals, they have shown a generous piety—a willingness to formulate universal declarations for the United Nations about the lack of scientific support for any unflattering belief that people have about each other. But aside from reference to "primitivism," "irrationality," and "neurotic narcissism," they have ignored the question of why individuals acquire a very salient set of beliefs about the unique virtue of national or ethnic identification.

The anger behind this piety is expressed most clearly by Erich Fromm:

This incestuous fixation not only poisons the relationship of the individual to the stranger, but to the members of his own clan and to himself. The person who has not freed himself from the ties to blood and soil is not yet fully born as a human being; his capacity for love and reason are crippled . . . The average man today obtains his sense of identity from his belonging to a nation, rather than from his being a "son of man." His . . . reason is warped by this fixation. . . . Nationalism is our form of incest, is our idolatry, is our insanity . . . Man—freed from the traditional bonds of the medieval community, afraid of the new freedom which transformed him into an isolated atom—escaped into a new idolatry of blood and soil, of which nationalism and racism are the two most evident expressions. (Fromm 1955, p. 58)

This is very close to a standard position on the question of nationalism. "Nationalism is in our day the chief obstacle to the extension of social cohesion beyond national boundaries. It is therefore the chief force making for the extermination of the human race" (Russell 1951).

Yet the psychological literature lacks a convincing and sympathetic explanation of why individuals in the modern world identify so strongly with their nations. Little discussion of the problem of national identity places the problem in the context of a more general consideration of social identity and the requirements of psychological functioning. Nationalism has been associated with racism and with religiosity (both positively and negatively (Fessler 1941) but rarely with family and occupational roles.

A PSYCHOLOGY OF NATIONAL IDENTITY

What does it mean to state that an individual is identified with a nation or that nationality is a component of his identity? What psychological functions are performed by this form of identification? Answers to these questions can only be formulated in the context of a more general psychological theory. The theoretical framework of choice for this task is social role theory (Sarbin and Allen 1968).

It is not necessary here to describe again the model of social identity that I have presented in the preceeding chapter of this volume. Suffice it to say that, in terms of that model, national identity falls near the granted end of the "granted-achieved" continuum. Hence, involvement with national identity is relatively constant and the contribution of national identity toward the evaluation of social identity has more to do with the maintenance of respect than the possibility of gaining esteem. Nationality, like other ascribed components of identity, is relatively resistant to change.

Social identity is a composite of that which a person is by right of birth and that which the person becomes through social promotions. That which one is, prior to the enactment of any achieved roles, is a result of the birthright. The nature of this contract is quite variable over time and cultures. Whatever its form, the birthright forms the critical basis for the social understanding of human nature. A child may be born slave or free, born as one of the "chosen" or one of the "heathen," born as an animal or as a human being with "inalienable" rights. In general, the terms of a birthright—rights, duties, or liabilities—are inalienable, for the granted component of social identity is a point of continuous involvement.

Not only does the nature of the birthright grant determine the respect in which a person is initially held (and, in turn, the self-respect that generates) but it also determines the possibilities for the individual to gain access to attained positions within the society, because of linkages that are explicitly or implicitly codified within a society to regulate the promotion process. Thus, the rule "no Irish need apply" constitutes a barrier to promotion resulting from the particular character of a granted component of identity.

The minimal characteristics of granted birthrights are not specified by role theory. Each society has some working definition of human nature that it uses as a basis for granting the charter of humanity to newborn infants produced within its domain. Whether there are universals of human birthrights is an open question. Certainly enormous variation is found over cultures. The Xavante tribe of Brazil practices infanticide, and doubtless with full moral justification, since the birthright grant is withheld from deformed children, excess females, or any child who cannot be supported by its mother (Neel 1970). The controversy over abortion laws in the United States devolves to a controversy over the arbitrary point in time at which a fetus may be regarded as a human being with inalienable rights to "Life, Liberty, and the Pursuit of Happiness." African slaves imported to the Americas were regarded by their European masters as chattel and as such entitled to humane but certainly not human treatment.

The rewards of respect that accompany a birthright are enormously important, but they are silent. The child growing up becomes fully adapted to the birthright. Since the child is born with the birthright but without knowledge of it, learning of it is the most powerful lesson about identity. A child must come to recognize membership in gender, caste, family, race, and nation. The description of this recognition process is an important subject of psychological research. (See Clark 1963, on race; Jahoda 1963, on nationality.)

Commonly, more than one social institution grants its charter to an individual at the same time. The terms of their charters under ideal circumstances are mutually consistent; the basic duties, rights, and obligations laid down may be compatible. But commonly the terms of institutional charters come into conflict with each other, particularly in societies that are undergoing rapid changes. The resulting conflicts generate intrapsychic problems with a clear social origin. For example, a child in the nineteenth-century rural United States was expected by the family to have primary responsibilities in working on the home farm, while the state, as represented in the schools, expected educational priorities to be more basic. Such conflicts may assume epic proportions, as in the case of a Thomas More or a Thomas à Becket.

Questions of conflicting institutional loyalties comprise a set of classical legal issues. Courts may, by what amounts to establishing a social convention (albeit a mightily significant one), determine the arrangement of priorities of conflicting granting institutions. For example, in a 1940 decision (*Minersville School District vs. Gobitis*), Justice Frankfurter declared:

The mere possession of religious convictions which contradict the relevant concerns of a political society does not relieve the citizen from the discharge of political responsibilities. The necessity for this adjustment has again and again been recognized. . . . We are dealing with an interest inferior to none in the hierarchy of legal values. National unity is the basis of national security. . . . The ultimate foundation of a free society is the binding tie of cohesive sentiment. (Walhke 1952, p. 25)

The issue was the school expulsion of a Jehovah's Witness student for failure to salute the flag and recite the pledge of allegiance. Just three years later a contrary opinion on the ordering of loyalties was expressed by Justice Jackson (*West Virginia State Board of Education vs. Barnette*):

[The] ultimate futility of such attempts to compel coherence is the lesson of every such effort from the Roman drive to stamp out Christianity as a disturber of its pagan unity, the Inquisition, as a means to religious and dynastic unity, the Siberian exiles as a means to Russian unity, down to the fast failing efforts of our present totalitarian enemies. Those who begin coercive elimination of dissent soon find themselves exterminating dissenters. Compulsory unification of opinion achieves only the unanimity of the graveyard. (Walhke 1952, p. 34)

No "natural" test can resolve the question of the relative priority between church and state, and, where the two institutions are not aligned, conflicts of the sort illustrated by this example are bound to arise. Membership in any other identity-granting group, such as a revolutionary political party or a hippie communal family, can and does produce similar conflicts among institutionalized rights and duties (Scheibe 1974).

In a society characterized by a high degree of institutional change and demographic mobility, a large number of individuals suffer considerable confusion about their birthright. In the United States, where one of three marriages ends in divorce, where one of five families moves every year, where religious institutions are often of vestigial importance, where material affluence creates the impression that the person is supported not by a social agreement but by money, and where the political structure for many provides only the vaguest sense of identity and basic human rights, it is not surprising that many authors should have noted a desperate search for "collective identity" (Klapp 1969; Lofland 1969). Bennis wrote in *The temporary society* (Bennis and Slater 1968): "Somehow with all the mobility, chronic churning, and unconnectedness we envisage, it will become more and more important to develop some permanent or abiding commitment. . . . This means that as general commitments become diffuse or modified a greater *fidelity* to something or someone will be necessary to make us more fully human" (p. 128). Keniston (1965) made a similar suggestion in *The uncommitted*. He notes a strong unconscious desire of youth to "merge, to fuse with, to lose themselves in some embracing person, experience, or group. This fantasy of mystical fusion involves the unconscious desire to lose all selfhood in some undifferentiated state with another or with nature, to be totally embraced and to embrace totally" (p. 190). As Kedourie (1961) has argued, this is precisely what nineteenth-century romantic nationalists promised: "that the state should be the creator of man's freedom not in an external and material sense, but in an internal and spiritual sense" (p. 47).

In classical nationalist doctrine, a primordial essence is supposed to manifest itself in language, culture, race, and religion; it is the true, the God-given nation. The psychological appeal of such an institution is the exact complement of the kind of identity-anxiety expressed by Bennis, Keniston, Klapp, and others. The early nineteenth-century philosopher and apologist for German nationalism, Schleiermacher, states the case as follows:

How little worthy of respect is the man who roams about hither and thither without the anchor of national ideal and love of fatherland; how dull is the friendship that rests merely upon personal similarities in disposition and tendencies, and not upon the feeling of a greater common unity for whose sake one can offer up one's life; how the greatest source of pride is lost by the woman that cannot feel that she also bore children for her fatherland and brought them up for it, that her house and all the petty things that fill up most of her time belong to a greater whole and take their place in the union of her people. (in Kedourie 1961, p. 73)

This declaration sounds archaic, and, given its national source, it resonates forward to Nazism. But if one attributes these words to a contemporary "Third World" statesman, they might appear to set a very proper sort of ideal.

Lest the point be lost in the examples, it bears repeating that the psychological mechanisms of national identification are presumed to be universal. In some manner the developing individual must seek to establish an identity by becoming aware of the nature of the birthright. Psychological problems result from conflict among institutions concerning the specific content of that birthright and also from ambiguity or vagueness about *any* birthright. When the individual conceives the question, "Who am I?" an answer is both expected and deserved. In some societies and under some circumstances, one hears nothing in reply or in reply one hears "nothing," so one has to seek out or build a social collectivity in which to find "the self."

The desire of the individual to find a common birthright or to seek a collective identity need not be construed as an attempt to obliterate uniqueness or individuality. Instead when a person finds a "natural" identity, he is redeemed from insignificance, and a basis is provided for the development of an authentic individuality. It is the sense of significance in the collectivity that gives importance to the individual—the person has a sense of the contextual meaning of individuality. The nature of this apparent paradox as it applies to the question of self-sacrifice is illustrated in an essay by George Orwell:

Brotherhood implies a common father. Therefore it is often argued that men can never develop the sense of a community unless they believe in God. The answer is that in a half conscious way most of them have developed it [a sense of community] already. Man is not an individual, he is only a cell in an everlasting body, and he is dimly aware of it. There is no other way of explaining why it is that men will die in battle. It is nonsense to say they only do it because they are driven. If whole armies had to be coerced, no war could ever be fought. (Orwell 1968, p. 17)

Of course, there are many occasions when appeals to duty and *patria* fall on deaf ears and arouse no response. People are not willing to die for institutions to which they feel psychologically alien. It is that dim awareness of being an organic part of an institution that makes legitimate, if not fully reasonable, its demands for loyalty. That awareness, in turn, must derive from having accepted a grant of identity from the institution (Scheibe 1974).

One consequence of this complex conception of social identity is that it is possible to envisage intrapsychic conflict as a conflict between components of the same social identity—as in some previous illustrations—traceable to conflicts between social institutions. In addition, the individual develops a self-conception connected not to a particular social institution but to a composite experience with the physical and social environment. William James (1890), besides describing the social self in its many manifestations, posited a material self—a psychological conception to be sure, but intimately tied up with the actual flesh of the body as well as its material possessions. Orwell expresses in vivid terms a conflict between this self and the part of a person that could respond favorably to a call to arms:

If you look into your own mind, which are you; Don Quixote or Sancho Panza? Almost certainly you are both. There is one part of you that wishes to be a hero or a saint, but another part of you is a little fat man who sees very clearly the advantages of staying alive with a whole skin. He is your unofficial self—the voice of the belly protesting against the soul. (Orwell 1941/1968, p. 163)

If most political rhetoric is of the Don Quixote kind, a good deal of the normative ethics emerging from psychological writing is partial to the interests of Sancho Panza.

The importance of national identity in one's psychological makeup depends on the composition of the remainder of self and social identity. Certainly there are other institutions—family, clan, race, church, university, or company—that might be the functional equivalent of a nation. The central psychological function of these institutions is seen here as the provision of a valid birthright to the person on which one can build the achieved components of one's identity. If competing birthrights are given or if the character of what can be "taken for granted" is never clear to the developing person, then the person may never have a sense of belonging to a human entity that extends beyond the limits of the physical self. In this condition, individuals will tend to seek or form collectivities with which to identify, so that a working birthright may be forged (Kanter 1972).

NATIONALISM

While there are certainly differences in the views of historians on the question of the social and ideological origins of nationalism, the consensus is that modern nationalism is a phenomenon of the nineteenth and twentieth centuries (Snyder 1968). The emergence of nationalism in the nineteenth century is often described as a transformation in consciousness or, on a different level, a transformation of collective identity. What were the preconditions for this transformation, and how may the change be characterized in functional terms? What follows here is an abstraction of what some historians have said, in psychological terms, about the emergence of nationalism (Hayes 1926; Kedourie 1961; Kohn 1962; Minogue 1967; Snyder 1968).

In primitive and stabilized cultures, social structures are supported by universal consensus within the community. In addition, a characteristic mythic and legendary tradition is passed on from generation to generation, providing the basis for the authority of the priesthood as well as functionally satisfactory answers to cosmic psychological questions concerning the origins of life, the meaning of death, the nature of purpose in the universe. Technically speaking, societies that are describable in these terms are also likely to be unprogressive and unsophisticated in their ability to use their own resources for development. Social strata are likely to be strictly demarcated, and positions in society are likely to be based upon heredity; hence there is discrimination exercised at the level of bestowing the birthright on newborn infants within the community.

Exogenous technological development, ideological change, and changes in mobility and communication tend to be destructive of this kind of stable psychological environment. Rationally, of course, little case can be made for the maintenance of such cultures, since it is often quite easy to see how they might be improved in a material sense, i.e., in terms of percentage of surviving infants, caloric intake per person, life expectancy, or incidence of communicable disease.

But the "satisfactoriness" of a given birthright depends upon the stability of the institution that bestows it. One does not have much confidence in a contract made with a company created yesterday, which is likely to be replaced next week. The destruction of feudal society left people free, but it also left them with deficient identities. While the medieval period is said to have terminated with the European Renaissance in the fifteenth and sixteenth centuries, it may be that the full psychological consequences of the disruption of medieval society were not generally felt in Europe until the beginning of the nineteenth century. The political revolutions in the late eighteenth century were truly fundamental challenges to the old order. People became aware that they were living in subjugation to myths of dominion, which could in fact be challenged. Of course, they might have discovered that same truth hundreds of years before; but it is one thing to know that the social institutions to which you are subject are not divine and quite another to believe that you have the power to overthrow those institutions.

What then is nationalism? I think there is good psychology in the following characterization by a political scientist:

The formula that I find most convincing is to say that nationalism provides an escape from triviality. Implicitly or explicitly, men suffering from a social upheaval put to themselves the question: what is happening to us? The nationalist answer is clear: our nation is struggling to be born; it is fighting for independence against its enemies. This answer is never the whole truth, and sometimes it has absolutely nothing to do with the truth at all. But that does not matter. The nationalist struggle is a noble one which dignifies a man's sufferings, and gives him a hopeful direction in which to work. (Minogue 1967, p. 32)

Nationalist struggles are attempts to be born or carried into a new identity. The dissatisfactions that fire nationalist movements often have purely material or economic aspects, but those who become revolutionary leaders are typically drawn from the classes most favored by the old established system. Nationalist ideology is romantic, transforming each prosaic setting into a stage of destiny. The German concept of *Volk*, championed by such writers as Herder, Schleiermacher, Fichte, and the Grimm brothers, comprised not only a collective folk name, but a mysterious *fons et origo*—an essential force that manifests itself in a particular set of great men, a distinct language, a folklore, artistic creations, and so forth. It hardly matters that such an idea is nonsense from a scientific point of view. The point is that such a conception provides a viable psychological reference for the most fundamental problem of identity—what is my birthright?

At times, the ideology of nationalism has been combined with that of racism, though such a connection is hardly a necessary one. Joseph de Gobineau (1816–1852) presented a thoroughgoing theory of racial inequality, which challenged political ideals of democratic nationalism as well as religious and moral values. His was an attempt to show that nobility inhered in the Aryan, who is ordained by nature to superiority.

A man is great, noble, virtuous, not by his actions but by his blood. The only test that our personal work has to stand is the test of our ancestors. It is his birth certificate that gives to a man the certainty of his moral value. Virtue is not a thing to be acquired. (in Cassirer 1946, p. 236)

But de Gobineau recognized that Aryans do not constitute a separate nation. Rather, he considered Aryans to be a kind of natural aristocracy—the only legitimate aristocracy—in whatever land they happened to live. While the ideological seeds for Nazism were clearly present in these ideas, it remained for later German ideologues to work out the theory that the Aryan race ought to be coextensive with the German nation, and that this nation should rule the world by natural right as manifested in their material power.

Early nineteenth-century German nationalists of a romantic persuasion were in favor of making political states coextensive with natural nations—indeed such was the major logic in European political partitionings throughout the nineteenth century and finally in 1919 in the Treaty of Versailles. But these same early nationalist writers were also universalists in that they respected the moral legitimacy of other nations and did not initially set themselves apart as superiors. This benign attitude led to a kind of appreciative descriptive anthropology, resulting in the collection of songbooks, folk tales, and typical artifacts by means of which other nations might be known. However, it was the clear duty of a person to cultivate those modes of speech and custom that are natural, and these derive from the nation.

It is but a short step from this cosmopolitan nationalism to a more "advanced" variety. Orwell describes a more vulgar nationalism as it was expressed in England:

All peoples who have reached the point of becoming nations tend to despise foreigners, but there is not much doubt that the English-speaking races are the worst offenders. One can see this from the fact that as soon as they become fully aware of any foreign race, they invent an insulting nickname for it. Wop, Dago, Froggy, Squarehead, Kike, Sheeny, Nigger, Wog, Chink, Greasers, Yellowbelly—these are merely a selection. (Orwell, 1939/1968, pp. 431–432)

Surely such attitudes must give tremendous satisfaction to those who hold them. All kinds of hardships might be endured with forbearance and patience if one has this kind of confidence in natural superiority—and that superiority is granted with the birthright, not attained by some test of performance or adequacy.

Individuals who do not possess any such natural surety of their own blessedness should be susceptible to appeals to seize the advantages of natural superiority. With rapid institutional change, the young find it difficult to engender such self-respect in themselves by imbibing the myths that nurtured their elders. It is the young, then, who will experience a need for a new nation. Kedourie notes that nationalist movements are dominated by the young:

Their very names are manifestoes against old age: Young Italy, Young Egypt, the Young Turks, the Young Arab Party. When they are stripped of their metaphysics and their slogans—and these cannot adequately account for the frenzy they conjure up in their followers—such movements are seen to satisfy a need, to fulfill a want. Put at its simplest, the need is to belong together in a coherent and stable community. Such a need is normally satisfied by the family, the neighborhood, the religious community. In the last century and a half such institutions all over the world have had to bear the brunt of violent social and intellectual change, and it is no accident that nationalism was at its most intense where and when such institutions had little resilience and were ill-prepared to withstand the powerful attacks to which they became exposed. (1961, p. 101)

If such a characterization applied to Mazzini and his Young Italy follow- ers, it applied with equal validity to the Woodstock Nation and its proph- ets—Jerry Rubin, Abbie Hoffman, or such academic apologists as Theodore Roszak and Charles Reich. During the Vietnam War, all the elements were present for the emergence of a new nationalism in the United States—rapid institutional change, affluence that allows a large segment of the middle class to discover their more fundamental poverty, and the strange meta- physical promise that you can be transformed and reborn into a natural human being if you will but "do it." A unique feature of this new national- ism was that the oppressor is not identified as a foreigner or alien influence, but as an endogenous entity—the Establishment, or Technocracy.

Another problem beset the new American nationalists. Revolutionary leaders knew better than to refer to some common origin of language or race as a way of creating a new mystique of nationality. Instead, reference was made to difficult abstractions such as "consciousness III" or the "psy- chedelic generation" or the "counterculture." Except for black revolution- aries, no radical political movement in the United States could hope to establish that romantic and mysterious sense of automatic brotherhood that characterized European nationalist movements in the nineteenth century. Such a mood might be established for brief intervals at music festivals or in a political campaign; but since no way was found to make such episodes a permanent feature of society there was no way of nurturing that mood from artificiality to reality.

The interpretation of nationalist movements that makes most psycho- logical sense is that they are searches for missing birthrights, or as replace- ments for birthrights that have been invalidated by the withdrawal of the granting institution or of the individual from the institution. As such, these human ventures affect primarily the granted components of social identity. The great facility with which one can "achieve" an identity in contemporary American society merely means that institutional deficiencies can be pa- pered over. But one's condition is much more significant for one's self-re- spect than is one's situation. Consequently, it is inevitable that there will be attempts, psychologically homologous to nationalist movements, to re-deem that condition.

For a long time now, but especially since the advent of nineteenth-cen-tury deterministic science into biology and the human sciences, the human birthright has been eroded away. Scientists have long ceased to regard birthrights as having any real meaning at all—anthropologists are forever giving assurances that fundamentally everybody is just like everybody else. Early nineteenth-century romantic nationalism did not destroy birthrights, yet this nationalism was compatible with universalism. Scientific univer-salism, on the other hand, gives to humans no sense of their own signifi-cance, except insofar as one can be a scientist, which, unfortunately, is an attained identity.

The novelist Kurt Vonnegut replied as follows when questioned about the impact of science:

When I went to school everybody was jeering astrology, congratulating each other on escaping these lies. Maybe we should get back to the lies and see if there is anything there after all. You have a problem in a lonely society. People think they are nobody, and somebody says when is your birthday. My God, this guy's a Leo, and pretty soon you find out who's compatible with him and life becomes very vivid because science has been abandoned and everybody's agreed to go nuts. (*New York Times Magazine*, January 24, 1971, p. 32)

For someone who has been reading about the history of nationalism, there is a familiar ring to these words. The excitement of self-discovery, the discarding of rational caution, the willingness to be guided by forces only vaguely understood—these characteristics appear to be common to cult initiation and participation in nationalist movements.

THE NATIONALISM OF INTELLECTUALS AND SCIENTISTS

The motto of my undergraduate college is *Pro ecclesia et patris*, a sentiment that must have seemed quite legitimate in the first quarter of the nineteenth century when it was adopted. But today, near the end of the twentieth century, such a motto is likely to appear at best quaintly absurd and at worst fiercely insulting to those who study and teach under the banner on which it is inscribed. Educated men and women in developed countries have for some time been in a profound dilemma with respect to the granted compo-nents of their identities. They have acquired the belief that the institutions into which they were born have been, historically, guilty of monstrous crimes while deluding themselves into self-righteousness. Much of the literature, poetry, and art of the modern era has been a steady work of breaking down illusions, of revealing hypocrisy, of demythification and deracination. It has become part of maturity to reject the naive myths of childhood.

Once disillusionment begins, the educated person develops an insatiable appetite for arguments, evidence, and illustrations on how political indoctrination "imprisons innocent children to lies." The educated person quite often succeeds in gaining liberation from the primitive emotional bonds into which he was accidentally born. But what is the psychological sequel to this liberation?

An example might be found in Orwell's characterization of the left-wing English intelligentsia:

Their obedience depended on the mystique of the Revolution, which had gradually changed itself into a nationalist loyalty to the Russian state. The English left-wing intelligentsia worship Stalin because they have lost their patriotism and the religious belief without losing the need for a god and a fatherland. (1943/1968, p. 286)

The Communist party provided intellectuals with something to believe in—something on which they could hang their identity. But this is only one of the many options that existed for intellectuals. One of the more attractive options is to become a heteronationalist, that is, an ardent nationalist for some country other than one's own. Emerging nationalism in Africa, in the Middle East, in Eastern Europe, in the territory of the former Soviet Union, and in Latin America not only fulfills economic and social needs for the regions directly affected by these changes, it also provides the observing intellectuals of developed countries a rich variety of causes in which to believe.

Another option for the redemption of a lost birthright is presented by science, which in the ideal is supposed to be no respecter of national boundaries or ethnic identity and hence is a universalist institution. Unfortunately, the plain facts of the history of scientific development spoil the illusion (Lasswell 1970). While it may be true that a small number of scientists in the history of the world have been true universalists working entirely without regard to national interests, it is surely safe to assert that most science has been and is being done as a means of promoting national interests, into which scientists have been willingly co-opted. In practice, most scientists willingly conform to the going political ideology in their countries since quite obviously they owe their very livelihood and "freedom of inquiry" to those political institutions. As Kedourie (1961) has said in a slightly different context, "It is not philosophers who become Kings, but kings who tame philosophy to their use" (p. 50). *Mutatis mutandis*, this certainly seems true for science.

Hitler was able to command the support of a large segment of the scientific community in Germany in the service of his war machine. He was even able to command congenial racial theories from his anthropologists, which, along with Lysenko's brand of genetics, we are quick to label pseudoscience. It is an open question as to how much of our currently accepted scientific dogma is similarly a matter of political conformity and expediency and might with equal rapidity be called pseudoscience from another national-ideological perspective.

If science has been guilty of facilitating the development of autonomous nationalism, while all the while posturing as something universalistic, history is guilty one hundredfold, if perhaps less pretentiously universalistic. The same is true for political science and the social sciences in general. The peculiarity of the practitioners of these arts is that they may maintain the illusion of gaining their birthright from their discipline and not from something so restrictive as a nation or a religion. Of course, the disciplines, themselves, are chartered by the nations in which they prosper, and their continued existence is at the sufferance of those nations; their efforts are largely in the national service.

NATIONALISM, RATIONALITY, AND THE PIETY OF THE SOCIAL SCIENCES

At the base of this formulation about the functional significance of nationalism is a psychological premise that may seem gratuitous from the rationalistic point of view characteristic of the social as well as the natural sciences. If people are viewed, correctly enough, as animals, it is not obvious from a comparative point of view why there should emerge with the human species a psychological need for a birthright—a fictional grant of identity that is supposed to remain with an individual throughout life. When psychologists speak of the most fundamental human needs, they are likely to present a list that can be coordinated with specifiable biological states, such as tissue deficits or optimal patterns of neural stimulation. Even such humanistic psychologists as Fromm and Maslow put such needs as hunger, thirst, and sex at the base of the hierarchy of human needs. Only in the last generation has attention been directed to the elaborate social organization of primates in their natural habitat (Goodall 1965; Washburn and DeVore 1961), so that one may begin to see some respectable evolutionary anchorage for such a phrase as the "need for stable identification with a social collectivity." For human beings it may be that motives deriving from the problem of identity are at least as fundamental as those drives that are customarily considered biological, such as sex. When a person's stomach is full, one has leisure to pursue a possible, unrewarding series of contemplations about such problems as the meaning of one's life and the importance of one's efforts. At the human level, mere organic survival potential is not the ultimate evolutionary value, however useful this concept may be when applied to the entire animal kingdom.

Nationalism is but one of the mythic enterprises by which men and women have been enthralled in what amounts, functionally, to attempts at detrivializing their existence. But because this special kind of human need frequently leads to behaviors that are noneconomic, from a narrower biological point of view (wars, crusades, religious movements, committee meetings, games, and sporting events) there has been a tendency for scientists to consider birthright needs as distinctly secondary or pathological, or both. Also, the monster serpent of superstition was supposed to have been laid to rest by the Enlightenment, by the industrial revolution, and by such intellectual companion movements as positivism. But the very success of these movements in serving humanity's tissue deficit needs has given the monster surcease from persecution, so that it may be in the ascendancy.

More recently, Freudian psychology has made the mistake of placing sex at the base of all human motives. Eighty years later a youthful revolutionary would proclaim, "General liberation is general copulation" (Jerry Rubin). Yet surely it is not a naive observation that human beings who copulate *ad libitum* discover that they have other problems. By a revision and extension of the "when a man's stomach is empty. . . ." cliche, it may be that the success of the sexual revolution exposes a much more fundamental and universal human problem—and I think that this will be the problem of the birthright grant.

This leads me to be highly critical of an easy liberal piety among social scientists. In the general introduction to the "World Perspectives" series of historical essays, Ruth Nanda Anshen asserts: "It is the thesis of 'World Perspectives' that man is in the process of developing a new consciousness which, in spite of his apparent spiritual and moral captivity, can eventually lift the human race above and beyond the fear, ignorance, and isolation which beset it today" (Kohn 1962, p. vii). Further, she states, "Beyond the divisiveness among men there exists a primordial unitive power since we are all bound together by a common humanity more fundamental than any unity of dogma. . . . Science, when not inhibited by the limitations of its own methodology, when chastened and humbled, commits man to an indeterminate range of yet undreamed consequences. . . ." (p. ix). These are phrases worth pondering, for they express the belief that if only people will be sensible, they can be led from fear, ignorance, and isolation into a condition of human fulfillment, with science the humble handmaiden to the enlightened progress of humanity.

These sentiments translate the hope that people will be sensible and see what is best for them into the expectation that they surely will. Such optimism is revealed even more clearly in Hans Kohn's conclusion to the same volume:

The 1960's are not a period of intellectual and spiritual sterility. Great works of art may not be created at present, but the treasures of many centuries in poetry, music and painting are today far more accessible to greater multitudes than they were in the past. . . . The rapid progress of science will not only change our knowledge and mastery of the outside world, it will refine and broaden our concern with our fellow man; it will alter and improve the scope and methods of human welfare and psychological understanding. In the 1960's, men are pushing forward, beyond any previous experience, toward higher forms of international integration—in the Inter-American Alliance for Progress, in Asian and African unity conferences, in the European Common Market, and the African unity conferences, and the North Atlantic Community, in the United Nations. No one foresaw these developments in 1940. They are experiments in building new frameworks for coexistence and cooperation, for mastering problems on the solution of which the survival of a great part of mankind may depend. (pp. 166–167)

In fairness to Kohn, these words must have had a different sound at the beginning of the Kennedy years. That most of the regional organizations to which he pointed would have come to grief along precisely nationalist lines could not have been obvious in 1960. But surely now our hopes for such a millennium should be chastened.

By returning once again to Cassirer, I think one may obtain a clearer vision of the future. It is indisputable that political myths, many of them in the form of nationalist doctrines, have been at the source of many of the great troubles of the twentieth century. Ample basis exists for fearing trouble again from this ideological quarter. But Cassirer notes his reservations about the facile combination of wish and reason:

It is beyond the power of philosophy to destroy the political myths. A myth is in a sense invulnerable. It is impervious to rational arguments; it cannot be refuted by syllogisms. But philosophy can do us another important service. It can make us understand the adversary. . . . To know him means not only to know his defects and weaknesses; it means to know his strength. All of us have been liable to underrate this strength. When we first heard of the political myths we found them so absurd and incongruous, so fantastic and ludicrous that we could hardly be prevailed upon to take them seriously. By now it has become clear to all of us that this was a great mistake. We should not commit the same error a second time. We should carefully study the origin, the structure, the methods, and the technique of the political myths. We should see the adversary face to face in order to know how to combat him. (1946 p. 296)

Among other things, this is a call for a certain kind of intellectual courage. Political and social developments that seem to be regressions to primitivism and myth are not to be reviled or dismissed as irrelevant because they do not appear to spring from respectable sources. It must be recognized that when people are in a certain condition, the invitation to danger and destiny is psychologically far more powerful than the invitation to a life of ease. Don Quixote awakens when Sancho Panza sleeps.

Orwell, to whom reference has been made several times in this chapter, displayed the kind of courage of which I am thinking. He was capable of seeing the evil in that which he loved—socialism—and the genuine appeal of that which he hated—totalitarianism.

Hitler, because in his own joyless mind he feels it with exceptional strength, knows that human beings *don't* only want comfort, safety, short working-hours, hygiene, birth-control, and in general common sense; they also, at least intermittently, want struggle and self-sacrifice, not to mention drums, flags, and loyalty parades. However they may be as economic theories, Fascism and Nazism are psychologically far sounder than any hedonistic conception of life. The same is probably true of Stalin's militarized version of Socialism. . . . After a few years of slaughter and starvation "Greatest happiness to the greatest number" is a good slogan, but at this moment, "Better an end with horror than a horror without end" is a winner. Now that we are fighting against the man who coined it, we ought not to underrate its emotional appeal. (1940/1968, p. 14)

Those who dare to look an enemy in the face are in danger of being suspected by more timid observers of being on the point of embracing their adversary. Certainly Orwell has been criticized in precisely this way. But his is a psychology less flawed by sentimental blindness and doctrinaire ideology than that produced by the bulk of psychologists and other social scientists. Not only do most psychologists refuse to take national identity seriously as a legitimate problem for research, those who do write on the problem seem bent on explaining it away in the course of preparing their moral case for universalistic utopianism. This is a condition that ought to be corrected, and this is a problem to which philosophers, in the broad sense of that term, can apply themselves to good effect and perhaps gain thereby some sense of legitimacy in their own calling.

NOTE

1. In 1945, there were 51 members of the United Nations. By September, 1992, there were 154 member nations. There is no sign that the number of nations on the face of the earth will be reduced by voluntary consolidation. Rather, divisive pressures of the sort evident in Northern Ireland or Quebec or Bosnia continue to have prominence. Whatever the psychological or social relief provided by the end of colonialism and of communism, in a certain rough empirical sense the world is much further away from universalism now than it was a generation or a century ago.

Chapter 6

Memory, Identity, and History

> We could not understand because we were too far and could not remember because we were travelling in the night of first ages, of those ages that are gone, leaving hardly a sign—and no memories.
> —Joseph Conrad, *Heart of darkness*

Living memory enables the binding of time and the realization of human identity. Yet as the experimental or physiological psychologist studies the problem, memory refers to a human capacity that stands outside of time. What are the informational limits of memory capacity? How does information pass from short-term to long-term memory? What are the relationships between sensory modalities and ease of information storage and retrieval?

The importance of these problems, and of the neurophysiology of memory, derives from the pervasive functional role played by memory in all intelligent behavior—speech production and comprehension, decision making, problem solving and the performance of complex motor activities. The term "memory" carries a hint of mentalism, and for this reason it was avoided or used with some embarrassment by strictly mechanistic behaviorists. But now that computer analogies have demonstrated the necessity of employing memory in a functional sense, all of this reserve has evaporated, and memory is here to stay as a central topic in psychology.

While the computer has helped in this way to restore and invigorate research on memory, the computer analogy has at the same time served to obscure the functioning of memory in sustaining human identity, for the memory of a computer does not perform this function. Similarly, the experimental psychology of memory is exclusively concerned with what the person *does* or can *do*. But the psychologist must ask also how memory operates in determining who and what the person *is*. The major purpose of this chapter is to elaborate upon the significance of memory in the development and maintenance of human identity.

In the course of this exposition, it will prove necessary to touch upon the nature of history and on certain problematic features of historiography. The significance of history in illuminating the problem of human identity is an obvious psychological problem, but one that is still a bit strange in contemporary practice. The fundamental premise is that human lives are lived in historical time and in the terms of that time they take their meaning. A particular person's self-understanding and identity is provided in historically particular terms—with proper names, specificity of time, an understanding of the particularity of circumstance.

This approach to identity leads inevitably back to the problem of conduct—of what people do. Actors on a historical stage do not just exist; they act, and they act out of the conditions of their character and circumstances. Of course, they must act in accord with the limits and capacities of the nervous and motoric systems with which they are endowed. In this way, the traditional experimental study of memory systems complements the study of memory as a means of developing and sustaining personal identity. Human life is biographical as well as biological, and it is clear that memory has sense from both of these perspectives.

The following section is an attempt to develop a sense of the role of memory from the biographical perspective. In order to illustrate this role, it will be useful to describe some reference cases.

MEMORIES AND IDENTITIES OF THE AGED: SOME CASES

I choose here to present records of the lives of old people—lives near the end of their biological course, but possessing a particular biographical richness. In the first two cases, this richness is diminished by impairments of memory function. These cases will be followed by a composite description of a set of old people with particularly vivid and active memories.

Marcus L: Alzheimer's Syndrome and the Fading of Memory and Identity

Alzheimer's syndrome has been identified for many years, but only recently has it received wide recognition as a serious problem for research. The most typical symptom of Alzheimer's syndrome is progressive memory loss, beginning in late middle age. The syndrome is evidently of neurophysiological origin, and recent studies have developed promising leads regarding neural sites and possible etiological factors, both environmental and genetic. The psychological side of the syndrome is of particular interest, for the memory loss is not typically accompanied by physical or motoric deterioration. At the present time, no therapeutic means exists to halt or reverse the progressive loss of memory.

The case of Marcus L. fits the general profile of Alzheimer patients.[1] A successful lawyer, widely read and well travelled, Marcus retired from the bar at age sixty-five. Since he and his wife were divorced, he lived after retirement with one or another of his three children, or with his sister and her family. This arrangement entailed a fair amount of travel, since Marcus would typically stay with one of these relations for less than a year, and in some years would visit all of them.

Memory loss became a serious problem for Marcus after retirement, but he often remarked before his retirement that he simply couldn't remember things. As a lawyer, this had bothered him considerably, for memory for case and procedure was vital to his practice. His awareness of memory loss was a factor in his decision to retire before he was required to do so. Memory lapses became most conspicuous in matters of travel and spatial orientation. Marcus would sometimes forget to pick up his suitcase after a flight or bus trip to a relative's city. Or he would forget where the relative lived in that city, and forget their name as well. After several misadventures, it became clear to all the relatives that he could not travel alone without having someone to send him off and to greet him at the terminal points of his trip, with instructions to attendants to insure his disembarking at the right point. Also, he began to wander off frequently from homes where he was staying and would be unable to report where he was staying to strangers or to police who picked him up. It became necessary to make for him an identification bracelet, including not only his name, but the name and address and telephone number of the relative engraved upon it. Thereafter, when he became lost, he would show the identification bracelet to someone and thus make contact again with his family. Over the years, these disappearances became increasingly frequent, for while his memory processes were evidently quite impaired, his physical strength and vigor were undiminished, and it was not possible to supervise him constantly or to confine him.

Parallel with spatial disorientation was a loss of memory for names and faces, as well as a loss of memory for matters of personal history. Once at a party, Marcus hastened to introduce one of the guests to "my old friend." The "old friend" was in fact his son, but he could not remember his name. The son's wife and children also lost their names in his memory, though he could still refer to them correctly on occasion as "the wife," "the older child" or "the husband."

In his early seventies, Marcus experienced problems of temporal disorientation and confusion about matters of personal apparel. He would sometimes arise in the middle of the night and get fully dressed. Or, he would go through his nightly retirement ritual at four o'clock in the afternoon. He also began to put on shirts over shirts, pants over pants, and socks over socks, apparently forgetting that he had already dressed himself with one layer of clothing. Sometimes he would put on as many as six or seven shirts, in summer as well as winter.

At about age seventy-four, Marcus had forgotten everyone's name but his own, which he would invariably pronounce with pride when asked to recite it, often adding a phrase or two about his early boyhood. By this time, he had forgotten that he had ever been a lawyer, and had no idea of where he had lived or what he had done for his entire adult life. He could not remember his age, the city where he was living, the day of the week, month or year. He would also sometimes report as real certain imaginary trips he had made to Russia, to Africa, or to the moon, in company with U.S. astronauts. He still recognized people he lived with, but not by name. At this time, he was admitted to a nursing home. While he was physically quite vigorous and healthy, his memory loss was so complete as to require twenty-four-hour supervision, which could not be provided in his family residences. After admission to the nursing home, which he accepted quite placidly, his mental condition continued to deteriorate. By age seventy-eight he could no longer report his own name and showed no sign of recognition to visiting relatives. The nursing staff would continue to call him by his name, and he did show some signs of recognizing it. For the last three years of his life, he was almost completely nonverbal, except for frequent bursts of song. During this period he was confined to a bed or to a closed chair, and his physical condition deteriorated markedly. He died at age eighty-two of a pulmonary condition.

Among Alzheimer patients, the emotional concomitants of memory loss are not at all uniform—some remain good-humored and placid, such as Marcus, while others become violently abusive or severely depressed. But it is remarkable that the emotional consequences for relatives and friends of the suffering person are common in nature and intensity. The failure of personal recognition is highly distressing to a wife or son or daughter. Relatives visiting Alzheimer patients in nursing homes become discouraged after failing repeatedly to obtain a flicker of recognition, and are loath to make further visits because of the emotional burden of such failure. Initially, family members react with anger to memory lapses, mistakes or failed recognition. Later, after struggling with the irreversible problem for years, the family suffers the inevitable guilt accompanying recognition that no amount of love or attention can succeed in restoring the sufferer to his previous condition. Commitment to a nursing home is almost invariably required, and this in turn leads to further feelings of guilt and depression on the part of the family. Their own identities are affected by the gradual disappearance of memory and identity in one who had been of central significance in their lives.

Sudden Stop: Anterograde Amnesia and Arrest of Identity

The case of Jimmy R. contrasts with that of Marcus L. in many respects.[2] Jimmy, who had been a chronic alcoholic, showed a symptom pattern consistent with Korsakov's syndrome. Jimmy had been in the Navy in the Second World War, continuing in that service until 1966, when his chronic alcoholism forced his retirement and his institutionalization. After his institutionalization, Jimmy's memory regressed back to 1945. A bright, energetic and physically able man, Jimmy's life story became permanently arrested at age nineteen. The continued aging of both himself and the world were quite unknowable to him. He had lost the capacity to transfer information from short-term to long-term memory.

As a consequence of this condition, Jimmy's institutional life was in many respects unusual. He could not remember names or faces of doctors, staff or patients in the hospital. On meeting his brother, whom he had known before the border date of 1945, he recognized him, but showed great puzzlement that he looked so very old. After leaving the company of his brother, he entirely forgot their first meeting, and meeting again, Jimmy showed exactly the same confusion.

Jimmy had an identity and a life story, but not one that corresponded with the chronology of his life. He could recall events of his early life in lucid detail, and had an uncanny knowledge of the current events of 1945. But after that, nothing. Were the time of the world to have stopped with Jimmy, there would have been no need to institutionalize him, for his knowledge and behavior were appropriate to that date. But given the arrest of his memory—his inability to provide new material to long-term memory—his identity-narrative was also arrested, with devastating consequences for his ability to get along in the world.

Unlike Marcus L., who showed until his last few years an awareness that his memory was progressively failing, Jimmy's arrest of memory included the limitation of not realizing that he had any memory loss at all. His case is analogous to that of a brain-injured patient, who in addition to the loss of vision, loses as well all visual memory—all recollection of ever having seen and all conception of what the faculty of vision might be. Jimmy was told by his doctor exactly what his problem was, and on the occasion of telling, apparently understood. But a few minutes later, it was as if he had never seen the doctor before, and had no remaining understanding of the limits of his memory, for he had forgotten. Jimmy was stuck in time, and so severely stuck that even the subsequent knowledge that he was stuck could not register.

The Richness of Mature and Intact Memories

Both memory and identity are in a strong sense social. Memory comes alive in the act of narration, and identity is realized when the self is presented to another. Memory is mere latent potential until it is recalled and retold in the form of story, and identity is reduced to the sadness of solitude for those to whom no attention is paid. It is one of the tragedies of our age that those old people who have the most to tell us about our world are left unattended, and their life stories, untold, lie inert and useless even to the beings who possess those lives.

The antithesis of this tragedy is illustrated in a remarkable book by Eclea Bosi (Bosi 1979), *Memoria e sociedade*, which recounts the life stories of eight old residents of São Paulo. The stories are composed narratives derived from prolonged series of conversations between Dr. Bosi and each of her informants. Here is represented a series of natural miracles. There sits an old man or woman, waiting in dim solitude to sicken and die. Here comes a researching psychologist, who turns out to be a genuine friend. For this psychologist did not come prearmed with categories and theories into which the stories of lives must be forced. Eclea Bosi presents the rare spectacle of the psychologist simply surrendering to her material, so that the material is in no sense subject to her, but is instead invested with full human dignity.

In these psychological studies, the "subjects" have real names, and the incidents they recount stand on their own terms, without tests of internal consistency, external veracity or interpretive significance. Think of the contrast of this style of report and the ordinary psychoanalytic case history, where real identities are shielded with an invented name, where nothing the patient says is taken at face value and where the sense or truth of the story is only revealed through the interpretations provided by the doctor. I think it is more than a question of psychological taste to prefer the former sort of story to the latter.

The stories told to Bosi all begin with a recounting of the time and circumstances of birth, proceeding in a roughly chronological way to recount the story of early childhood, the critical transition phase involving the dissolving of the home and family of youth and the formation of the home and family of adulthood. Here are stories of first loves, of disappointments, of successes, of deaths, accidents, marriages, births, travels, adventures, engagement in public life, economic hard times, times of happiness, of sorrow, of folly.

The narrators manifest a joy in the telling, and are often pleased and astonished as memories come into fresh life in the revivifying light of Dr. Bosi's attention. It is as if a sudden egress into consciousness were provided for narrative material that had been smoldering in silence for years. One consequence of this outpouring is an obvious and developing affection of the old people for their interlocutor. One cannot help but conclude that the narrators also come to feel better about themselves as a consequence of this opportunity to replay their life stories in sympathetic conversation.

There is, finally, an unexpected benefit: Since these eight narrators all lived at roughly the same time in roughly the same place, the reader is provided a rare composite portrait of the ambiance of the city of São Paulo in the early twentieth century. This is a history from the inside out, not from the outside in. The ordinary historian is a recorder of events and circumstances, a chronicler of the public and observable. By contrast, we have in these narratives eight separate and distinct views of Paulistana life and culture in the form of personal memories. In some cases entire wars and major crises are passed over, quite unperceived. On the other hand, great importance may be attached to the form and feel of the cobblestones of a particular street. Since all views of history are incomplete and partial, a multiplicity of perspectives provides the best hope of attaining historical truth. These internal stories provide a salutary complement to the formalized external accounts provided by historians. The feel and smell and taste of life are conveyed in these stories with a poignancy that is unattainable for most social histories.

Experienced or psychological time is not at all a constantly flowing stream. Major attention is lavished on the events of a few days; decades are accorded scarcely a word. Commonly, a narrator is able to identify something of an ideal period in the course of the life—the period from which one would select the photograph representing for the narrator a kind of idealized permanent picture of the self. It would be uncharitable to say that the narrators do not think of themselves as they really are, for in this sense we are all guilty of autobiographical distortion. We have, after all, the general custom of giving our ages as our previous birthday, not our next one; except for children, who have an interest in presenting themselves as older than they are. Memory jumps about, is fleeting, ever selective, ever flexible regarding objectivity; now it is blocked, now it flows smoothly, now it cycles and returns to the same point; now it finds a peaceful haven of the harmony of life, now it is drawn irresistibly into dark chambers of horror.

MEMORY AS ACTIVE CONSTRUCTION: IMPLICATIONS FOR IDENTITY

The accepted view within experimental psychology on the basic nature of memory processes has changed considerably in the last generation. In some ways, this change represents a return to the views of earlier writers on the topic, particularly Bartlett (1932), whose studies led him to view memory not as a process of passively storing information, but rather as involving the active organization of mental content around implicit mental structures, or schemata. Before Bartlett, James (1890) had considered the essence of memory to be the active organization of content into semantically ordered structures.

The conception of memory as active construction rather than as passive registration works both for and against the mere efficiency of memory as measured by the ability to recall with accuracy. Memory is partly a matter of recalling that which once was. But in addition, we remember that which never was and forget material which was most concretely and palpably presented to the senses.

In effect, recent studies of memory represent a restoration of meaning to the problem. Over one hundred years after Ebbinghaus' invention of the non-syllable, psychology has finally regained an appreciation of the importance of meaning in memory. As a consequence, there have been many recent studies of memory for prose passages, a tradition that really owes its beginning to Bartlett's work in the 1930s. A general conclusion of this work is that one remembers extended prose in terms of some overall pattern, structure, organization or schema (Thorndyke 1977). The dramatic studies of Bransford and Frank (1971) showed that subjects reported with high certainty having seen sentences that in fact they had never seen, on condition that those sentences were logically implied by a general story framework provided by other sentences.

That all of this has much to do with the identity problem is shown most clearly in the spate of work on "self as narrative" (Mancuso and Ceely 1980; Spence 1982; Mancuso and Sarbin 1983; Gergen and Gergen 1983). If memory for external stimuli is selective, constructive, and subject to the organizational constraints of predispositions to certain kinds of meaning by observers, then memory for one's own story must *a fortiori* obey the same principles.

Certainly the evidence favors the conclusion that memory for self is selective, constructive, and subject to organizational constraints of predispositions to certain kinds of meaning. I do not assert that memory is somehow tailored by individuals to produce for themselves a life story that is singular and integral in its meaning, or polished of flaws, blemishes, and contradictions. Rather, I propose the more modest claim that we do not simply register and preserve our life experiences as they are given, but rather take and ignore such experiences selectively, and from them construct narratives of who we are. As we have more than one audience for which such narratives might serve, so we have more than one story. And as we are ourselves a kind of audience-of-one for ourselves, we may be expected to have a special and allowably complex version of our story for internal consumption. The twin questions of *agency* and *interest* must for the present remain open. Even though the self is author and agent of narrative construction, it is clearly not able to construct anything at all by way of a story—but must obey requirements and compulsions seen and unseen. Clearly also one does not always observe some easy hedonic calculus of self-interest in constructing or narrating one's story. Oddly enough, pre-writing of one's story may include one's own suicide, as in the cases of Anne Sexton, Sylvia Plath, Robert Barryman, Ernest Hemingway and other self-tortured poets. Sometimes the scripts of other lives are taken as models for our own stories, so that the identities taken on are adaptations or versions of stories first lived or invented by others, a phenomenon which

Sarbin (1982) has discussed under the heading of the Quixote Principle. These transformations of art to life and back to art provide matter of which psychologists must take account, however complicating they might be to simple theory.

The two cases of memory pathology presented in the previous section are interpretable from this view of memory for self as construction. In the case of Marcus L., the gradual fading of memory over time amounted in functional terms to a gradual fading out or diminution of his identity. It is as if the moment of death were extended for him—played out in slow motion—over a period of fifteen years. As his memory was reduced, his ability to sustain his own story in the company of his family and former associates was likewise diminished. In the end, his own story was obliterated in him, while it continued and doubtless continues to exist in the living memory of those who knew him. Similarly, for Jimmy R. there came to exist a radical disparity between his story as he could retell it and his story as it was understood by the hospital staff and others in his surroundings. For Jimmy was unable to continue to refine and extend his own narrative in tempo with the rest of the human company. And as his identity strayed away from acceptable or tolerable limits of distortions, he was effectively disabled as an actor on the normal human stage.

The cases recounted by Eclea Bosi serve equally well as illustrations of the connection between reconstructions of memory and the representations of one's own identity. In particular, these stories show the import of what Bartlett referred to in his studies of memory as conventionalization. The story of an old citizen of São Paulo is necessarily told in terms of the conventionalized social institutions, categories and customs particular to time and place. These stories all begin with reference to the birth of the story-teller. But these beginnings are never described abstractly, as "I was born." But rather, "I was born on August 15, 1902, on Rua _____, in the city of São Paulo." Then begins an account of who the father and mother were, again not abstractly, but in terms of particular historical facts and circumstances. These narratives are intelligible only in contextual terms. Someone knowing nothing of the religious, political, cultural, and familial traditions of Brazil in the early twentieth century would find these stories quite unintelligible, and were they to be retold by such a person, they would of necessity be conventionalized in other and alien terms. Thus one might consider rendering a version of the life of St. Augustine in Marxist or Freudian terms, but in so doing, one must recognize that such an exercise is an enormous biographical crime, for it implies a magisterial negation of the conventions of Augustine's own time and context, however remote these might be to us. One of Bosi's informants asserts, near the end of her story, that she has always been a rebel, has always "rowed against the current." But even though she defined herself in contradiction to the dominant conventions of her time, still her identity takes its true meaning only by relation to those conventions.

Bartlett was hardly thinking of the problem of identity when he wrote of the operation of memory. And yet we can make a ready application of his characterization:

It looks as if what is said to be reproduced is, far more generally than is commonly admitted, really a construction, serving to justify whatever impression may have been left by the original. It is this "impression", rarely defined with much exactitude, which most readily persists. So long as the details which can be built up around us are such that they would give it a "reasonable" setting, most of us are fairly content, and are apt to think that what we build we have literally retained. (1932, p. 176)

Similarly, Tversky and Kahnemann (1973) have demonstrated the enormous significance of vividness of imagery in facilitating and also in distorting memory. One's memory is selectively retentive for particularly vivid or meaningful material, or for material that "fits in." The act of recalling is not a matter of simply reproducing that which was presented, but of reconstructing what must have been presented, in order that some meaningful or vivid image of a story might be supported. Studies of factors influencing the accuracy of eyewitness testimony likewise have demonstrated convincingly the importance of the observer's particular patterns of meaningful construction in determining what is observed, or what is remembered as having been observed.

The most general point I wish to make is given clear illustration by Bartlett's series of original studies on remembering. Using the method of "serial reproductions," Bartlett demonstrated that visual and prose material tended in their successive reproductions by memory toward simplification, conventionalization and sharpening of detail, in accord with the selective principles of the observer. Thus, a very irregular face mask is sifted through memory and emerges as an ordinary and highly simplified sketch of a human face. Odd and incongruous elements are dropped out of stories; in successive repetitions, stories are told in such a way as to make sense from the framework of the culture from which the original story was taken. Bartlett commonly observed in these successive retellings of stories a complete reversal in the main point or moral sense of a tale. For example, a folktale emphasizing the deep respect the young have for the wisdom of the old is transformed in its retelling into a story describing the relief of a youth in escaping the punishment and domination of his father.

The sort of life story told by an old person is a construction, a fabrication that reveals certain truths both about the agent of construction and about the world from which the materials of construction are borrowed. In the case of a failing or arrested memory, the power to construct and maintain a narrative is diminished or destroyed. In the case of intact and functioning memories, we observe arrangements of details of life lived around some central self-impression, which, as Bartlett observes is "rarely defined with much exactitude." But the details and their arrangement reveal two sorts of reality—one inner and one outer. The inner reality, itself without articulate voice, is revealed by the conformation of arranged detail—a kind of visible shell constructed over an invisible and impalpable core. The external reality, of course, is revealed by the very substance of the details appropriated by the storyteller from that person's providential location in time and circumstance. The "I" is unintelligible out of its circumstances. And circumstances can only be understood from the tacit position of "that which they are about." This is, I believe, what is meant by Ortega y Gassett's enigmatic expression, "I am I plus my circumstance."

Another of the conceptions of contemporary cognitive psychology is of great use in illuminating the relationship between identity and memory. Tulving (1972) first coined the distinction between episodic and semantic memory. Episodic memory is located in time, is tokened by the recall of specific events in specific historical context, as in "Last February, just at the end of a bitterly cold and snowy month in Connecticut, I embarked for a week's vacation in the Caribbean." Semantic memory is of a different sort, and has to do with the recognition of conventionalized patterns of meaning, quite apart from historical or temporal context. Thus, Jimmy R., no longer able to register episodes into a continuing story of his life, could nevertheless remember quite well that the food on his plate is for eating, the bed for sleeping, and language for talking. He used language with great precision of meaning, and could solve difficult puzzles if they did not require memory for events as opposed to memory for meaningful relationships. While recent interpretations suggest connections and certain grey areas in these two types of memory, it is generally accepted that the functional distinction is useful. In describing cases of damaged or disordered identities, the distinction has obvious applicability. For a semantic sense of identity may remain after one literally has become disconnected from time through destruction or atrophy of episodic memory.

Even though one's chronological story might effectively cease to be known or controlled from the inside, it is not proper to conclude thereby that an inner sense of identity does not exist. In this condition, "I am I plus my circumstance" would mean that I am able to understand and be related to the palpable and immediate reality of the present—that episodes of the past and possible episodes of the future do not form part of these circumstances. Even though identity is thus reduced in the dimension of time to an apparently motionless present, it cannot be said to disappear, for it can retain its own existential semantics. "A man does not consist of memory alone. He has feeling, will, sensibilities, moral being, matters of which neurophysiology cannot speak" (Luria, in Sacks 1983, p. 12). In this statement, Luria is referring directly to loss of memory of the episodic kind, suggesting that a continuous sense of existence remains in someone like

Jimmy R., even though that continuity has nothing to do with what is ordinarily thought of as a historical line.

Bosi employs a distinction between *information* and *narration* in a way that parallels the distinction between episodic and semantic memory. Semantic memory allows for the processing of information and its effective and correct interpretation. Computers process information—they register it, store it, manipulate it, transform it, retrieve it and reproduce it. Human beings are simulated by computers in these functions, but only insofar as their semantic memories are concerned. When it comes to episodic memory, the computer analogy becomes strained and awkward. For human beings are not mere processors of information, they are inventors and makers of narratives, including narratives about themselves. Human episodic memory is a means by which selves are related to history and to the particularity of circumstance. This process is creative, original, constructive and not always subject to the constraints of realism.

Human episodic memory makes it possible for a person to continue the development and refinement of his self-narratives. This in turn makes it possible to retain a knowable social identity and thus to enter into normal social interactions, conversations and relationships that are conceived as transcending the limits of the present (Scheibe 1979). The truncation of episodic memory entails a corresponding truncation in social identity, or the development of what sociologists refer to as socially atomized persons. The socially atomized person retains semantic memory, and thus is able to function meaningfully in the present. But relationships—such as marriage, filial identity, brotherhood, loyalty to clan, religion, race, nation, employer, or to any social entity remote in time or place—all of these are impossible to the socially atomized person. The socially atomized person is unloosed from all historical connections through the disappearance of episodic memory.

MEMORY, HISTORY, AND THE QUESTION OF CONTROL

> Who controls the present controls the future, and who controls the past controls the present.
>
> —George Orwell, 1984

The previous section suggests some of the ways in which an individual's capacity to remember is related to that individual's ability to construct and maintain an identity. In this section, I propose to examine the extension of this argument to the memory of collectivities of individuals—that supra-individual memory known as history.

It is, of course, outrageous to regard history merely as that which happens to be remembered. But a psychological perspective on the meaning of history enables us to set aside for a time all the vexed questions of what history might be, in favor of a straightforward functionalist view of the matter. What provides an outside frame and context for the meaning of the story of the individual is not history as it may have really happened, or history as it is recorded in the most authoritative books, or history as it is revealed in the interpretative modes most in current vogue, but rather history as it happens to be transmitted to and understood by the individual. We can see from this perspective another outrageous fact: As the narrative form and content of history can be revised or renegotiated by those in a position to control the telling of history, so can the meaning and content of an individual's life be radically reconstrued by such changes. The life of Napoleon was whatever it was. But the way we regard the life of Napoleon—who we think him to be, and of what quality—is very much a function of the historical frame in which his life story is placed. This is no fixed matter, but a matter of continual negotiation and interested change.

The pigs in *Animal Farm* crawled up on the side of the barn at night and revised the principle of universal equality by introducing the qualifier, "but some animals are more equal than others" (Orwell 1946). Similarly, in *1984*, the work of the Ministry of Truth was to comb published historical records and to delete inconvenient passages, making revisions according to the needs of the moment (Orwell 1949). These caricatures were meant by Orwell to represent a real danger—that of allowing historical memory to be controlled by a single interested group. Indeed, the controllers of history can turn the truth inside out, upside down or simply obliterate it. Just as Bartlett demonstrated the strong effect of social conventionalizations in the operation of individual memory, so is collective memory—history—conventionalized by the currents of present interests. Totalitarianism, in this interpretation, is simply the centralization of the control of transmitted history. The meaning of the present is controlled by the memory of the past. In turn, the options for future courses of action are limited and defined by the sense of present reality. If this control is centralized and complete, then War can become Peace, Freedom can become Slavery, and Love can become Hate. Examples of these perverse transformations are all about us, as when armies are called, "Peace-keeping forces," when harbors are mined by the United States in Central America in order to preserve "democratic choice," when concentration camps are referred to as "reeducation centers," etc. Somehow Christianity, a religion based on brotherly love, love of one's enemy and turning the other cheek, is used as a basis for justifying genocidal campaigns; and Marxism, a doctrine committed to the elimination of all forms of human oppression, becomes, in interested hands, a doctrine most flexibly applicable to the justification of mighty and generalized oppressions.

Our present view of history, while it does contain vast margins of doubt and ignorance, is nevertheless quite fixed in many of its central features. Yet what is now taken as given—the sanctity of the U.S. Constitution for instance—was once a matter of urgent debate and honest doubt. The genius of Gabriel Garcia Marquez's (1970) *One hundred years of solitude* is that he manages to demonstrate through a work of fiction the way in which history has been made and remade and remade again in Latin America. Somehow, in Macondo, the mythic bedrock of history has not yet been touched.

Of course, what seems to be historical bedrock sometimes turns to sand. Why should King Henry VIII have cared greatly whether or not he was to be excommunicated on account of his desire for divorce? What is status in the Roman Church but a matter of established and mutable convention? And what is marriage, after all, but a fictive arrangement of convenience that may be nullified at any time? To ask such questions seriously, of course, is to betray an enfeebled sense of the enveloping power of historically carried beliefs and conventions. "What the whole community comes to believe in grasps the individual as in a vise," said William James (1910/1984, p. 358). The most powerful controllers of our lives are such deeply engrained conventions that they seem not to be conventions at all, but immutable truths. Money, for example, is nothing at all unless it is conventionally agreed to be a legal medium of exchange. And neither has gold any intrinsic value, apart from common assent. The Indian has a full right to his belief that land is not ownable by mere men, but belongs eternally to the Great Spirit, but this view is laughable in our courts. Slavery, where it exists, is justified by a congenial history. Hitler, in mounting with insane racist ambition the program of a thousand-year Reich, tried to command into existence a history and a prehistory, supported by scholarly and anthropological authority, to make fully reasonable and legitimate his program. Now in the United States, historians have discovered to their chagrin that the country's story has been transmitted with overwhelmingly powerful biases against women, blacks and other minorities, so as to provide a tacit justification for the continued social deprivation of such groups. Now that social historians are trying to provide a corrective to the errors of the past, they are themselves charged with using history as polemic or apologia for some desired social change. Meanwhile, prominent figures of the past are not even free in death from changes in the historical frame. Corpses in Moscow are hefted about—to and from less and more honored sites. Mao Tse Tung is now built up as a saint, now derided as an evil menace, now redeemed again. Thomas Jefferson is drawn as a slave-owning philanderer, and not even Abraham Lincoln is free from the reconstructors of his story.

In Brazil during the era of military rule which ended in 1985, the government wanted to have people believe that the twenty years of military rule produced an enormous surge of prosperity and development because of the sure and firm hand of the benevolent and far-seeing military leaders. But as soon as this government allowed an "abertura," it became possible to counteract this official story with other and less flattering versions of the historical forces that have been flowing and acting for the twenty-year period. The film *Jango* is an attempt to provide a rereading, not only of the character and quality of the last elected president of Brazil, but also of the entire flux of the historical currents that led to his downfall and to the establishment of the military government. Now, after a decade of civilian rule and accompanying economic social and economic turmoil, the idea of military rule is looking better and better.

Such examples can be multiplied at will. Indeed, it is the daily work of newspapers, journals, scholarly reviews, and political and historical writings to remake and reread the past. From whatever systematic or haphazard contact the developing person has with all of this historical working and reworking, the terms of one's own story are defined and provided. The story of a particular person's identity must be worked out with the materials that are given to it on a particular stage of history.

Given the conditions of a particular stage of history, individuals come to enact a particular form of story, or become a particular kind of person. Sometimes this is described as learning of one's vocation or calling, as if there were some voice out there making heard its claim for a particular form of service. Indeed, there are many such voices. The developing young person is not allowed to drift passively into the future, but must perforce have a plan, a program, a profession, a career, or plans for an adventure or for a family, or even for a life of reflection and meditation. The social nexus will not rest until the developing young person has covered the nakedness of a vacant life with some serviceable story, entailing some sort of progression or dramatic development.

Russell Baker's biography, *Growing up*, contains a description of how Baker acquired a legitimate career story for himself:

The only thing that truly interested me was writing, and I knew that sixteen-year-olds did not come out of high school and become writers. I thought of writing as something to be done only by the rich. It was so obviously not real work, not a job at which you could earn a living. Still I had begun to think of myself as a writer. It was the only thing for which I seemed to have the smallest talent, and silly though it sounded when I told people I'd like to be a writer, it was one way of thinking about myself which satisfied my need to have an identity. (1983, p. 121)

Fortunately, the world was sufficiently cooperative with this protean self-definition to allow its full realization. The consolidation of a presentable life story is always a joint product of internal interests and external forces. In the best of cases, these pressures converge to produce roughly the same story.

Life is begun without a story. Even so, the fundaments of the developing person's story are laid down before that person knows of them. These fundaments are matters of sex, social class, kinship, national, religious, and racial heritage. These form the conditions of the birthright grant, upon which a large but limited number of life stories can be erected. Normally, individuals integrate these historically-given conditions into their life stories effortlessly, and memory has no trouble in preserving them. As the story of one's life develops, the historical ambience plays an equally important role, but now it is the provision of opportunities or possibilities for movement into the future.

Neither the conditions of birthright grants nor the opportunities provided by the current historical ambience are constant, though like the clouds on a still summer day, they may seem to be so. By appropriate revisions of the dominating views of the past, a present institution such as slavery can be undermined. Once destroyed, a new birthright is conferred upon individuals who were once condemned by the vagaries of history. And once liberated, these individuals have a new range of choices for the development of life presented to them. Sadly, the movement that abolished slavery did not at the same time accomplish the sort of historical transformations that would result in the provision of opportunities for life development commensurate with opportunities offered to others. A lived life is a story traced within the confines of historically-given circumstances. Both the continuity of the tracing and the giving of historical circumstances are ultimately dependent upon fallible human memory.

CONCLUDING CONSIDERATIONS

> People awaken to consciousness in a society, with the inner story of experience and its enveloping musicality already infused with cultural forms.
>
> —Stephen Crites (1971)

If the facts of collective history and individual memory are secular matters, the facts of *having* a collective history or of *having* an individual memory most assuredly are not secular, but universal. The particular dramas we enact, the dances we dance, the music we know, the language we speak—all of these derive from particular historical episodes of invention, transformation and propagation. But *that* we enact dramas, know music and speak in languages—these are universally given as part of the human condition. Moreover, the basic forms of language, and of drama, art and music are timeless—given to us as universal (Crites 1971).

This point allows us to see the profoundly social bias of all the preceeding discussion of the relation between identity and memory. Memory of the nonepisodic sort might not even be socially acquired, but might simply be given as a natural endowment. To be sure, the nurturance of the socius is required in order for this protean or inchoate endowment to be realized in any particular way. Carl Jung (1965) describes his main reality as inner and timeless. For Jung, commerce with the socius was always regarded as a kind of concession to necessity.

Jung developed and used a striking metaphor to describe this relation of the temporal and the timeless. The collective human nature, product of millennia and without consciousness or voice, is like a vast perennial rhizome (root mass), lying beneath the surface, invisible. An individual human life is like a single green shoot growing upwards into light and air from this vast subterranean rhizome. For its brief period of life, these historically particular growths are able to see and have commerce with their contemporary neighbors. But the possibility of this social commerce is dependent upon the common but invisible nature shared by individual forms. Much of Jung's interest was in plumbing the depths—in vertical exploration. Commerce with his fellows was mainly an auxiliary to this major interest.

Jung's memories, then, are of two kinds. Conventional memories are of going to school, of parents, of medical school, of his relations with Freud, of his patients, of his writings, of his wife and family and so on. These memories comprise his conventional social identity. But Jung gives great importance to less time-bound memories—memories of particular dreams, particular obsessions, achievements of insightful and arresting interpretations, fruits of solitary meditations. These are Jung's attempts to gain an understanding of universals, or in different terms, the sacred or the primordial. Without question, the category of "vertical" or timeless memories had priority for Jung, while he realized full well the utter necessity of an ordinary secular existence and memory to enable his exploration of the timeless and the sublime (see Juhasz 1983, for an exposition on timeless polarities of human nature).

What sort of evidence is there that we should take seriously these half-mystic ruminations of Jung? To the already convinced, no evidence is needed, and to the skeptic, no amount of evidence will suffice. But I offer at least a shred of an observation which seems consistent with Jung's conception of a nonsocial but human identity.

Jimmy R., whose temporal memory was permanently arrested at age nineteen, could still participate meaningfully in Catholic Mass.

If he were held in emotional and spiritual attention—in the contemplation of nature or art, in listening to music, in taking part in Mass in chapel—the attention, its "mood," its quietude, would persist for a while, and there would be in him a pensiveness and peace we rarely, if ever, saw during the rest of his life at the Home. (Sacks 1983, p. 19)

The coherence of this sort of experience for Jimmy could not depend upon memory of a secular kind, but rather upon memory derived from some universal sense of semantics, of significance. Music, the Mass and art can be seen as particular secular expressions of universal forms, and the appreciation of these forms could just be given in the nature of things, and not be a matter that is dependent on secular memory. Both Jimmy R. and

Marcus L. seemed to have lost their sense of temporality. But it is by no means certain that this rupture of the temporal also entailed for them a loss of their "vertical" consciousness, their inner sense of timeless identity. We can say of the aged and the senile that their temporal stories are finished— that nothing more of consequence will happen to them, save their death. But while life remains, it is presumptuous and inhumane to affirm that, with the disappearance of chronology, their identities in the inner and vertical sense are also thus dissolved. Something there is of the sacred in human life. Of course, in temporal and historical terms, I am now talking nonsense.

The thinker is the thought, said James. And the thought, in turn, is not some fixed and formed entity, but a process —an on-going, ever-shifting and continual reforming of content. Thus, thought is like a stream, and memory allows one to have a sense of the stream of time and a sense of continuous identity in that time. But the streams are surrounded by oceans, and these are timeless, eternal. Our identities are stories told in terms of the streams of our thought, as these streams are conducted through the courses of grounded circumstance. But the streams presuppose both an origin and destiny in their endless cycles, and these are not matters of story, but of voiceless and universal verity.

NOTES

1. I maintained personal contact with Marcus L. and his family over a number of years. I have modified certain identifying details in this description. The description is based on my own observations.

2. This summary report is based upon a fuller presentation of the case of Jimmy R. in Sacks (1983).

Chapter 7

Fugitive Identity: Self-Control and the Spy

Oh, what a tangled web we weave
When first we practice to deceive.

> —Sir Walter Scott

It is an essential to the spy to seem to be one person while secretly being someone else. Unlike the stage actor, whose assumed identity is not taken seriously to represent the self within, the spy must convince skeptical and suspicious others of the reality of an assumed identity, when that assumed identity is in fact false. Thus, the spy poses an interesting case for a psychology of self and identity, especially when the possibilities of double agents or counterspies are considered. The notion of a hierarchy of identities is suggested, and the significant question has to do with which identity is ultimately in control of the others.

Social control and self-control are the general headings under which the psychology of espionage might be considered. This chapter examines how identity and control are related to each other, using the case of the spy as an example.

I begin by examining three cases in which the relation between control and identity seems to be a central issue.

1. A Marine guard assigned to the U.S. Embassy in Moscow is befriended, then becomes romantically involved with a "swallow"—a Russian woman who is in fact a KGB agent. He is persuaded by her to provide access to secrets, such as personnel lists.

2. A forty-year-old married man, after many failed attempts to break his dependence on alcohol, enters a one-month treatment program. On release from the program he joins an Alcoholics Anonymous group, continues going to meetings regularly, and remains abstinent for an entire year—for the first time in his adult life.

3. A student attends a stage demonstration of hypnosis on a college campus. After
    a series of preliminary exercises and demonstrations, the student finds herself
    on stage with twelve other students. Together they experience a trip to outer
    space, responding to changes in gravitational pull, heat and cold, and other
    suggested environmental changes in a way that appears to be entirely genuine.
    Later, the student is "regressed" to the age of five and acts and talks like a
    five-year-old child.

These cases are but a small sample of problematic cases of conduct
control—a perennial and vexing challenge to psychological explanation
and understanding. The common element in these cases is the transfer or
exchange of control. The Marine ceases to be controlled by ordinary conceptions of professional duty or national loyalty and is controlled instead
by an alien agent. The alcoholic comes to gain control over his drinking by
adopting and adhering to the standards of conduct prescribed by Alcoholics
Anonymous. The college student temporarily assigns complete control of
her actions to the stage hypnotist, and in this condition is made to act in
ways that seem bizarre and uncharacteristic. At a minimum, these cases
testify to the possibility of transferring the locus of control of human
conduct. Admitting this possibility opens a host of questions concerning
self-control, social control, and the causes and conditions under which the
control of conduct is gained, sustained, and modified.

The main topic to be examined in this chapter is espionage, of which the
first case above is an example. The claim is that this understanding will be
advanced by first broadening the problem to include a range of cognate
cases, thus gaining perspective on the common and fundamental psychological questions involved. Espionage inevitably involves a concealment of
control; so that an agent's "control"—that is, the person or entity to which
the agent is truly responsive and responsible—is not evident in the agent's
ostensive real life. The spy appears to be serving one master while really
serving another. But so too the alcoholic, the bulimic, the compulsive
gambler, the cocaine addict, or the athlete who "throws" a contest at the
behest (or hire) of some interested party. Concealment of control is common
to all of these cases. In hypnosis, or in other forms of "influence communication" (Sarbin and Coe 1972), the person effectively chooses to be controlled by the suggestions or instructions of another person, under the terms
of a brief social contract. Often by tacit common consent, the control is
mutually attributed to a "state of hypnosis"—and this is a concealment of
control as well.

In earlier times, the fundamental psychological problem involved in all
of these instances would have been that of volition, or the will (James 1890).
Indeed, in everyday parlance we still hear of "strength of will" as a condition of character which enables one to resist the temptations of espionage,
substance abuse, or any of the so-called appetitive disorders. Hypnosis is
also considered in some way to involve manipulation of a weaker will by

a stronger one. Whatever its merits, the psychology of will is a topic that has not yet been revitalized from a long sleep induced by the adoption of a mechanistic world view in twentieth-century psychology (Sarbin 1976), nor is this the place for such an undertaking. But anyone reading William James' long chapter on the will must recognize that it has some relevance to the topic at hand, for the central concern of that chapter is an analysis of the means by which certain ideas which predispose to action acquire dominance in the consciousness of a person. In a more contemporary idiom, the problem is that of the control and direction of conduct—how influences from within (self) and without (society) operate in the control of a person's thinking and action.

Some of the cases falling under the rubric of conduct control seem to be problems of self-control and others appear to be problems of social control. In the former category are the so-called appetitive disorders (Mule 1981; Orford 1985)—eating disorders, alcoholism, sexual promiscuity, drug dependence and compulsive gambling. In the category of social control are treason and betrayal, religious fanaticism, nationalistic loyalties, racist programs, identification with ideologies, or prescriptive utopian doctrines. This distinction is not always clear, for the problems of self-control and social control are often co-mingled and interdependent. One may see the self-control of the chocolate fancier break down as the Christmas candies are passed around. The social control which keeps a person from engaging in criminal acts often breaks down under conditions of extreme hunger or privation. Even so, for heuristic purposes it is useful to discuss self-control and social control separately and then to explore some of the complexities of their interaction.

SELF-CONTROL

The model expression of the problem of self-control is Paul's plaint in Romans 7:19: "For I do not do the good I want, but the evil I do not want is what I do," and later (verse 24), "Wretched man that I am" (Revised Standard Version). Psychological versions of this problem will differ in choice of language—speaking of resolution of moral dilemmas or of intrapsychic conflicts between id demands and superego strictures—but the phenomenon is recognizable in many forms and seems endemic to the human condition. Freud was right in this sense: A single human psyche always has the potential for civil war.

Individual differences exist in the ability to control behavior in a way that is consistent with superordinate goals. Moreover, reliable individual differences are to be found in separate domains of appetitive control. The propensity to chronic alcohol dependence seems influenced by genetic disposition; eating disorders are far more common among females than among males, and among the young rather than the old. The compulsive gambler is no more likely to be an alcoholic than the nongambler. All of these observations suggest consistent individual differences in separate domains of self-control. Certainly it is possible that some general trait of self-control can be identified. Paper-and-pencil scales of self-control, such as the SC scale of the California Psychological Inventory, have acceptable levels of reliability and construct validity (Gough 1957). On the anecdotal level, examples are plentiful of individuals who seem to have high generalized levels of self-control—Thor Heyerdahl sailing the Kon-Tiki across the Pacific, Olympic athletes making enormous personal sacrifices in order to continue their training, and so on.

Reliable individual differences in hypnotizability are also well established (Shor and Orne 1962; Hilgard 1965). It is instructive to explore the conceptual relationship between hypnotizability and self-control. Whether hypnosis is regarded as a special trance state or is more skeptically regarded as an enactment respecting the specific and peculiar requirements of the hypnotic role, it is undeniable that the key behavioral issue in hypnosis is that of control. The very content of the induction ritual centers about control. Typically, "Listen only to my voice. Try to put everything else out of your mind. Relax. Do those things I ask you to do. Allow yourself to have those experiences I suggest you will have. Just let happen whatever happens. Pay attention only to my voice," etc. Hypnosis is achieved when the subject is eventually induced to be in the control of the hypnotist—giving up self-control for heterocontrol, at least within broad limits. In hypnosis, the subject's exercise of initiative is reduced to a minimum; the subject responds instead to the initiatives generated by the hypnotist. In the terms of nineteenth-century psychology, hypnosis involves a transfer of will from the subject to the hypnotist. In contemporary language, the hypnotized subject assigns limited control over thoughts and actions to the hypnotist.

It is perfectly consistent with this interpretation that the vast majority of cases in which clients seek the help of a hypnotist for therapeutic purposes involve problems which might formerly have been attributed to weakness of will and are now seen to be problems of self-control. Hypnotists and other therapists commonly treat manias, phobias, obsessions—all problems of self-control. Their help is sought to break dependence on alcohol or tobacco, to aid in programs of weight loss, or as a way to control fingernail biting, tics, or obsessive thought patterns.

This is not the place to evaluate the effectiveness of hypnotherapy. Rather, the objective here is to depict in broad strokes the progression of events in an idealized case of hypnotherapy. First a person is forced to admit helplessness to control some particular kind of conduct or thought—for example, periodic and extravagant food binging. The suffering individual then arranges to gain the strength needed to control the disruptive problem by intentionally assigning control to another—in this case, the hypnotist.

The hypnotist arranges an entrance ceremony into a role relationship and in this manner invokes the terms of the special brief social contract known as hypnosis. These terms allow the hypnotist to command obedience for the present, and to suggest an extended form of obedience in the form of post-hypnotic suggestions. The effect of these commands and suggestions is to increase the power of the individual to control that which previously could not be controlled. Through this newly acquired power to control, binge eating may now disappear, as counter-suggestions occupy the attention of the client. In effect, self-control is enhanced through the expedient of borrowing control from a creditable and powerful other (Haley 1961).

The transferability of control is illustrated in two ways by this sequence of events: First, the weakened subject intentionally assigns authority to the other to control all thought and action within the confines of the brief social contract. Secondly, the greater power of the other is internalized by the subject—and thereby new strength of control is achieved. It is as if the required additional control of thought and action is somehow yoked to the weakened subject. Thus fortified, the subject is now able to control rather than be controlled by circumstances.

This therapeutic sequence can be generalized to much of psychotherapy. The psychotherapist is someone who is willingly allowed into a position of control in the life of a patient, who is having some difficulty with control in his or her life. The objective is for the therapist to act for the benefit of the patient or client, and not to exploit the relationship for personal advantage. However, it is important to observe that the hypnotic or the therapeutic relationship can be abused so that the interests of the therapist are served at the expense of the interests of the client. To return to the case of espionage, the Marine guard, under the "spell" of a "swallow" as a relief from the boredom and tedium of duty, might easily be exploited. The guard, like the patient in therapy, has bartered away some amount of autonomous control. Reports suggest that the guard's KGB controller, known as "Uncle Sasha," exploited the relationship in this sense—control was exercised in a way that was not in the subject's interest.

Another quite different mechanism for increasing self-control deserves mention. This involves the idea of metacontrol, or achieving control over circumstances which are likely to lead to difficulties in self-control. This might be called the Ulysses solution. Upon being warned by Circe about the seductive power of the Sirens' song (the Siren was half-bird and half-woman), Ulysses ordered his sailors to bind him to the mast and to tamp their ears with wax, so that their ship could sail safely by the treacherous shores of Scylla, the helmsman impervious to the Sirens' song and to the pleas of Ulysses as well. Thus was Ulysses able to anticipate and guard against a temptation which he would otherwise be unable to endure, and which would, with certainty, drive him and his men to their doom. Ulysses was fortunate in being able to exercise this meta-control without the advantage of a single previous aversive trial, thanks to the timely counsel of Circe, functioning as the ideal therapist. The same principle of metacontrol is exercised by alcoholics and drug addicts who have the sense to avoid circumstances in which they are likely to be tempted beyond endurance. We might think of the phrase "lead us not into temptation" in the Lord's prayer to be an example of meta-control, for here the agent does not take responsibility for avoiding tempting circumstances, but rather by imprecation hopes not to be led into such circumstances by external forces.

It is misleading to think of self-control as pure and isolated from social reference. Indeed, one becomes a Stoic through a process of socialization. Having no more self-control than a jellyfish is also a product of socialization. G. H. Mead (1934) argued that the self arises out of social commerce, and no exception to that position is taken here. Even so, the perspective to be discussed next in conduct control is more obviously and explicitly social than that which has been presented above.

SOCIAL CONTROL

If self-control is manifest in conduct which is consistent with previously internalized standards or long-term goals, social control is characterized by an individual's obedience to role demands which are more immediately present. The key to the distinction is remoteness in time of the standards of conduct. The priest who remains true to the vows of his order throughout his life, despite many temptations and opportunities for sinful deviation, demonstrates enormous self-control. So does the scientist, who in the hope of making a fundamental discovery about the order of nature, resists all distractions and minor pleasures—adhering instead to the strict discipline of research.

Social control, by contrast, is illustrated clearly by the famous Milgram obedience studies (Milgram 1964). The essential elements are a) the individual, b) a social entity—not just the generalized socius, but a defined social entity such as a family, a tribe, a school, a military unit, or a psychological researcher—and c) some kind of co-presence, so that the individual is with the social entity, at least in a psychological sense, but usually in an obvious physical sense. Social control in operation is pervasive and simple: The individual acts in conformity to the norms, values, and standards of the salient social entity. This is normatively what happens all the time. We are conforming, we are obedient, we observe and respect social conventions; we are largely—all of us—under social control most of the time.

On occasion, social control becomes conspicuous and psychologically interesting. The Milgram studies are interesting because of the disparity between actual conduct and what is considered in the abstract to be proper individual conduct, respecting standards of human caring, charity, and decency. Milgram succeeded in showing that for most people, the wind of social control is far more powerful than the straw hut of self-control. One might say that this is the general lesson to be taken from a long tradition of studies in social psychology on social influence. Sherif's (1935) studies of the autokinetic phenomenon showed that social norms come to dominate individual perceptions of an ambiguous stimulus. Asch's (1952) conformity studies showed that an erroneous group consensus can pull an individual away from stating the simple truth. In these studies, naive subjects conformed to clearly erroneous perceptual judgments made by confederates posing as subjects. Milgram's (1964) studies extended this phenomenon to include not just statements of opinion or belief, but to entail the performance of potentially harmful and inimical actions, such as delivering painful electric shocks to innocent victims. The Stanford simulated prison study demonstrated the extraordinary power of artificially imposed rules on the beliefs and actions of participants (Haney, Banks, and Zimbardo 1988). Subjects arbitrarily assigned to the role of guard acted in a repressive manner to subjects arbitrarily assigned to be prisoners. Sherif's (1966) naturalistic studies of the influence of group membership on the conduct of boys in a summer camp setting can be added to this list. Boys arbitrarily assigned to different camp groups developed strong cohesion within their groups and strong hostility to competing groups. Here again, social control simply dominated any individual dispositions to think and act independently of group norms. More recently, Tajfel's (1982) experiments on minimal groups demonstrated a similar point. The major generalization from these studies is that the mere arbitrary assignment of an individual to a group produces an automatic and immediate identification of the individual with that group, bringing about a tendency for in-group cooperation and out-group competition. In these experiments, what begins as an entirely arbitrary group assignment quickly becomes an essential element in the identity of group members, and becomes a powerful determinant of their conduct.

The potential conflict between social control and self-control produces conspicuous and psychologically interesting cases. The attempts at "thought reform" during the Korean War pitted the immediate social force of enemy interrogators against the frail or sturdy commitment of prisoners of war to remote values and standards (see Lifton 1956). Galileo's obligation to scientific truth had to withstand the pressure of ecclesiastical inquisition to force his recantation. The Polish Cardinal Mindzenty was stubbornly controlled by his conscience and resisted until death the inducements of his prison keepers to make him capitulate in his religious principles. The quasi-legendary Sir Thomas More defied his king and the example of many of his nobel peers in refusing to sanction the marriage to Anne Boleyn, out of loyalty to the principles of the Catholic Church. Even earlier in English history, Thomas àBecket was canonized for his martyrdom on behalf of the right of the Church to maintain control against secular authorities. This is the stuff of drama, for in epic confrontations of individual conscience and immediate social forces, both uncertainty and heavily weighted consequences are present. These same elements are present in the drama of espionage. The stories of Nathan Hale, of Alger Hiss, of Harold "Kim" Philby and their fictional counterparts, presented in the works of John LeCarré, Ian Fleming, and others are but variations on these same simple elements and themes.

In order to appreciate the interplay of self control and social control more fully, it is necessary to employ a serviceable conception of human identity. The claim is that the composition of a person's identity is a major determinant of conduct control, both self-control and social control. In describing this conception of identity, I will rely heavily on the model of social identity presented by Sarbin and Scheibe (1980; see chapter 4, this volume), and with particular application to the question of the legitimization of aggressive actions, relying on an argument presented more fully in Scheibe (1974; see chapter 9, this volume).

SOCIAL IDENTITY AND LEGITIMIZED AGGRESSION

The concept of identity bridges the gap between the individual and the social reference groups from which identity is given and claimed. If the continuity of self is experienced internally as an undivided and ever-flowing stream of consciousness, one's social identity allows the perception of continuity for the person by others, and allows constancy in the perception of particular others by the person. To recognize someone is to connect a present impression with a previous impression or set of impressions; and this recognition is mediated and labelled with identifying terms—names ("This is Raymond Danzer"), roles ("That is the clerk at the bank"), or other markers ("That is the woman who lives down the street and who drives a blue Buick").

Elsewhere, Sarbin and I (Sarbin and Scheibe 1980) have argued that one's social identity is a composite of validated statuses, and that statuses fall along a continuum of grantedness or attainment. Sex, race, and nationality are relatively granted, whereas occupational status or socioeconomic standing are relatively attained. It is important to make use of this distinction in the present discussion, for the ways in which one's conduct is controlled depends strongly on the composition of one's identity. While attained statuses characteristically require repeated performances of some kind in order to be sustained, granted status normally is sustained passively. But since granted statuses are more fundamental, comprising what might be termed the person's birthright, they are immensely powerful in legitimizing conduct which cannot be brought about in any other way.

Pascal has said, "Never is evil done so thoroughly or so well as when it is done in a good cause." This does not refer to reflexive crimes of passion, or to an inebriated person running amok and causing great damage. Neither does this refer to the work of mercenaries, hired assassins, or self-serving criminals. Pascal refers instead to the sort of aggression represented by an Irish Protestant throwing grenades into a crowd at an IRA funeral, or by British soldiers being trapped and killed by an IRA mob, or by the exchange of rocket fire against the cities of Teheran and Baghdad, or by the stoning of Israelis by Palestinians, or the beating of Palestinians by Israeli soldiers. In each of these latter cases, aggression is legitimized—it is neither impulsive nor paid for. The terrorist acts out of a sense of identity and of a sense of the absolute rightness of the causes connected with that identity. In this way, terrorist acts are legitimized by the people who commit them and by their supporting reference groups. The mechanism of legitimization hinges upon granted roles—upon what a person most fundamentally is.

It is necessary to conceive of and understand the moral balance of power in any conflict—something which is entirely independent of a physical balance of power. One index of moral imbalance is the extent to which the parties to a conflict are willing to risk their lives. Individuals or groups can be so committed to a cause as to make martyrdom legitimate. When seen from the other side, such martyrdom can seem irrational or bizarre. It is common to hear of an enemy that they have no regard for human life, not even their own. This was said of North American Indians during our Indian wars. It was said of the Japanese during World War II, of the North Koreans and Chinese during the Korean War, of the North Vietnamese during the Vietnam war, of Muslim fundamentalists in the war between Iran and Iraq. Russians have said this about the Afghan rebels, for the force of their resistance was far beyond what was called for by practical reason. It can be taken as given that every collectivity on the planet cares to live. But human beings do on occasion so identify themselves with a superordinate social entity—tribe, nation, creed, ideology—that they are willing to sacrifice themselves for its sake. The social psychology of legitimized aggression is concerned with defining the circumstances and contexts within which such sacrifices are likely to occur.

It must have seemed in the nineteenth century as if human civilization would evolve away from "primitive" ties to blood, soil, and creed; that the growth of science and technology might usher in a new millennium; that as practical and material causes of international tension disappeared with increases in global productivity, no one would be so foolhardy as to engage in wars. The lessons of twentieth-century history are a sobering correction of this naive hope. Our wars have to do with the conflict of religions, races, and nationalistic ideologies, and not generally as a way of reducing material disadvantage or of annexing additional material advantage. As Orwell observed, "Human beings only started to fight each other in earnest when there was no longer anything to fight about"(1946/1968, p. 249). Material progress does not necessarily produce in its wake a more enlightened way of managing ideological conflicts—the contrary seems to be the case. Isaiah Berlin suggests that two factors have shaped the twentieth century. The first is the growth of science and technology.

The other, without doubt, consists in the great ideological storms that have altered the lives of virtually all mankind: the Russian Revolution and its aftermath—totalitarian tyrannies of both right and left and the explosions of nationalism, racism, and in places, of religious bigotry, which, interestingly enough, not one among the most perceptive social thinkers of the nineteenth century has ever predicted. (1988, p. 11)

The twentieth-century phenomenon of decolonization is strongly motivated by emergent nationalism; but it is nationalism which has been at the root of some of the most bloody and insane conflicts (Scheibe 1983; see chapter 4, this volume). Even so, the moral rightness of decolonization is unmistakable and often irresistible. Fanon's (1962) *Wretched of the earth* is an instructive example. Fanon was from Martinique, studied medicine in France, went to live in Algeria, then a French colony, and wrote books about the oppression of the Algerians. The book conveys a sense of the absolute moral rightness of the cause of Algerian liberation. In this context, it is understandable that Algerians should appear to be indifferent to death. The point is to escape the oppression of a diabolical and corrupt power. The plea for action is not mercenary, not rational, not economic, not even ideological in the narrow sense of commitment to some single world view. The struggle has to do with the redemption of identity. Such a transcendent objective confers a distinct advantage in the moral balance of power, for the adversary in these cases is much more practical and fights only to retain the material and economic advantage of colonial possessions.

Those who have for a time enjoyed the material benefits of economic prosperity and advantage do become less enthusiastic about transcendent principle and the like, unless perhaps these principles are somehow at a distance. In this way, prosperity seeks to subvert itself. The intellectual of the First World is free to identify with the oppressed of the Third World. In fact, this seems at times the only way of redeeming the identity of the prosperous from utter vacuity.

This argument does not lead to an easy meliorism or predict some state of political or economic equilibrium. Rather, the implications are for continued cycles of disequilibrium; as moral advantage produces material advantage, it loses its force, preparing the way for others to assume a moral advantage, and so on continuously. The sequence of events over the last 40 years in the struggle between the Israelis and the Palestinians is a clear example of this shifting disequilibrium.

The concept of social identity provides a way of connecting the problem of conduct control with the legitimization of extreme actions—aggression, martyrdom, or spying. Not everyone is susceptible to the appeal of risk and sacrifice. One's birthright grant contains privileges, but also the implied responsibility of responding positively to appeals for the defense of that birthright. The Israeli is loyal to Israel because he is an Israeli, not because in some abstract and detached way he has decided that, all things considered, the Israeli cause is right. The Palestinian is likewise controlled by being a Palestinian. Different identity grants, then, dispose the individuals bearing those grants to a particular and defined range of social control initiatives. Even so, individual differences will be found in the tenacity and loyalty displayed by people within the same collectivity. But the power of the defining collectivity over the individual is enormous. The next section consists of an examination of the mechanisms by which that power is exercised.

MECHANISMS OF ACHIEVING COMMUNITY CONTROL

Kanter (1972) has presented a useful and instructive discussion of mechanisms involved in the establishment and maintenance of control within communities. Her analysis is based on historical records of successful and unsuccessful utopian communities established within the United States in the period between the Revolutionary War and the Civil War. Her inspection of the historical record results in the conclusion that the employment of six theoretical mechanisms is more characteristic of the communities that survived for at least a generation than for shorter-lived communities.

Successful communities showed greater evidence of *sacrifice* and *investment*, where sacrifice refers to giving up of individual property or financial resources, and investment means placing resources at the disposal of the community. Investments for successful communities tended to be non-recoverable, so that if a person or a family were to decide to leave the community, they could not simply withdraw their investment. This tends to ensure continuity of membership.

Cohesion is achieved by the twin mechanisms of *surrender* and *communion*. Surrender refers to the cutting off of ties to relatives and friends outside the community. Communion refers to a ceremonial celebration of bonds to members of the community—common songs, rituals, meals, work. Utopian community members often refer to each other as "brother" or "sister," while ceasing to regard actual biological relatives as having any special importance for them. These mechanisms also entail surrendering the possibility of forming special relationships of coalitions inside the community which might in some way provide a competing focus for individual loyalty. Successful communities tended more often than unsuccessful communities to prohibit permanent and unique marriages, and instead encouraged either celibacy (the Shakers) or a form of temporary and provisional mating (the Oneida community).

Finally, control of the community over individuals is achieved by *self-mortification* and *transcendence*. Self-mortification typically involves a communal criticism of individual initiatives, traits, false pride, and the like. The drill instructor in the military provides a ready example of the mortification process. Jesuit novices who must prostrate themselves, give up their names, wear black, and become "dead to the world" as part of their training also illustrate the process of mortification. Transcendence means taking the self to a higher and more sublime level. Transcendence is illustrated by the charismatic leader—Mother Anne for the Shakers, John Humphrey Noyes for the Oneidans, Jim Jones for the People's Temple experiment, David Koresh for the Branch Davidians. All of these leaders offered the promise of spiritual transcendence.

The effect of the three negative mechanisms—surrender, sacrifice, and self-mortification—is to erect a barrier between a community and the surrounding world. The positive mechanisms—investment, communion, and transcendence, all direct the energies of the community inward. The result is to create a functional island of culture—internally homogeneous and alien to the rest of the world in its ways and customs.

This schematic characterization of community control mechanisms is relevant to the temptations of espionage in two ways. First, espionage is predicated on the idea of separation of collectivities—and that separation is achieved and maintained by control mechanisms such as these. Nation-states are not communes, but resemble them in varying degrees. The greater its autonomy and internal commitment, the more a nation might be perceived as a threat by others. Secondly, the conditions that produce commitment to a community are the same ones that produce the sort of loyalty in a community member required for spy work, if the spying is to be for the home side. The obverse propositions are: To the extent that societies are open, not cohesive and individualistic, collective commitment will be weak and also nonthreatening. And, to the extent that an individual is not bound psychologically to collective identity in this fashion, the more likely the person is to be responsive to material rewards for services rendered, rather than being bound to some transcendent loyalty to the collectivity. Such unbound individuals are likely recruits for espionage for the adversaries of the collectivity to which they nominally belong.

CONTROL AND COUNTER CONTROL: SPY AND COUNTERSPY

It can be seen that there is a roughly inverse relationship between the social conditions likely to produce loyal agents to a country and those likely to produce agents who are subvertible, who might become counterspies or double agents. What are the conditions and mechanisms of subversion?

Within large collectivities, it is a simple matter to form internal coalitions—institutional arrangements more intimate and potentially more compelling than the large community. In a group hypnosis demonstration, the stage hypnotist takes pains to prohibit whispering, giggling, and commentary among members of the audience, on the grounds that this would break the attention of others. School teachers are intent on breaking such subversive coalitions within their classes. The right of free association, granted in our Bill of Rights, can be a threat to centralized power—which is precisely why this provision was added to the U.S. Constitution.

Another means of weakening community control is by creating openings in boundaries and frontiers. The followers of the Rev. Moon are not supposed to travel outside of their compounds unaccompanied, for free movement would lead to more defections. The physical isolation of China for a generation created enormous collective control, a control now weakened and compromised by openings and exchanges with the West.

Loyalties to transcendent and nonlocalized doctrines or entities—e.g., religious faiths—can also subvert immediate community control. Lifton (1956) reports that thought-reform programs during the Korean War were most successfully resisted by prisoners who had especially lively and strong religious beliefs, family ties, or a sense of patriotism. Once again, the mechanics of the soul depend largely on ascriptive ties provided by the birthright grant.

Since the birthright-granting entity is always a large collective social entity, the character of that entity is a major determinant of the power of the loyalties adhering to it. It is important that birthright-granting entities possess a moral constancy. The Church must maintain the impression that it is fundamentally immutable—not subject to secular pressures and human aberrations. In actual fact, the Church does adapt, if slowly, to historical change. But it does so while retaining its storied claim to universality. Nations must not betray their most fundamental principles. This is not so much a matter of maintaining a kind of absolute institutional purity as it is a matter of assuring that a proper story—a morality tale—can be told and sustained. If the nation appears to act in such a way as to betray its own legend, then the moral legitimacy of the nation is undermined, and the ability of the nation to collect on the duties entailed in the birthright grant is severely impeded. Every citizen of the United States is given a birthright by the nation—equality under the law, the right to the pursuit of happiness, and so on. The reciprocal of this birthright is the duty of individuals when called upon to protect and defend common interests. But if the nation acts in a way that appears to be subversive of its own moral history, then it can lose its right to call citizens to its defense. James Wilkinson (1985) makes the point that war is not only made possible by the cultivation of a proper national history, but that the national history battens on the stories of heroism deriving from war:

Since the advent of mass education in the late nineteenth century, most modern nations have . . . attempted to inculcate a version of their collective pasts that might be termed "official history." Its chief function is to promote a sense of patriotic duty and to inspire national self-respect through a series of carefully selected heroes (and, more rarely, heroines) and monitory tableaux. Founders, leaders, benefactors, and martyrs are commemorated on holidays, eulogized in speeches, and studied in schools, thereby becoming exemplars for the citizen in search of values or an identity. He or she shares something with these heroes, if only a common homeland, and hence views their deeds as a source of personal pride. War, in turn, is a privileged arena for much official history—a heroes' nursery that over the centuries has provided many of the most enduring figures in the national pantheon. (p. 334)

The Vietnam imbroglio was a failure in two respects: First, the story legitimizing our entry in the war was not universally compelling, so that significant numbers of young men did not answer the call to duty but took refuge in Canada or Sweden. Secondly, and of more lasting importance, Vietnam and the contemporary Watergate scandal did not provide an enrichment of our official history. If anything, the decade from 1964 to 1974 brought credit to unofficial versions of history—with investigative reporters taking on a kind of heroic significance.

Decisions and judgments are made on the basis of what seems to be true, not what proves ultimately to be true. This is illustrated by the possibility that politicians can be corrupt and still honorable. This is only an apparent contradiction. Corrupt politicians might have the wit and decency to maintain good cover stories about themselves and their activities. During the last 15 years this has been an increasingly difficult achievement in the United States. The failed political ambitions of Gary Hart are due not so much to his weakness and peccadilloes as they are to a spoiled story. On the other hand, the capacity of Ronald Reagan to maintain a good story about himself and his deep inner commitment to American values made it possible for the American people to overlook a number of contradictions: he was our first divorced president and gave little attention to his children, while professing the values of the family; he professed a dedication to strict enforcement of the law while blithely ignoring it in the case of the Iran-Contra affair; he professed a dedication to fiscal restraint while accumulating the largest deficits in U.S. history; he espoused Christian principles and was supported by the fundamentalist right, but he was not a churchgoing man. The question of how one manages to maintain a good story, despite many potentially ruinous episodes and defects in actual performance, is a fascinating problem, but is not a matter that can be pursued further in this essay.

The point is that the quality of the sustainable story is enormously important as a determinant of perceived legitimacy, and in turn of the conditions that facilitate or inhibit the turnings of loyalty, including the turnings of spies. If the actor becomes disillusioned about the moral quality of the collectivity of which he is a member, then an act of treason does not appear to be treason at all. The treason against England of our eighteenth-century American revolutionaries was palpable and real. But victory in the war gave the rebellion historical legitimacy, and as a consequence the loyal Tories who were forced to flee to Canada came to be known as traitors. The story of the Pollards, convicted of treason for their sale of secrets to Israel, is another case in point, for according to their own testimony they seemed to be acting out of a sense of self-justification, against a background of what they considered to be a corrupt and morally defeated nation.

WHY SPY?

A book by a former KGB agent (Levchenko 1988) presents four basic modes for the recruitment of agents. He organized his observations according to the commonly used acronym MICE, for money, ideology, compromise, and ego. Each of these modes can be considered in relation to the foregoing arguments about self-control and social control.

Money is an obvious inducement for spying. The arguments about the determinants of control have two implications with respect to the power of money. First, financial inducements will be most effective in recruiting agents if the person to be recruited is already among the alienated or the disaffected. One could look upon spying as just another job—a job entailing certain risks and providing certain benefits. Such a view is not sustainable by someone who has vestigial romantic ideas of patriotism or of abstract loyalty to principle. By no means does this suggest that one looks for psychopaths or sociopaths for hire as spies. Freedom of all conscience is not necessary—just freedom from that part of conscience having to do with the nation. Sarbin's inquiry on the way in which treasonous acts are perceived on a scale of seriousness suggests that the special opprobrium customarily reserved for traitors to the nation is waning in our populace, corresponding to a general cynicism about politics in our time. The second implication is that no amount of money paid to government employees with security clearances is sufficient to guard against the temptations of financial inducements for employment as a spy. The precondition for the effect of financial rewards is not so much financial privation as it is the freedom from conscience just described. To be sure, massive debts due to gambling or other causes have been the background condition for the recruitment of some agents, and impoverished individuals are vulnerable. However, the general point is that no amount of money will ensure loyalty. Loyalty is established most strongly with respect to granted components of identity, and these have little to do with wages.

Ideology is a second mode of agent recruitment. The principle is this: A transfer of ideology from the host collectivity to another collectivity entails a transfer as well of social control. Herbert Philby became a potential recruit for loyalty and control by the Soviet Union because he first became ideologically committed to communism. Similarly, Stanislav Levchenko as a KGB agent became a candidate for defection and betrayal of the Soviet Union as he lost his ideological commitment to communism and became attracted to the economic and social system of the West. The appeal of defection in these cases is not so much material or financial as it is ideological.

The third mode of recruitment is compromise, by which Levchenko means the sort of device used to recruit the Marine guard, Sergeant Lonetree. This is a problem of self-control. Lonetree's self-control was severely compromised by his falling in love with a Russian woman, and this lack of control proved to be his undoing because she was a "swallow," a KGB agent. The control of romantic and sexual impulses is a classical appetitive problem, and for young men with remote and lonely assignments, the conditions for compromising this control are optimal. Viewed out of context, it seems incredible that anyone would be so careless and injudicious as to allow a Russian woman to have access to the U.S. Embassy in Moscow. However, just as is the case in hypnosis or in Milgram's obedience experiments, one has to be in the context of control in order to realize the full power of the compromising conditions. Just as the hypnotic subject might be surprised at being made to hop around the stage as if he were a huge frog, so the compromised agent has a difficult time explaining to others why such improbable and foolhardy actions were undertaken. Sex is, of course, not the only appetitive means of compromise. Drug and alcohol addictions can be equally compromising. These are merely other examples of transferability of control.

Finally, Levchenko focuses on the fourth recruiting mode—ego. He means by this the acceptance by certain individuals of spying as a personal challenge—an adventure, an opportunity for excitement. A fascination with taking risks and the possibility of a glamorous life-style is nowhere better illustrated than in the James Bond spy novels. Their enormous popularity attests to the pervasiveness of boredom as a negative motivating condition in our society. There are those who are not satisfied with the vicarious adventure and excitement to be had by being a James Bond fan, but who feel themselves compelled to imitate the James Bond role. Some of the soldiers of fortune who have been identified as participating in the conflicts in Central America seem to be motivated not by money, ideology, or compromise, but rather to be filling out their identity by this particular form of adventure. As in the case of the mercenary mode, the background condition for choosing espionage as a way of exercising one's ego must be a certain indifference or alienation from ordinary patriotic sentiments—certainly not a rare condition.

A final implication of these arguments does have some practical application. Because of the extraordinarily low base rate of occurrence of recruitment into a career in espionage, no specific prediction of individuals who are likely to be susceptible to appeals to betray their country will be of any particular value. But while prediction is not possible, prevention is. Recruitment into a career in espionage is facilitated and motivated by background conditions that are, to some degree, controllable. The base rate of defection is low, but it is not constant. The increase in the number of security breaches in the United States seems to be a systematic phenomenon and not a mere statistical aberration. If it is systematic, then it must have derived from some change in the moral climate within the United States, a moral climate which is to a degree under the control of those with political power, including many with institutionalized power outside of the structure of government, such as information media. Prevention of security defections, would, according to this argument, be achievable by improvements in the moral quality of the national story.

A POSTSCRIPT ON SPIES IN A PLURALISTIC WORLD

Espionage is part of the drama of international conflict and confrontation. The moral evaluation of an act of espionage is problematic; it is largely determined by the perspective with which the evaluator is identified. If the spy is on our side, the act of spying is justified; if spying is for the other side, it is bad. However, even spies for the right side live in a morally cloudy region, since their profession obliges the use of protracted subterfuge, deceit, and possibly criminal action. One way of eliminating this entire range of shady activity is to achieve a world order in which serious international conflicts cease to exist. No sober student of politics thinks this is possible, and some do not think it desirable—for the achievement of such a "final solution" would entail such horrors and genocidal campaigns along the way to the achievement of perfection as to make present levels of gratuitous harm-doing pale by comparison. (See Berlin 1988, for a superb essay on the unacceptable cost of "The pursuit of the ideal.") So espionage will forever remain a part of the human drama.

Throughout this essay, it has been argued that espionage entails a transfer of conduct control. Examining some analogous cases of transferring control—in hypnosis, in social psychological experiments, and in communal experiments—provides some clarification of the mechanisms of conduct control, the limits of conduct made possible (and legitimate) by control transfers, and the institutional conditions that work for and against recruitment into the role of agent.

A pluralistic society and a pluralistic world must forever live with differing and seemingly incompatible values. Liberty is good, and so is security. But liberty for the foxes compromises the security of the chickens. Justice is good and so is mercy. But justice for the victims of crime puts limits on the mercy extended to criminals. The right to life is important but so is the ability of a woman to choose whether or not to bear children. The most enduring conflicts in our world are not between good and evil but between good and good. Such hard conflicts of values will continue to exist and will produce in their train both suspicions and fears of the other. The spy may be someone who passes into the control of the other. Or, the spy may be someone who enables us to neutralize the threat of the other to us.

This complex argument leads to an unconventional conclusion. The conclusion is that the spy is a useful and even helpful creature in the general round of existence. For the possibility of recruiting an agent for the Other from among the faithful attests to the possibility of an escape from universalism, and so from the sacrifices this would require of our species. Isaiah Berlin states certain theoretical problems with universalism, but he notes practical and historically evident difficulties as well:

Marxists tell us that once the fight is won and true history has begun, the new problems that may arise will generate their own solutions, which can be peacefully realized by the united powers of harmonious, classless society. This seems to me a piece of metaphysical optimism for which there is no evidence in historical experience. In a society in which the same goals are universally accepted, problems can only be of means, all soluble by technological methods. That is a society in which the inner life of man, the moral and spiritual and aesthetic imagination no longer speak at all—is it for this that men and women should be destroyed or societies enslaved? (1988, p.16)

In practice, the activities of spies do as much to neutralize the potential for harm-doing deriving from a concentration of power as they do to facilitate it. Somehow spies, ferreting and burrowing in all directions, work collectively to keep too much power from being concentrated in any small set of hands. Agents and objects of transfer—of identity, of loyalty, of control—they in some ways represent the possibility of appreciating more than one good value at the same time. If then we are to live in constant political and social disequilibrium, these changelings will have their work to do. Should this intrusive work cease to be done, our collective danger might thereby increase rather than decrease.

Chapter 8

Self-Narratives and Adventure

Though man lives by habit, what he lives *for* is thrills and excitement.
The only relief from habit's tediousness is periodical excitement.

—William James

Those naked little spasms of the self occur at the end of the world, but
there at the end is action and character.

—Erving Goffman

As psychology loses its ahistorical and universalistic pretensions, it becomes not harder but rather easier to recognize the commonness of certain
forms. Near the end of his life, William James prepared a series of essays on
the paradox of modern wars, where civilized and rational societies are
brought to engage in barbaric and primitive acts of destruction. "The Moral
Equivalent of War" (in James 1911) is the best known of these essays. In it,
he makes a case for the commonness of the impulse to war. He argues also
that the war mentality is resistant to reasoned argument:

"Showing war's irrationality and horror is of no effect. . . . The horrors make the
fascination. War is the *strong life*; it is life in *extremis*; war-taxes are the only ones men
never hesitate to pay, as the budgets of all nations show us" (p. 350).

In presenting an argument against our customary modern wars, James
departs from the premise that wars are representative of a much more
general class of psychological activity. For this class he suggested no generic
name, but its function is the production of thrills and excitement: indeed,
he suggests that history and human life itself are interesting because of large
and small glories, and that in the past wars have been the chief means for
the generation of glory.

Erving Goffman's 1967 essay, "Where the Action Is," takes up this same theme, but in an entirely different context. The quotation at the head of this chapter about action and character refers specifically to the conduct of idle youths in amusement park arcades, as they pit their little skills against the determined responses of coin-operated machines. It is a pathetic little adventure to see whether the polished steel ball will strike the light post and thereby register a score. If it seems an absurd stretch to connect the amusement park arcade and the battlefield, a visitor to an arcade will be somewhat reassured by the ubiquity of the battle theme in the names and symbols displayed by the machines.

My claim is akin to that of James and of Goffman—that a large class of human activity is functionally common, and that the range of this class is suggested by the examples of war and amusement park games. But I wish also to connect this idea with that of "identity as narrative." I suggest that the form of human activity known as adventure has a central role to play in the construction and development of life stories, and that life stories, in turn, are the major supports for human identities.

A claim for the commonness of adventure as a mode for the construction of life narratives should not be misconstrued as a claim for universality. Let it be admitted that in Western culture the idea of adventure—whether it is manifest in sport, in gambling, in the exploration of nature, or in exposing oneself to risk of injury—is strongly associated with the role of male. That this association is largely cultural in origin rather than biological is taken here as an article of faith, but the attendant controversy about origins is in any case not essentially important to the argument to be developed. As a further qualification to the scope of the present treatment, I note that much of the following discussion refers to two stylized forms of modern adventurous activity—sport and gambling. The objective is to establish interpretive commonality within a class of human activities, of which sport and gambling are representative, and for which *adventure* seems the best generic label.

The contextualist view of human conduct is the point of departure for the argument to be developed (Sarbin 1976). Human identities are considered to be evolving constructions; they emerge out of continual social interactions in the course of life. Self-narratives are developed stories that must be told in specific historical terms, using a particular language, reference to a particular stock of working historical conventions and a particular pattern of dominant beliefs and values. The most fundamental narrative forms are universal (Crites 1971), but the way these forms are styled and filled with content will depend upon particular historical conventions of time and place.

As a justification for devoting special attention to sport and gambling in this treatment of human adventure, I offer the well substantiated observation that such activities are growing all around us—in magnitude, intensity, and variety. Survey data in the United States show that ninety-six percent of the population is at least minimally involved with sports. About eighty-five percent of Americans are in some fashion involved with sports every day. Finally, sport is no longer a male domain. Women are participating in sports at a rapidly accelerating rate. Barriers to the participation of women in some sports formerly dominated by men are quickly disappearing (Miller Brewing Company 1983). Similarly, studies have shown beyond all doubt that legal and illegal gambling are becoming ever more popular in the United States, with most states now running legal lotteries. Casinos, horse and dog tracks, jai alai frontons and off-track betting facilities show a steady rise in popularity. Also, there is no sign that illegal gambling activity is in decline.[1]

My fundamental thesis is that people require adventures in order for satisfactory life stories to be constructed and maintained. The variety of adventures has no obvious limit—participation can be direct or vicarious, the venture can carry one no farther than one's garden or to the ends of the earth. Adventures can be conducted in fantasy, as in the case of Walter Mitty, or in hard reality, as in the case of the bullfighter. Such activity can be carried on with a collectivity, as in nature study groups, or individually—the solitary bird-watcher comes to mind. Sport and gambling are singled out here merely as particularly prominent and common examples of the larger class of human activities suggested by the term adventure. The objective is to display the functional significance of adventures in the development, maintenance, and occasional metamorphoses of human identity.

THE ADVENTURE THESIS

In *Meditations on Don Quixote*, Ortega y Gasset (1961) credits Cervantes with the invention and development of the figure of the hero in modern fiction. Cervantes, in the boredom of his prison cell, was inspired by reading the legendary tales of Amadis of Gaul, recounting the chivalrous deeds of medieval knights-errant. Don Quixote is now an ineradicable historical reality—fevered brain and all. It is well to remember not only that he once was not, but also that the entire imaginative tradition he represents—the fictional hero—once was not among the presences on life's stage. To be sure, he was preceded by heroes of legend and epic: by Ulysses, by Beowulf, by King Arthur and Sir Lancelot, and many others. But Don Quixote is, of course, only a single expression of a more general historical and cultural development; other representations of this same development are the Age of Exploration, the Renaissance, the extension of European imagination and presence over the world. No claim need be made about cause and sequence here—only the observation that in the general round of things, these events occurred in relation to each other. We might say that the sixteenth century ushered in an age of adventure, and that as a sequel, Don Quixote represented the new and pressing role for adventure in the construction of life narratives.

Along with Don Quixote, Cervantes created Sancho Panza: a creature as material, hedonistic, and realistic as his Quixote is ethereal, idealistic, and surreal. In the Western psyche a polarity was established, again in the round of things, without claim that Cervantes is responsible for it. About this polarity, George Orwell observed:

The two principles, noble folly and base wisdom, exist side by side in nearly every human being. If you look into your own mind, which are you? Don Quixote or Sancho Panza? Almost certainly you are both. There is one part of you that wishes to be a hero or a saint, but another part of you is a little fat man who sees very clearly the advantages of staying alive with a whole skin. (1941/1968, p. 163)

This duality is dynamic. While Sancho is in the ascendant, Quixote recuperates his strength, so as to assume control again when Sancho's vigilance wanes. While the period of oscillation here is not at all precise, the fact of alternations between belly-to-earth realism and starry idealism is easily verifiable in ordinary life. And it is these variations that provide the stuff of life story. In literary terms, Don Quixote without Sancho Panza as counterbalance is not a good story. In terms of psychological biography, a life lived on a single plane is simply insufficient as a story—it doesn't go anywhere, it doesn't move. The socius is constantly testing the individual for the satisfactoriness of the unfolding life narrative, and the particular socius in which we are immersed wants change, wants variation, wants dramatic build and decline.

The sort of self-narrative which this sequence produces is what Gergen and Gergen (1983) call the *romantic saga*, a series of progressive and regressive periods repeating over time. The timing, amplitude, and possible overlay or relation of these cycles with other narrative progressions is not a matter of concern here. Rather, the point to be established is that repose and adventure are inherently unstable states; the sequencing or progression of these states produces the material out of which narrative constructions of the self are developed.

The need for change and novelty or for repose and redundancy must be understood contextually. That is, the extent to which the environment is seen as noisy and too busy will depend not only on the distal environment, but upon the state of the person who is in that environment. Similarly, the felt need for change and novelty is not merely endogenous but depends upon the amount of variation occurring in the stimulus world.

In John Steinbeck's version of the Arthurian legend, the king is puzzled at the unrest of his castled knights who, "eat well, sleep in comfort, make love when and to whom they wish. They feed appetites only half awakened—and still they are not content. They complain that the times are against them" (Steinbeck p. 249). Here is laid out the fundamental motivational dynamics of one-half of the adventure cycle. The contextualist part of the argument is supported by the observation that not all those in the castled circumstances feel restless—just the knights. The other half of the cycle is also amply illustrated in the Arthurian epic, where Lancelot and his mates leave the docile pleasures of the castle for the unpredictable adventures awaiting in the wild. They continue their quests until their resources for adventure are simply used up, and the wild life becomes intolerable. Although their tolerance levels differ, all knights must return again to haven. We can conclude from the enduring charm of the Arthurian legend in all its many forms that the repetition of this cycle makes a very strong story. So strong is this story, I hold, that our current attempts to construct self-narratives are still pulled and formed by its mythic forces.

The literary theme of adventure and return, as old as Homer and therefore as old as literature itself, has emerged in myriad guises throughout the modern era. Character, as Goffman has it, is built out of repeated exposures to trials, risks, and uncertainties of venturing forth. Withdrawal to domesticity is both a recuperation from the effects of such exposure and a preparation for the next adventure. In specific cultural expression, these venturings range from the "naked little spasms" at the end-of-the world arcade described by Goffman, to the grandiose venturings forth of Napoleon, seeking to establish his character by the conquest of Europe. We hear two major chords of the human song—risk and accompanying fear, certainty and accompanying security.

Concerning the taking of risks there is, of course, a substantial and informative body of psychological research (Kogan and Wallach 1964). However, the focus here is not on the social determinants or individual correlates or risk-taking behavior, but rather on the contextual significance or participation in risk for the construction of self-narratives. A sense of the psychological consequentiality of risk and uncertainty emerges more clearly from literary sources than it does from the social psychological laboratory.

Thought and attention are wasted in the contemplation of the certain, the fixed, the still. Tours through museums are quickly tiring, and the nostalgic contemplation of the past brings slight satisfaction. If the past can be made to come alive, it is through exploring its interstices of mystery and uncertainty, or by somehow bringing the past to bear upon the mystery and uncertainty of our own lives, as when Herman Melville's Pierre examines the evidence of the past to determine whether his lover might also be his half sister. The exploration of this past mystery is but another instance of adventure—in this case a value-freighted exploration of the unknown. Once the mystery reaches resolution, the story is over, and our attention turns elsewhere, seeking always and relentlessly, if in multifarious ways, to reencounter some interesting uncertainty which will repay our watching.

THE SPORTING LIFE AND CONSTRUCTION OF SELVES

Common games of sport and gambling are but stripped down, stylized and abbreviated dramas, inviting the direct or vicarious participation of masses of people seeking some adventure, no matter how minuscule, to provide story matter for their lives. The temptation is strong simply to regard sport and gambling as expressive of the ludic impulse—forms of play motivationally *sui generis*, as Huizinga (1949) would have it. Without denying that sport and gambling are developmentally related to the ludic impulse, continual adult involvement with sport and gambling cannot be accounted for in this reductive fashion. An alternative interpretation is that participation, direct or vicarious, in sport or in gambling provides occasion for what Goffman (1967) refers to as "the generation of character," or for the development of what Mancuso and Sarbin (1983) call self-narratives. Children perhaps begin to play at sports and games of chance for the same motives as kittens playing with a ball of yarn. But transformations can occur from the ludic base. "To display or express character, weak or strong, is to generate character. The self, in brief, can be voluntarily subjected to re-creation" (Goffman 1967, p. 237). Somewhere in the developmental sequence a transformation occurs, so that activity once pursued out of blind motive is now engaged in with reasoned purpose, however miscalculated that activity might be as strictly hedonic rationalism (compare Allport's 1937 concept of functional autonomy). The guaranteed payoff for sport and gambling activity is that they provide a venue for stylized and reasonably safe adventures, and so provide sequence and story for the lives of the participants.

This argument can be usefully elaborated by considering the self-transforming functions associated with each of the four forms of play identified by Caillois (1961). These are:

Agon   Games or sport played against an opponent involving the possibility of victory or defeat. All professional sports fall into this category, as do such confrontational gambling methods as poker or backgammon.

Alea   Games in which the outcomes are determined entirely by chance—craps, roulette, lottery games, bingo. In sport, chance is not supposed to play much of a role, except in coin flips to determine who gets the ball and other minor intrusions.

Mimicry In this form of play, the actor imitates another person, role, or object—as when children play cowboys and Indians or pretend to be an animal. Adult theater is mimicry play. Another case of mimicry play is that of the football fan who identifies with the team and symbolizes this identification through use of the pronouns "we" and "our," or perhaps by using team emblems as a part of personal apparel.

Vertigo Amusement park rides provide a clear example of this form of play. Long-distance running also belongs. Fights and sentimental betting are also classifiable here, for this sort of betting is instrumental in producing a greatly heightened sense of the dramatic impact of the events in question.[2]

All of the sporting events, gambles, and other forms of play here mentioned have the character of being closed or finished dramatic episodes. These events have a conventional beginning, a middle, and an end. And all are in some way value-weighted. The yield is victory or defeat in the agon category. It is monetary wins and losses for chance games. The value weighting for mimicry, I suggest, is one of direct identity enrichment through an amplification of one's repertory for role enactments.

The value of vertigo is revealed through an examination of the nature of the thrill; that which James said we live *for* even as we live *by* habit. Balint (1959) suggests that the thrill involves three essential elements: fear, voluntary entry, and hope for survival.

A Ferris wheel has just these characteristics, as does a fox hunt, a bobsled run, or skydiving. The value of such action is that the consequences of having enjoyed such thrilling experiences flow beyond the bounds of the occasion. One tells stories about these events, "dines out" on them, elaborates and embroiders on successive retellings. The telling of a joy is the fulfillments of that joy. In this fashion, the life story of the participant is enriched.

These elements of the "thrill" are present in the three other forms of play as well. For certainly in agonistic play there is fear, voluntary entry, and hope for survival. Similarly, entry into aleatory games is voluntary, involves fear of loss, and even in the case of Russian roulette one hopes for survival. Mimicry involves the fear of embarrassment, of being caught out, of having one's identity improperly read. Here again one decides to enter the play and one hopes to overcome or master stage fright, or the risk of being exposed.

The thrill is the expected product of adventure. Engagement in the types of thrill-producing play here outlined offers the same kind of potential for self-construction as outlined previously for adventure. Here are confected episodes which are bound to produce swings of value, and thus is time filled and punctuated—existing becomes living. This theoretical view is strongly supported by observation. Guttman (1978) provides a summary of empirical investigations of athletes. The protocols overwhelmingly support the positive self-construction effect of sports participation; "feeling that one exists," "discovering myself," "realizing oneself," "finding an expression of the self," "knowing oneself," "communicating nonlinguistically," "obtaining recognition from others," or "dominating others."

Guttman (1978) quotes from Roger Bannister's description of his feelings as he neared completion of the first four-minute mile:

I had a moment of mixed joy and anguish, when my mind took over. It raced well ahead of my body and drew my body compellingly forward. I felt that the moment of a lifetime had come. There was no pain, only a great unity of movement and aim. The world seemed to stand still, or did not exist. . . . I felt at that moment that it was my chance to do one thing supremely well. I drove on, impelled by a combination of fear and pride. (Bannister 1976, p. 77)

This is a literary reconstruction of a fleeting moment, but one that succeeds well in showing the dramatic and self-constructive potential of a single agonistic sporting event. The context for this performance was unique and transformed it into the thrill of a lifetime. The accomplishment was ratified by a huge public, waiting anxiously to see who would be the first human being to cause two completely arbitrary metrics, 240 seconds and 1,760 yards, to converge by unaided human pace. Roger Bannister, physician, has a place in the annals of history far more distinguished than that of later and faster runners. As a component of individual biography, surely Bannister's record-breaking run occupies for him a more central place than is commonly the case for middle-aged men who happened to have competed in athletics in their youth.

Direct participation in sports is extremely common among young people. James Michener (1976) makes the point in his compendious survey, *Sports in America*: "Young people need that experience of acceptance. . . . In the United States it is sports that have been elected primarily to fill this need" (p. 19).

Sports in the United States constitutes one of the chief means, if not *the* chief means, by which a young person might construct a life story that is generally considered to be full and complete. As noted previously, sports involvement by means of spectatorship virtually permeates the entire U.S. population—with the vast majority of the population devoting daily attention to occurrences in the world of sport.

Gambling activity in the United States is extremely common, accepted, and shows every indication of a trend toward increasing volume. A recent report states that in 1983 $132 billion was wagered, with about twenty percent of that amount lost to the gambler. In other words, in 1983, something like $26 billion was paid in voluntary taxation and contributions to the owners of legal and illegal gambling enterprises. This figure might be considered to be the price tag attached to the aggregate of aleatory thrills purchased by the U.S. population this year.

Participation in sporting activity, as player or as spectator, and in gambling activity is pervasive in our world, and at the same time is noneconomic in the narrowly rational sense of that term. Moreover, both of these classes of activity are so heavily stylized and rule bound as to produce events that are aesthetically uninteresting and intrinsically boring. Slot machines cycle in about five seconds. A hand of twenty-one is often completed in less than a minute, and almost all casino games complete a cycle in less than five minutes. Baseball, football, and basketball games might be said to command some interest for their pure beauty or intrinsic dramatic quality, but I argue that this appeal is slight and fleeting. Extrinsic context in the form of league or national competitions or comparisons with existing records does contribute to the interest of what is going on, as does a complete knowledge of the intricate possibilities diverging from each moment of play. But the crucial element in a sporting contest is that its outcome is not known ahead of time; and more, that there are those on and off the competing teams who look to the final result with personal interest. Attending an adventure in the small, one might redeem the empty time by investing attention and perhaps money in the unfolding of the minor fates involved. Aleatory gambling events are totally devoid of interest unless one buys part of the action. Then there is thrill to be had, if only the downward thrill of disappointment. Poker is a game of the utmost mechanical simplicity, and is therefore entirely without interest unless enriched by the exchange of tokens of value. When so enriched, poker is one of the few human activities that is commonly sustained over periods as long as 24 hours or more, with few or no interruptions for sleeping, eating, or any purely ludic diversion. These contrived adventures are important. Out of their combination and repetition elements are acquired for the construction and sustenance of suitable self-narratives.

CONSIDERATIONS OF CONTEXT

I have already suggested how the particular web of meaning woven about the four-minute mile barrier imparted a special historical significance to Roger Bannister's accomplishment in 1954. Neither the performance nor even the result of the sporting event determines the power of that event in the construction of self-narratives. Rather, the entire configuration and meaning of a sporting event determines what is to be made of the result. The second Louis-Schmeling heavyweight match, in 1938, was not just a boxing contest, but an event that came to symbolize in complex ways the struggle between U.S. democracy, where a poor black man could become champion, and Nazi Germany, with its arrant claims of racial superiority. This match was cast dramatically as a confrontation of champions, with the victor to carry the day not just for himself but for his entire nation. Never mind that racism was still rampant in the United States, or that Jack Johnson had been heavily abused just twenty years earlier for his effrontery in becoming the first black U.S. heavyweight champion. The Louis-Schmeling bout was witnessed with devout and partisan excitement by the entire Western world. The drama of the 126 seconds it took Louis to knock out his opponent became part of the life story of millions of people. On a similar scale, the finals of a World Cup football (soccer) match draws the attention and anxious interest of everyone in the participating nations. Few could resist the pull of the Italy-Germany final match in 1982, for it seemed within these nations as if something large and fateful were at stake, without anyone being able to specify exactly what it was. Historical and dramatic context often provides sporting events with a rich, if ephemeral, significance. The history of sport is full of thrilling moments, with more to come.

If the significance of sporting events to the individual must be understood in a wide context of meaning, then the very institution of sport and attitudes toward sport must be addressed as a major problem in social history. Indeed, a major new field of history has developed and is devoted to the development of just such understandings (see *The Chronicle of Higher Education*, June 8, 1983).

Sport provides adventure, a euphoric release from drudgery, tedium, and the gracelessness of ordinary domestic life. Where routinized and confining dreariness are prevailing conditions of life, interest in sport should be strong when the option is presented. Thus, it is not mere coincidence that the country whose oppressive industrial scene inspired *Das Kapital* should also be the universally acknowledged source of competitive sports the world over (Weber 1971; Guttman 1978). In the context of English life, sport takes a special and very strong meaning:

It may be precisely for their power of contenting some souls that anachronistic English recipes appeared exciting. Action, liberation, adventure and the heroic life were what the colonies seemed to promise. So did sports. Both proposed a way of escape from the drudgery, stultification, and repression of everyday life. Both hold out the opportunity to assert oneself, to expend energies little needed or rewarded in the stagnant situation at home. Both reflected, evident in the little reviews or in the new artistic venture of the *fin de siecle*, against an aging, listless way of life, but largely in terms of a fat boy's revolt rather than a rebellion of the downtrodden. (Weber 1971, p. 98)

Games do provide an outlet for emotional display in boring or confining worlds, as Elias and Dunning (1970) argue in their essay, "The Quest for Excitement in Unexciting Societies." It is not just excitement that is provided by sports, but an ongoing series of adventurous episodes, a source of mystery where one's attention and conversation might truly become engaged. The Marxist analysis of competitive sport as escapist, and of professional sport as a capitalistic abomination is limited in that it does not grant legitimacy to the self-narrative producing function of sport (Guttman 1978).

Competitive sports, it would seem, cannot forever coexist with a system of artificial social elitism. Sooner or later the physical superiority of athletic talent must come to embarrass and cast into ridicule those who would serve as the gatekeepers of traditional privilege. Since raw physical talent is no respecter of arbitrary social classes, sport can indeed serve as a wedge for upward social mobility. One of the great psychological satisfactions of an agonistic sports encounter is the lack of ambiguity in the final result, together with the realization that the final result depends primarily on the quality of play within the frame of the game and not on any inherited privilege. Competitive sports are in this sense democratizing.

Because the results of competitive games bear these features, Hitler's decision to host the 1936 Olympic Games in Berlin is curious and problematic. First, his embracing of competitive sports was conceived as an outrage by the nationalistic Turner movement, for the Olympics were seen as totally alien to the German spirit and to nineteenth-century romantic ideals. Hitler took a calculated risk, for he hoped to show to the world the superiority of the fruits of his system in fair competition, and thereby to reap a huge propaganda advantage. For this he was prepared to sacrifice the noncompetitive character of traditional German sport. But the vertigo element of sport participation did not suddenly disappear with Hitler's decision. Leni Riefenstahl's brilliant film documenting the 1936 games makes this abundantly clear. Riefenstahl's camera is focused on the beauty of form: runners train on winding forest trails in the crisp mountain air, and their splendidly formed bodies luxuriate in a steamy sauna where limber fronds are applied to naked backs to stimulate circulation. The film shows horses magnificently clearing water hazards in the pentathlon. In another sequence, divers in majestic slow motion seem to defy the law of gravity; in one long montage, many divers are shown in airy freedom, never striking the water. Grace, majesty, harmony, the perfection of the human form—these are the qualities dominating Riefenstahl's film, and only incidentally do we learn of winners and losers. Not once is there mention of the numbers of medals won by the various nations. Even so, it is a work of propaganda for the Third Reich, but more subtle and artful than that which would have been produced by Goering. Of course, for Americans the 1936 Olympic Games are remembered for the astonishing four victories of Jesse Owens. Like the Louis conquest of Schmeling to come later, these victories were savored by Americans as a kind of divine signal that in any serious confrontation our system would prevail over theirs. In this as in many other cases, Hitler's strategic decision brought his followers to ultimate defeat. This illustrates a danger of vertiginous play, for from an exalted state of transcendence, one may utterly misjudge one's capacity to prevail in agonistic confrontation.

That the United States has always been in the thrall of the Anglo-competitive mode of play is illustrated by the strategic decisions of another prominent national leader, John F. Kennedy. Gary Wills (1982) has convincingly shown the dominance of raw adventurism in the Kennedy style of government. The New Frontier presented the kind of challenge Americans could understand—missile gaps, space races, the man-on-the-moon program. The Kennedy crowd was young, partied dangerously and often to excess, and played touch football for recreation. Robert Kennedy was a ruthless opponent of the Teamsters Union, Jimmy Hoffa, and many other real and imagined arch-villains. The Cuban missile crisis was broadly played up as a triumph of superior grit, and we came to expect the repeated thrills of "brinksmanship." All of this excitement was created against the background of the Eisenhower decade, which became ever more dull and grey in retrospect as the brilliant sporting and gambling of the Camelot years claimed excited and breathless attention, not only in the United States, but around the world. On the national level, this is an example of a "good opening" period (Klapp 1978) emerging from one of ennui. Stories are made of adventures for nations as well as for individuals.

Another instance of the same U.S. thirst for adventure is richly presented in Tom Wolfe's (1979) book *The right stuff*, describing the pioneering space program. The constant tension of this story is sustained by combinations of all four basic forms of play. The astronauts are not interested in being mere passive riders in a traveling can, but want to engage in continual agonistic play, controlling or piloting their craft against the force of natural gravity. The press agentry surrounding the man-in-space program is an instance of mimicry play, for here the astronauts are blown up as superhuman heroes, the elite of the elite, trained to the finest edge of physical and mental perfection, devoid of ordinary and debasing human appetites. *The right stuff* as a concept is bound up with vertigo and transcendence in the escape from earth's bondage. If you have the right stuff you are in harmony with the sublime. And involving as it did a game with ever-fallible machines, large elements of aleatory adventure were involved in the initial space flights, with back-up systems helping to favor the odds of survival while at the same time certifying a real possibility that the gamble could fail calamitously. But with all this complexity, the agonistic element prevailed in the program to conquer space. The United States was first in the imaginary race to the moon, to the incalculable relief and satisfaction of millions of Americans.

The death of the crew of the Challenger spacecraft in 1986 provided a reminder that the game of space exploration can have deadly consequences. Now that the United States and the Soviet Union no longer are involved in a struggle for world domination, the glamour of the space race has lost much of its allure. This, coupled with the Challenger disaster, makes the space adventure less attractive and less likely to receive substantial financial support.

The end of the Cold War in 1991 has produced something of an adventure vacuum. No longer can Russia be represented as "the evil empire." The major premise of enmity between world powers provided an easy theme for hundreds of spy stories and novels, and now all of that has changed. But the thirst for world drama continues unabated.

No strictly rational argument existed for maintaining a cold war, striving in an arms race, or attaining nuclear superiority. The game was not what it seemed. These adventures were required not logically but dramatically—

the requirement was that some sort of reasonably coherent and compelling political story line be sustained. The demand for this story line allowed talk of "domino theories," "imperialist expansionism," and so on to be taken seriously. The rationale in Orwell's *1984* for the continuing, unstable competition among Oceania, Eastasia, and Eurasia is the same as that being described here. The need for a continued story is paramount, and the government-media combine is insatiable and remorseless. Since story does not emerge from a condition of prosperous security and stability, it is necessary to manufacture insecurity and instability. It is not that the leaders of the world know this in a way that common citizens do not. It is not that world leaders cunningly devise these adventurous shows to keep the masses from falling into an existential abyss. Rather, world leaders are caught up in the texture of the drama in a way that prohibits this cool perspective. Ronald Reagan was so involved in his role as president of the United States, and so aware of the glare of lights on the stage of history, that he had perhaps less capacity than his citizenry for gaining a clear view of the arbitrariness and absurdity of the drama in which he was participating as a chief protagonist. The hungry media are also largely incapable of gaining a saving perspective on the adventures they so yearn to describe.

World politics is a game, a drama, a series of adventures; it is uncertain, risky, and fraught with weighty consequences. The requirements of adventure for actors on the stage of world affairs is imperative, for it simply will not do to let the narrative collapse. This electronic age could never begin to tolerate a Calvin Coolidge. That this insistence upon action involves certain dangers is quite obvious, but I shall defer further consideration of those dangers until the final section of this chapter, after picking up again in the following section the significance of individual adventures of the sporting and gambling sort in the construction of life stories.

SOME ISSUES AND PROBLEMS IN THE CONSTRUCTION OF SELF-NARRATIVES OUT OF REPEATED ADVENTURES

The biographical aspect of life is not coterminous with the biological. Narrative constructions are the socially derived and expressed product of repeated adventures and are laid over a biological life progression that often extends beyond its storied span. Obviously, this is a social problem of increasing significance in the United States, where a growing proportion of the population encounters retirement while in possession of full physical vigor. Kurt Vonnegut states the problem nicely: "If a person survives an ordinary span of sixty years or more, there is every chance that his or her life as a shapely story has ended and all that remains to be experienced is epilogue. Life is not over, but the story is" (1982, p. 208).

The problem of one's life story being prematurely over is particularly pronounced for the athlete. Two stanzas from Housman's "A Shropshire Lad" will illustrate the phenomenon:

The time you won your town the race
We chaired you through the market-place;
Man and boy stood cheering by,
And home we brought you shoulder-high.

Now you will not swell the rout
Of lads that wore their honors out,
Runners whom renown outran
And the name died before the man.

The problem with athletic fame is that it often sets impossibly high standards for developing the rest of one's life story; indeed such a standard can be sustained through the period of young adulthood only with great difficulty. As matters stand, many young lives suffer the brutal, definitive, and unanswerable fate of "not making the cut," of not seeing their names on the list taped to the locker room door and thus being consigned to the sidelines, or worse. Difficult as this can be, things become more difficult still for the athlete who has survived many cuts and has even achieved stardom on the local teams; for the day will inevitably come, and it will not be long delayed, when the local star will find that the competition is too tough and retirement is the only option. Even for the greatest of professional sports stars, age or injury or a combination of both will bring about an end to the active athletic career.

The image of vulnerability is apt, for the athlete retiring after a long and successful career is often ill-prepared to meet the challenges of continuing to structure a life story. After all, an admiring public has largely ceased to be interested in the day-to-day activities of the retired athlete. The wise athlete will be prepared for the transition, with recourse to family and occupational preparation that offers entry into a sustaining and sustainable life story. But because the demands of time and attention are so great for high-level athletic performance, it is more commonly than not the case that financial, educational, occupational, and familial preparation for assuming a post-athletic life will have been slighted. The failures in retirement are more common than the successes, particularly in sports such as boxing, where educational background is commonly minimal. The typical dramatic narrative progression is that of tragedy (Michener 1976).

It is possible to overestimate the traumatic effect of athletic retirement, for with a minimum of prudence, the athlete will be reasonably secure financially; and there are, after all, records. Athletic records serve as a kind of mnemonic for revivifying and improving the past. The notion of "living on one's laurels" is not altogether absurd, for records of past accomplishment can serve as a kind of narrative capital which can be drawn upon again and again. The ex-baseball star who opens a package store or restaurant emblazoned with his name is borrowing on that capital, but it is perhaps a kind of borrowing that need never be repaid.

The cash value of adventures, after all, is only partly enjoyed at the time of their occurring or being suffered, but realizes itself later as the survived adventure becomes the stuff for enriching one's story. Travel to remote and foreign places is partly done for the intrinsic pleasure of beholding the strange and unfamiliar. But without the possibility of redeeming the travel by showing photographs and souvenirs, and telling stories to interested friends of how it was—without these possibilities the traveler is cheated of the major value that can be realized from the trip.

Stories, of course, are often improved in the retelling. Eclea Bosi (1979) remarks on the pleasure with which old people she interviewed regarded their youth. Bosi notes that periods of childhood were often objectively characterized by poverty, deprivation, limitations of freedom, and sickness. And yet the old person often views such a miserable childhood with great pleasure and warm nostalgia. Bosi remarks that the reason for this historical foreshortening has to do with the character of youthful perceptions of the world—perceptions that are fresh and full of adventure. No matter how hard the external conditions, the playful gathering in of fresh perceptions of the world comprises essential features—the fundaments—of the life story as it is to develop. Because the role of early remembered experience is necessarily constructive in this sense—even if the experience itself was negative—it is carried forward into the present as something valuable.

The memory of past adventures is not a faithful transcript of the past, since the memory-record serves a constructive purpose. Even so, the keeping of formal and exact records in modern sports has a very important function, for in this fashion comparative possibilities are afforded which greatly enrich the meaning or significance of present accomplishments. Record and history keeping in sports is a modern phenomenon—basically restricted to the twentieth century (Guttman 1978). We cannot compare the performance of today's runners or swimmers with those of ancient times, but we can make direct comparisons that go back 75 years or so. In baseball, the keeping of records reaches manic proportions, and there is an avid interest in the most arcane statistical data; playing with this information becomes itself a sustaining adventure for groups of aficionados (Angell 1977).

Similarly, horse players are given an overrich supply of information in the standard racing form. For the adept horse player, it is truly fascinating to study the myriad details of past performances of all the horses in a race. The twenty minutes between races seems to the neophyte an eternity, while to the experienced player the whole time is filled with study: hardly enough time to produce a reasoned prognostication and get down a bet. The reconstructions offered by horse players after the race are creative narrative refinements, for the player will typically report having been led away from the correct pick in the last race only at the last minute, having been beguiled by some quirk or whim to follow a loser. Even losers have satisfying stories to tell about their day's adventure. Over the long term, the dedicated horse player develops a scholarly erudition for the chosen subject, and the narratives are densely packed (Herman, 1976).

Narrative enrichment occurs both retrospectively and vicariously. Retrospectively, one revises and selects and orders details in such a way as to create self-narratives that are coherent and satisfying and which will serve as justifications of one's present condition and situation. The autobiographer must describe a story line that somehow or other concludes and coincides just exactly with the known present. Vicarious narrative enrichment is accomplished by the act of identifying with or devoting attention to the myriad adventures occurring or being invented in the world around us. There are sports events, novels, opportunities to gossip with friends, plays and films to attend, and here and there are famous people who sometimes allow themselves to be touched. These are common varieties of vicarious narrative enrichment.

The possibility of retrospective narrative enrichment makes understandable a range of adventurous activities that are otherwise puzzling. Sir Edmund Hillary is said to have responded to a question about why he climbed Mt.Everest with the famous retort, "Because it was there." But he might have replied, somewhat more accurately, I think, "Because you are here and are asking the question." Imagine how few mountains would be climbed if the story of climbing the mountain could be told to no one, and if memory could not somehow contrive to select and keep positively valued adventures and to delete or evaluatively transform the unpleasant adventure, for there is much pain and hardship in climbing. An unpleasant episode is suffered, and in time is converted into a diverting tale, as it is selectively revised, burnished, and served up for the delectation of self and others. Chaucer's *Canterbury tales* are truly delicious. That their trek could have been thus distilled into pleasure would doubtless have astonished the original pilgrims who were the subjects of the tales.[3]

ADVENTURE AND THE SERIOUS

Leaving the castle to go questing normally involves a cost or a burden to those left behind. Someone must mind the castle while the knights are gone. And here we see an essential element in the feminist protest, for it has traditionally been the role of the male to go questing, while the women are left behind to their domesticity. Increasingly today it is the ideal to provide equality of opportunity to the sexes in just this sense—to provide women with the opportunity to leave the castle for the challenge of the wild unknown, and to challenge men to take their fair turn at mopping up the castle. I argue that this can be read as a move to provide equality of seriousness to the possible life stories of women and men.

The athlete who trains for a sport is thereby drawn away from domestic responsibilities and chores. The gambler is as likely as not to play with the rent money, with only secondary thought given to who will pay the cost of losses. Those who seek cheap thrills by experimenting with drugs, engaging in profligate sexual adventures, or simply bumming around the land are imposing some increment of cost on the collectivities of which they are a part, with such benefits as accrue from these adventures going mainly to the adventurer. Touching another facet of seriousness, the scientist, the literary scholar, or the explorer engage in their quests and searches at the expense of the large social collectivity. Here the hope is that benefit will eventually return to the collectivity in the form of advanced knowledge, new discoveries, and fresh insights—or at least in the form of a diverting tale.

Since adventures are in this sense costly, it follows that societies will generally consider it in the collective interest to regulate access to certain forms of adventuring. The ancient Hebrews had no use for pagan sport. Neither did the Puritans. Sport for both societies was considered to be unproductive, costly, and therefore not serious. Recreational drugs are commonly banned, not out of arbitrary meanness, but because of the cost their use brings to the collectivity. Gambling has a truly ancient history of conflict with the rules of the collectivity, and more often than not is banned. The Crusades of the Middle Ages can be seen as adventurous escapades, the legitimacy of which would have been quite suspect had they not been framed in the context of high religious purpose. Adventures that can bring no rewards to the collectivity are commonly regarded as not serious.[4]

Goffman describes the Calvinistic solution to life's problems as dividing one's activities into those which can have no harmful effect and those which are sure to produce some small gain. On such a plan nothing can go wrong. The problem with this in our current era is purely psychological. We are likely to regard a life lived on Calvinistic principles to be overly serious and very dull.

It is an open question how much the sense of a need for the wild and unpredictable is a matter of individual temperament and how much a matter of the temper of an age. I suspect it is both. The compulsion to avoid complete domestication is neither a cultural nor an individual constant, but something that is itself freely varying and unpredictable. The compulsion to adventure is in a sense a compulsion to play, and is often an avoidance of seriousness. The reciprocal compulsion is the compulsion to seriousness. It is possible to have both.

Some forms of staged or play contests pretend to great seriousness—perhaps the bullfight is the most conspicuous example; but grand opera is contrasted with light opera, and serious music is distinguished from music that is merely entertaining. Goffman (1967) cites Hemingway's description of bullfighting as a kind of ultimate action, complete with the inevitable moment of truth, real swords, real blood, and so forth. But still, I would argue that the whole elaborately staged frivolity is nothing but another example of a domesticated public adding excitement to their lives through vicarious enrichment. I suspect that real struggles to the death normally have a rather different tone, and for the dying person at least, the struggle does not really count as an adventure, for unlike other thrilling experiences, the hope for a return is here quite reduced.

Conrad's description in *Heart of darkness* expresses the nonsportive character of the struggle:

I have wrestled with death. It is the most unexciting contest you can imagine. It takes place in an unpalatable grayness, with nothing under foot, nothing around, without the great desire of victory, without the great fear of defeat, in a sickly atmosphere of tepid skepticism, without much belief in your own right, and still less in that of your adversary. If such is the form of ultimate wisdom then life is a greater mystery than some of us think it to be. I was within a hair's breadth of the last opportunity of pronouncement, and I found with humiliation that probably I would have nothing to say. (1981, p. 119)

This is serious. But it is not a permanent or stable seriousness, at least for Conrad or Marlowe, who lived long enough to write about this gray mortal struggle, even finding thought and voice enough to make considerable pronouncements. So it is that just about anything can somehow be assimilated into one's self-narrative, should the adventure be one that is survived.

Adventure is truly described as an escape, as a release from the dead and deadly. It is creative and constructive, even as it is sportive and risky. It is life-creating and enhancing, even as it departs from the hard material seriousness of the rational world. Adventure creates story and contributes to the realization of completed identities. Seriousness is at risk in every venturing forth. But without the venturing forth there is no seriousness. Without the possibility of adventure, domesticity becomes a ludicrous reduction of life, and cannot be serious. Also, seriousness reasserts itself inevitably at the last to characters constructed by even the most frivolous series of naked spasms. Some see this restoration to seriousness as one of the moral advantages of death and war. The search for equivalents continues.

NOTES

1. The source of this and much additional information in this chapter concerning gambling is the report of the U.S. Presidential Commission on the Review of National Policy Toward Gambling, based on survey research conducted in 1974 (Kallick, Suits, Dielman, and Hybels 1979).

2. See Herman (1976) for a description of the relevance of vertigo for gamblers.

3. The necessity of *relating* the adventure leads to the observation that the photographic industry has probably done more to promote the tourist industry than the tourist industry has done to promote photography, which is the usual way of regarding the matter.

4. It is interesting to note that hunting and fishing, skilled activities which once constituted the most serious human work, and war, the most serious of human conflicts, have been transformed into sports in the modern era. And activities performed purely for pleasure, such as playing baseball, football, or racing horses have become serious professional businesses. These are further examples of transformations to and from the ludic.

Chapter 9

Legitimized Aggression and the Assignment of Evil

If the war didn't happen to kill you it was bound to start you thinking.
—George Orwell

War is still a paradox to psychology. Psychological accounts of this spectacular and particularly human form of aggression have mostly been exercises in instinct naming, in the manner of Freud, or else attempts at explanation in terms of abstract social structure, in the sociological tradition. The first kind of exercise is merely another example of the nominal fallacy, and the latter has the disadvantage either of offering no concrete deductions or else yielding deductions that are clearly at odds with the facts.

But if psychology is ever to contribute to our understanding of human destructiveness, now might be a time for optimism. The Vietnam War was an enormously powerful stimulus for thinking about aggression. Masses of vicarious participants were attracted by the emotional force of the longest and most fully reported war in modern history. A large number of people throughout the world are true survivors of the war and became aware of its contradictions. Over the last generation, the United States has experienced at first hand the domestic equivalent of war. The 1960s and 1970s produced an ubiquitous crescendo of violent protests and riots. In the 1980s and 1990s our cities and our highways have become even less secure from individual violent crimes, with rape, homicide, and armed assault statistics on the rise, abetted by traffic in crack cocaine and other drugs. So there is plenty of material on hand for study. Quite a large number of behavioral scientists—psychologists, sociologists, criminologists, and political scientists—are working actively on aggression and related problems and the outpouring of published research is impressive. The journal *Aggressive Behavior* was founded in 1975 as the organ of the

International Society for Research on Aggression. Dozens of books appear annually on the topic, their extensive reference lists crowded with recent publications. Finally, optimism about developing a psychological understanding of aggression is warranted because a certain conceptual and linguistic liberation has occurred within psychology. In token of this liberation, I use the word "evil" in my title, a term that psychologists in the past have thought suitable only for theologians and philosophers of ethics.

This essay has a very modest objective in relation to the magnitude of the problem and also in relation to the progress that may be anticipated in the future. My objective is to delineate the essential features of a certain form of human aggression, of which wars are one representation. In my view, the major psychological work involved in this form of aggression is performed and completed before the execution of a single violent act. This work consists of transforming individuals into agents of aggression, plus indicating and degrading the object of aggression. In this manner, legitimized aggression is potentiated, or armed.

Before discussing this process it is necessary to lay some conceptual groundwork by successively excluding forms of putative aggressive behavior that are not within my central focus. A starting premise is that the topic of aggression as it is currently considered in psychology is inconsistent and logically disjunctive. In good representative books on aggression, (Archer and Browne 1989; Groebel and Hinde 1989; Johnson 1972; Klama 1988) we find discussions of a loosely related family of phenomena—the agonistic behavior of Siamese fighting fish, the My Lai incident, the predation of animals, the bombing of cities, the use of drugs and brain stimulation in eliciting aggression, and the laboratory administration of pseudoshocks. In causal patterns or in observed behavior, these examples have little in common. The application of a few conceptual distinctions will render this amorphous family of events more coherent and allow us to focus on one psychologically uniform subtype of aggression.

REASONED VERSUS CAUSED AGGRESSION

In *The concept of motivation*, R. S. Peters (1958) makes a distinction between reasoned acts, in which an individual guides his behavior according to purposive rules, and caused behaviors ("happenings") in which the person is psychologically passive. What appears to be the same behavior may be included in either category, depending on the mode of participation of the actor in the direction of the behavior. The quivering and half-falls of the high wire walker may be the result of lack of skill or a sudden wind, or they may be part of the production—purposive, rule-following behaviors, done for a reason rather than for a cause. Staying to see the act a second and third time will support one or the other of these interpretations, and an interview with the performer will further clarify whether the behaviors in question were purposefully done or merely suffered.

It will be objected by those with a great passion for unity and smoothness in matters of explanation that what are here called reasoned acts of aggression must ultimately be explained in causal terms. This is a good rhetorical point, but one that must be rejected on functional and pragmatic grounds. Plans and reasons appear commonly as the background conditions for human aggression. To claim that such reasons never enter into the actual determination of events is merely to beg the question and to hide in equivocation, for the actual mechanics of the causal process are never fully displayed.

The suggestion by Peters and other "action theorists" that the distinction between causes and reasons be accepted as part of motivational psychology has met with great resistance. Behaviorism, as well as classical psychoanalysis, has modeled its motivational principles on an imagined version of physical science that permits explanations only in causal terms. Unfortunately, the acceptance by psychologists of this conceit has resulted in a kind of enforced ignorance. Confidence in reasons is abandoned in favor of motive-based interpretations.

Even such a thoughtful and comprehensive treatment as Fromm's (1973) *Anatomy of human destructiveness* does not avoid confusion on this issue. Fromm accepts a category of aggressive acts that are instrumental to other objectives, such as acquisition of territories or resources. These are set against aggressive acts that have no instrumental significance—and are irrational. The "psychical motivation" of German opinion leaders prior to World War I is described as a "mixture of group narcissism, instrumental aggression, and the wish to make a career and to gain power within and through this nationalistic movement." But in the subsequent chapters on "malignant aggression" he shows how what appear to be the reasons for aggression in this composite may be interpreted in terms of motives such as sadism, masochism, pathological boredom, necrophilia, or characteristics of either "character structure" or the nervous system. Thus, Fromm first accepts the proposed distinction between reasons and causes, then collapses it and regains the psychologist's advantage as the unique provider of explanations. To show how much he despises human aggression, Fromm goes so far as to set the reasoned-caused distinction on its head by arguing that only human aggression is truly malignant and irrational—our destructiveness is rooted in our condition as civilized beings.

A consistent distinction between reasons and causes avoids obscurantism and the accompanying temptation to show disapproval of aggressive acts by demonstrating their base motivational origins. Without denying the problematic status of the reasoned-caused distinction, I hope to illustrate its utility by a few examples.

It has been shown that rage behavior in cats, rats, and monkeys can be reliably elicited by electrical stimulation applied to portions of the hypothalamus or amygdaloid structures of the brain. In such elicited rage attacks, a purpose is to be found in the antecedent chain of events, but only in the head of the experimenter and not in the head of the stimulated animal. The experimental animals fall outside the range of docility that Edward Tolman prescribed as a necessary condition for the application of purposive behavioral analysis. However, the experimenter is also engaged in aggressive behavior as an active instigator of violent attacks. But if asked about purpose, the experimenter would probably reply that the production of violence is quite incidental to ultimate objectives, which have to do with the development of new knowledge, or the perfection of techniques of control, or grinding out another publication.

A purposive actor is not necessary to the production of aggressive behavior. Hydrophobic ("mad") dogs have not been instigated by any purpose to run around biting people. At the human level the same kind of caused aggression occurs. A good case has been made that Charles Whitman, perpetrator of massive indiscriminate killing at the University of Texas in 1966, was literally compelled to this violent culmination. His autopsy revealed a malignant tumor in the amygdaloid structure of his brain. His written self-description prior to the shootings is psychologically consistent with such a physical condition:

I don't understand what it is that compels me. . . . I don't really understand myself these days. . . . I have been a victim of many unusual and irrational thoughts. . . . After my death I wish that an autopsy would be performed on me to see if there is any visible physical disorder. I have had some tremendous headaches in the past. . . . It was after much thought that I decided to kill my wife. . . . I love her dearly and she has been a fine wife to me. I cannot rationally pinpoint any specific reason for doing this. (Johnson 1972, p. 78)

It is as if Whitman was caused to engage in violence despite his conscious desire to avoid this course of action and the lack of any reason for violence.

A different sort of explanation is called for by the murders committed by guerrillas in the Middle East conflict. Members on missions of violence know very well what they are up to, and the reasons for their actions are shared and applauded by a large reference group. It is a gross mistake—but not one that psychiatrists and psychologists are beyond making—to label such individuals "paranoid schizophrenics" or as otherwise mentally deranged. Militancy in the Irish Republican Army, in Serbs or Croats or Muslims in the former Yugoslavia, in Palestinian youths or in Jewish settlers is similarly characterized by certifiable acts of violence. Those who say that these acts are evidence of illness simply reveal their disagreement with the political objectives of the perpetrators, or else they fail to understand those political objectives. The difference between barbarity and heroism lies more in the observer's point of view than in the content of the acts themselves. Such acts fit the paradigm of purposive, rule-following behavior. An analysis of the acts themselves involves finding the sets of beliefs and values that provide convincing explanations.

The distinctions between caused and reasoned aggression has additional implications. It has been suggested that capital punishment has no effect on homicide rates precisely because murderers usually do not make rational decisions to kill. Most reported homicides in Western nations are impulsive acts rather than planned liquidations. In the present terms, enraged or impulsive homicides are caused and operate independently of regulative social norms.

The reasoned-caused distinction also sheds light on the proposition—popularized by Konrad Lorenz (1963) in *On aggression*, that humans are unique among species of the animal kingdom for engaging in the killing of their own kind. While it is true that reports by ethologists of conspecific killing are rare, we may doubt the satisfactoriness of the comparative base line. As Johnson (1972) has noted, "If a baboon came to Boston disguised as an anthropologist, he might prowl the city for several months without ever seeing a single killing. He might then go back to Africa and report that humans are unusually peaceful and rarely kill each other" (p.18). Indeed, most people can say that they never have seen one human being kill another one. Yet because of the human ability to symbolize remote events and the modern capacities for mass communication, it might seem as if we are constantly observing human conspecific killing. On those rare occasions when observers of nonhuman animals have truly extensive contact with their subjects, they too find instances of conspecific aggression and killing. Such killing has been observed in lions, in various insects, in lizards, elephants, baboons and hippopotamuses (Johnson 1972; Huntingford and Turner 1987).

Nevertheless it is quite likely that conspecific killing among human beings is more common than among lower animals. For caused aggressions—impulsive fits of rage, reflexive reactions to releasing stimuli—it may be speculated that the number of potentially fatal instances is about the same for man and for the higher primates. However, because of our sophisticated technology of killing—our weaponry—a far larger proportion of these events result in death. In the United States, over 37,000 persons were killed by guns in 1990. More than 200 million guns are in the possession of private citizens in the United States (Bureau of Alcohol, Tobacco, and Firearms).[1] If these weapons did not exist, would the assailants go to the trouble of stabbing, or, more work still, of killing with bare hands? I know of no experiments in which higher primates have been equipped with deadly weapons, but if this line of thinking is correct, such a modification would greatly increase their intraspecific homicide rate.

Self-assertiveness versus Self-transcendence as Reasons for Aggression

"The crimes of violence committed for selfish, personal motives are historically insignificant compared to those committed *ad majorem gloriam Dei*, out of a self-sacrificing devotion to a flag, a leader, a religious faith or a political conviction" (Koestler 1970, p. 26). Whether or not Arthur Koestler's assertion about the relative prominence of these two types of reasoned aggression is correct, the distinction is a psychologically valid one. Reasoned acts of aggression fall into two subcategories—those in which the reason is narrowly economic for the individual agent of aggression, and those in which an agent transcends narrow economic interest for the sake of some collective interest or ideal.

Again, those for whom parsimony is the dominant methodological principle will resist the distinction between selfish and altruistic motives for aggression by insisting that ultimately what appears to be altruism must be explained in terms of self-interest. Of course, if self-interest includes all possible benefits to the individual, both material and abstract, then such an argument is in principle irrefutable—but it is also without scientific interest.

The intended distinction is well illustrated in the standard social psychological experiments on competition and cooperation. In "prisoner's dilemma" games or in the experimental games of Morton Deutsch (1973), a subject makes a choice between a competitive option, by which one hopes to improve one's relative position among players of the game, and a cooperative option, in which the relative advantage of the subject is not improved but in which favorable results accrue to all members of the microcollectivity comprised by the players of the game.

An example of assertive aggressivity would be a violent act committed by a bank robber or other privately operating assailant. The same acts, if committed by a revolutionary group in the interest of obtaining funds or displaying strength, would be of the self-transcending kind. The anonymous air pirate who parachuted to earth with a very large ransom was apparently motivated only by self-interest. On the other hand, airliners have been commandeered by individuals from terrorist organizations to bargain for the release of prisoners or to collect ransoms to finance revolutionary operations.

The diagnostic problem posed by this distinction is not always an easy one—certainly no simpler than the earlier problem posed by the reasoned-caused distinction. During the Mexican Revolution, marauding groups engaged in robbery and destruction throughout the countryside were considered by some as mere opportunists and common criminals, while others saw them as attacking the established landholders and thereby furthering the revolutionary cause. Yet in principle, such difficult questions are resolvable—given sufficient information. What happens to the spoils of such raids? Are the bandits identified with some revolutionary leader? Is the choice of targets and methods consistent with either the self-serving or self-transcending hypothesis? *Qui bono?* Given this information, a plausible historical judgment could be made.

It cannot be denied that service in collective causes provides a special kind of individual gratification. André Malraux has spoken of the Spanish Civil War as "a most profound experience of brotherhood." Shakespeare's Henry V exults just before the battle of Agincourt, "We few, we happy few, we band of brothers." Fidel Castro's speeches are full of the glory of the struggle against imperialism. The common travail of the English people during the last world war produced a kind of elevated national morale that seems afterwards to have vanished. The story of nationalism is at once a romance and a chronicle of fire and blood. The kinds of rewards derived from participation in these experiences, as well as the honors and accolades given to heroes, are a product of self-transcendence, but they are not necessarily its objective. The collectivity bestows its rewards on individuals because they are seen as having sacrificed their own interests to those of the collectivity.

So the subtype of aggression that forms my principal topic is aggression which is reasoned rather than caused, and for which the reasons are self-transcending rather than self-assertive. As a shorthand expression for this category the term "legitimized aggression" will be used.

Elements of Legitimized Aggression

A critical element in all cases of legitimized aggression is the social collectivity. Such collectivities may be real and visible, such as an immediate family or tribe. They may be real but invisible, such as a nation or a trade union. Or, they may be theoretical abstractions, with varying degrees of manifest reality, such as social classes, *volk*, races, or the "community of saints." The relationship of the individual to such collectivities determines the potential for legitimized aggression.

Social collectivities are a means of establishing, maintaining and extending social identity. The collective aspect of human life begins at the moment the newborn infant is bestowed with a name and grants of membership in racial, national, kinship, gender-specific, and perhaps religious and occupational groups. Social identity develops as the person discovers what has been initially granted and accepts the duties and responsibilities entailed in this grant. In addition the person acquires new group memberships— new components of social identity—with maturation, the development of requisite skills, and the reciprocal process of social selection.

The relationship between the person and each of the social collectivities by which one is defined may be seen as an implicit two-way contract. The person performs valued services in achieved roles and is recompensed with social prestige, power and money. For granted components of identity, the content of the contract is different. The duties required for maintenance of valid identity in nation, kinship groups and the like are normally minimal. But these entities, which provide the initial grants of identity, have the authority to require much more of the individual, on occasion. Employers must use positive social incentives to make legitimate new requests for worker performance. Identity-granting institutions—nation, church, family—can require much more of the individual, and without promise of compensation. Instead, they characteristically rely on the loyalty that is the product of the initial grant of identification. An individual can refuse such requests only at the cost of being labeled traitor, heretic, or prodigal.

In functional terms, all of the collectivities in which the individual has valid membership do not have equal power in commanding loyalty. In general, it can be said that identity-granting collectivities have greater power in commanding loyalty than do collectivities in which membership is achieved.

However, even among granting collectivities, an ordering must be established on the occasion of conflicting demands. When a conflict occurs in the dictates of the church and the dictates of the nation, the individual will decide in favor of the institution that is of more fundamental importance. Thomas More and Thomas à Becket opted to be labeled traitors to England rather than heretics to the church. Henry VIII made a different decision. The choices made in such situations reflect the master element of the person's social identity. Two Italian reporters were once excommunicated for having recorded and published a number of confidential confessions. The excommunications, however, mattered little, since both had declared themselves atheists. Thus, canceled loyalty left these persons free to betray the church in favor of a more material master.

Nations normally have the legitimate authority to call citizens away from their occupations, communities, and families to defend common interests. It is important to recognize that this power is based primarily on legitimized authority and not on coercion or material incentive. In terms of the selfish interests of soldiers, fighting battles cannot appear rational without enormous or highly specialized rewards. But it does not appear irrational from the standpoint of the collectivity for individuals to sacrifice their interests for the sake of the collectivity to which they owe their being.

Wars are not waged and crusades are not started for the sake of the narrow self-interests of the individual soldiers. Recruits are obliged to transcend selfish concerns for the sake of the collectivity in which identity is claimed. Agents of legitimized aggression are activated not by physical coercion but by a contractual moral obligation. The extent to which physical coercion or material incentive must be used as a way of goading individuals into fighting is a gauge of the extent to which the collectivity lacks legitimate authority in commanding the loyalty of its members. A collectivity that has to depend on slaves and mercenaries for its aggressive force is morally bankrupt. A collectivity in which soldiers fight without being forcibly conscripted and without hope of financial reward is displaying a high degree of legitimate moral authority.

Conflicts between management-hired strikebreakers and union strikers, between government mercenaries and local liberation movements, or between hired bank guards and bandits representing revolutionary movements are characterized by an imbalance of moral authority. Such moral mismatches can be compensated only by an imbalance in the opposite direction in numbers and weaponry.

Conflicts between two morally legitimate collectivities are of a different kind. Examples are tribal wars, many international wars, family feuds, racial wars, some genocidal campaigns and wars of conquest. Unless there is a great imbalance of material force, such conflicts tend to last a very long time—even over several centuries, as witnessed in the struggle of self-sacrificing and totally committed warring factions in Northern Ireland or the Middle East.

The way in which legitimate authority can function as a social lever—turning the individual into an aggressor—can be illustrated on a small scale in laboratory experimentation. In Milgram's (1964) studies of obedience, the implicit contract of the psychological experiment is used as a means of compelling subjects to engage in ostensibly harmful behaviors that would, in the abstract, be considered repugnant and morally unjustified. The subject, in order to continue his self-identification as a "good subject," must accept the legitimate authority of the scientist-experimenter. Within the actual situational constraints of the experiment, individual choices are not made on the basis of some general conception of right and wrong. Instead, given the provisional social definition of "subject in a psychological experiment," behaviors are legitimated by the apparent sanction of the defining authority—the experimenter. In fact, the actual power of the experimental situation for the potential personal harm is not demonstrably great. In fact, the "shocks" delivered by the subjects were not real and the cries of pain and anguish from the experimenter's accomplice were also part of a performance. Similarly, Orne and Evans (1965) have shown that a variety of antisocial and apparently harmful acts (picking up a poisonous snake, dipping a bare hand into boiling liquid, throwing a beaker of acid at another person) can be elicited by hypnosis or by special instructions to simulate hypnosis. In all cases, subjects are responding obediently to apparently legitimate requests from a recognized authority—the experimenter or hypnotist. Also, in all cases, the subjects are in a fundamental sense correct in their assessment of the situation. Events that are contrived to look harmful are in reality completely safe.

These experiments demonstrate how an occasional and transitory social contract can be used as a way of legitimizing behaviors that are at least potentially harmful and that are not normally considered legitimate acts.

That the experimenters arranged things so that nobody would really get hurt is a fact, but not a necessary fact, in the causal pattern of the behaviors themselves. In the nonlaboratory social world, it often is otherwise. In order for aggression to be legitimized, it must be given that individuals are reciprocally involved with some social collectivity or collective ideal. Usually, this component of identity is granted rather than acquired. The collectivity then has the moral authority to ask that the individual give up narrow interests in favor of those of the group in which membership is claimed.

The Assignment of Evil

This call to self-abrogation is often accompanied by the indication of the enemy—another collectivity which is portrayed as threatening the welfare of the home group. This process may be called the "assignment of evil," for the enemy is not seen merely as a spirited competitor or an ambitious stranger. Rather, in order for their elimination to be made psychologically legitimate, enemies must be depicted as subhuman, bestial, unworthy of basic human rights and privileges. When these phases are completed, the psychological work of aggression is done. The rest is merely a mechanical and well-determined process of acting out the conflict.

The potentiation of aggression is a social process consisting of two kinds of preparation—one general and one specific. The general process is accomplished by socializing bonds of identity between the individual and the social collectivities that might later command loyalty. Specific direction is given to aggressive acts by the indication of a suitable enemy—another collectivity which is defined as both menacing and degraded.

When these subprocesses are completed the results are powerful: justified hatred of the enemy and comradeship in arms. Marc Antony's funeral oration illustrates this transformation. Initially the citizens of Rome are urged to sublimate their individual small-mindedness and selfishness and to look on the great and noble Caesar. In this state of heightened communion, the enemy—Caesar's murderers—are indicated. The call for battle is issued and all respond happily, joyously, to the invitation.

In a northeastern Brazilian city, a family feud is proceeding after more than forty years of activity. According to reports, the Alencar and Sampaio families have been shooting each other since 1949. The story is a familiar one—the scenario would be found in hundreds of other examples. After a death on one side, the other side goes about the identification of the killers and forms its own list of prime targets. When one of these is eventually killed, the stalemate moves one step further. Along the way, the initial justification for the feud is forgotten, just as nobody could quite remember how the United States came to be so involved in Vietnam.

In other cases, the material or economic reasons for the initial conflict remain in evidence. From the sixteenth to the twentieth centuries, it has been in the economic interests of the expanding nations of European origin to take possession of the lands in the Americas occupied by the indigenous populations. In the portion of this conquest enacted in the United States, from the seventeenth to the nineteenth centuries, the Indians were depicted as primitive savages, who achieved virtue only with death. Once evil is assigned, the extirpation of the malignancy becomes an act of courage and heroism. General Custer, in his time, was being seriously considered as a candidate for the presidency of the United States. His Argentine counterpart, General Roca, who commanded the liquidation of the Indians of Patagonia, was richly praised. His equestrian statue is still pointed out with pride to visitors to Buenos Aires.

When Pascal said "Never is evil done so thoroughly or so well as when it is done in a good cause," he was referring to harmdoing of the reasoned, legitimized kind. The major intent of this discussion has been to delineate the social-psychological antecedents of this kind of aggression. Social identity is a necessary mediating link between the goodness of causes and the destructiveness of consequences. Just causes are framed in an understanding of the welfare of the collectivity which provides fundamental grants of identity to its human elements. To see justified harmdoing as evil requires only a slight shift in perspective—a shift that is not possible if one's identity is anchored in the acting collectivity.

This kind of argument, linking the justification of massive aggression to social collectivities, is hardly original, for this is a major ingredient in anarchist thinking. The next step is to identify all extended collectivities as evil. When this step is accomplished, the use of terror and acts of violence against established social institutions, in the manner of Bakunin, is justified. Thus, an ideal or a single charismatic personality may provide the functional equivalents of the collectivity in terms of justifying aggression. But still the concept of identity is central. Still the potential for legitimized aggression follows from what are for the person the most fundamental elements of identity—be that anarchist, patriot, man, Christian, German, black, family member, woman, member of a tribe, communist, fascist, democrat, or free spirit. The constant element of this argument is that identity extension, or self-transcendence, is linked to the potentiation of legitimized aggression.

This idea conflicts sharply with what is commonly considered to be positive socialization. In Kohlberg's (1969) progressive stages of moral development, or in the description by Piaget that provided the inspiration for Kohlberg's work, the general direction of moral socialization is seen as progressing from egocentrism to identification with more and more extended and abstract entities. At the last stage of moral development, the individual no longer makes moral choices on the basis of conformity with existing law and custom, but in accord with abstract conceptions of justice, fairness, equity and freedom. Such individuals are notably immune to being manipulated into fighting over some just cause. However, the saints, and religious and political leaders who attain this degree of detachment from secular concerns have the capacity to inspire the loyalty of disciples and followers, who may be called upon to defend the faith in very material ways. A self-appointed prophet, such as Charles Manson or David Koresh, makes his own rules about right and wrong, and respects no subsidiary human law. His followers, once identified with him, do his bidding without moral qualm—as a proof of fealty and a celebration of community. The murders committed by Charles Manson's followers fit well the paradigm of reasoned, legitimized aggression. First a grant of identity is accepted from a collectivity. Next, enemies are indicated and the subjects are called to show their loyalty, which they do with commendable spirit.

The Missing Content

This discussion is meant to provide a general characterization of the major psychological features of legitimized aggression as it occurs in a variety of settings and circumstances. As a rough analogy, the potentiation of legitimized aggression is like the arming of a weapon, while the assignment of evil is like pointing it at a specific target. An order is then given and the harm is done.

Such a conception is both nonreductive and virtually empty of cultural content. No appeal is made to physiological processes, instincts, or learning paradigms. Also, the major concepts—social collectivity, social identity and self-transcendence—are vague in that no necessary roles are given to institutions such as family, nation, church, or organization. Obviously, for such a model to be useful, it must be fitted with content by some supplementary discipline. The choice is obvious; this kind of psychology needs to be filled by history.

When the story is told of an individual or any group, we may learn specifically what collective entities have provided functional grants of identity. We must look to history to fill in the skeletal description of how enemies are made—how evil is assigned. And we must recognize that the marching orders that convert the armed potential for harm into an actual physical result can take many forms—forms that will be determined by the historical meanings of the moment. Nevertheless, psychological order and coherence is discernible in that all of a variety of historically determined forms are homologous in function. The test of the utility of this conception will come in attempts to fit in to a very wide set of historical cases, without forcing or distortion.

In this way, psychology can be of real service to history. Historians and observers of human affairs often must stop with the recognition of paradox. For example, Orwell (1946/1968) has noted in connection with modern warfare, "Human beings only started to fight each other in earnest when there was no longer anything to fight about" (p. 249). By employing the present psychological model, in specific historical content, it is possible to say what men are fighting about and to show that the reasons for their fighting each other have great consistency over time and space.

Psychology needs contact with the content of history. We do not need pseudoexplanations of legitimized aggression nearly so much as we need a filled-out acquaintance of this process as it has occurred and as it continues to occur. As Philip Hallie (1971) has said in a very similar context, we need heuristic models that allow observation and conceptualization of the branchings and flowerings of our subject, not root models that force us into oversimplification and invite a false security.

NOTE

1. Figures obtained from Handgun Control, Inc., June 1993.

References

Adelson, J. (1982). Still vital after all these years. *Psychology Today* 16: 52–59.

Adelson, J., Green, B., & O'Neil, R. (1969). Growth of the idea of law in adolescents. *Developmental Psychology* 1: 327–332.

Alexander, F. (1941). The psychiatric aspects of war and peace. *American Journal of Sociology* 46: 504–520.

Allen, V. L., & Scheibe, K. E. (1982). *The social context of conduct: Psychological writings of T. R. Sarbin*. New York: Praeger.

Allport, F. (1927). The psychology of nationalism. *Harpers* 55: 291–301.

Allport, G. (1937). *Personality*. New York: Holt.

Angell, R. (1977). *Five seasons*. New York: Simon and Schuster.

Appel, K. E. (1945). Nationalism and sovereignty: A psychiatric view. *Journal of Abnormal and Social Psychology* 40: 355–362.

Archer, J., & Browne, K. (1989). *Human aggression: Naturalistic approaches*. New York: Routledge.

Ariès, P. (1962). *Centuries of childhood*. New York: Knopf.

Arons, S. (1972). Compulsory education: The plain people resist. *Saturday Review* (January 15): 52–57.

Asch, S. (1952). *Social psychology*. New York: Prentice-Hall.

Baker, R. (1983). *Growing up*. New York: Norton.

Baldwin, J. M. (1897). *Social and ethical interpretations*. New York: Macmillan.

Baldwin, J. M. (1930). Autobiographical statements. In C. Murchison (Ed.), *History of psychology in autobiography* (vol. 1). Worcester, MA: Clark University Press.

Balint, M. (1959). *Thrills and regressions*. London: The Hogarth Press and the Institute for Psycho-Analysis.

Bandura, A. (1977). Self-efficacy: Toward a unifying theory of behavioral change. *Psychological Review* 84: 191–215.

Bandura, A., Ross, D., & Ross, S.A. (1963a). Vicarious reinforcement and imitative learning. *Journal of Abnormal and Social Psychology* 67: 601–607.

_____. (1963b). Imitation of film-mediated aggressive models. *Journal of Abnormal Social Psychology* 66: 3–11.

Baron, R. A. (1970). Attraction toward the model and model's competence as determinants of adult imitative behavior. *Journal of Personality and Social Psychology* 19: 345–351.

Bartlett, F. (1932). *Remembering*. Cambridge: Cambridge University Press.

Bennis, W. G., & Slater, P. E. (1968). *The temporary society*. New York: Harper & Row.

Berkowitz, L. (1964). Aggressive cues in aggressive behavior and hostility catharsis. *Psychological Review* 71: 104–122.

Berkowitz, L., Corwin, R., & Heironimus, J. (1963). Film violence and subsequent aggressive tendencies. *Public Opinion Quarterly* 27: 217–229.

Berlin, I. (1988). On the pursuit of the ideal. *New York Review of Books* 4: 11–18.

Berne, E. (1978). *Games people play*. New York: Ballantine.

Blanchard, E. B. (1969). Relative contributions of modeling, informational influences, and physical contact in extinction of phobic behavior. Ph.D. dissertation, Stanford University.

Bloom, A. (1994). The body lies. *The New Yorker* (July 18): 38–49.

Borgida, G. (1972). National identity and the draft. *Journal of Clinical Child Psychology* 1: 8–9.

Boring, E. G. (1950). *A history of experimental psychology* (2nd edition). New York: Appleton-Century-Crofts.

Bosi, E. (1979). *Memoria a sociedade*. São Paulo: T.A. Quieroz.

Boswell, D. A. (1983). *The construction of self as a textual process*. Lecture delivered March 7 at the Center for the Humanities, Wesleyan University, Middletown, CT.

Bransford, J. D., & Frank, J. J. (1971). The abstraction of linguistic ideas. *Cognitive Psychology* 2: 331–350.

Breakwell, G. M. (1992). *Social psychology of identity and the self concept*. London: Surrey University Press.

Bronfenbrenner, U. (1972). *Two worlds of childhood: U.S. and U.S.S.R.* New York: Clarion.

Bryan, J. H., & Test, M. A. (1967). Models and helping: Naturalistic studies in aiding behavior. *Journal of Personality and Social Psychology* 6: 400–407.

Buss, A. H. (1980). *Self-consciousness and social anxiety*. San Francisco: W.H. Freeman.

Caillois, R. (1961). *Man, play, and games*. New York: Free Press.

Cassirer, E. (1946). *The myth of the state*. New Haven, CT: Yale University Press.

Catholic dictionary. (1885). New York: P.J. Kennedy & Sons.

Clark, K. B. (1963). *Prejudice and your child*, 2nd ed. Boston: Beacon Press.

Comstock, G. (1991). *Television and the American child*. San Diego: Academic Press.

Comstock, G., & Strasburger, V. (1990). Deceptive appearances: Television violent and aggressive behavior. *Journal of Adolescent Health Care* 11: 31–44.

Condon, T. R. (1982). Trance personality: Language and hypnosis in everyday life. Paper presented to the Southwestern Anthropological Association, Santa Fe, NM. Cited in *Psychology Today*, March 1983, p. 26.

Conrad, J. (1981). *Heart of darkness*. New York: Bantam.

Cooley, C. H. (1902). *Human nature and the social order*. New York: Scribners.

Cooper, D. G. (1970). *The death of the family*. New York: Pantheon.

Crites, S. (1971). The narrative quality of experience. *The Journal of the American Academy of Religion* 39: 291–311.

Crowne, D. P., & Marlowe, D. (1964). *The approval motive: Studies in evaluative dependence.* New York: Wiley.

Daniels, A. K. (1983). A tribute to Erving Goffman. *ASA Footnotes* (January): 1.

DeMause, L. (1982). *Foundations of psychohistory.* New York: Creative Books.

Deutsch, M. (1973). *The resolution of conflict: Constructive and destructive processes.* New Haven: Yale University Press.

Duval, S., & Wicklund, R. A. (1972). *A theory of objective self-awareness.* New York: Academic Press.

Elias, N., & Dunning, E. (1970). The quest for excitement in unexciting societies. In G. Luschen (Ed.), *The cross-cultural analysis of sport and games.* Champaign, IL: Stipes.

Ellenberger, H. (1970). *The discovery of the unconscious.* New York: Basic Books.

Emerson, R. W. (1883). *Emerson's works.* Cambridge, MA: Riverside Press.

Erikson, E. H. (1950). *Childhood and society.* New York: W.W. Norton & Co.

———. (1958). *Young man Luther.* New York: Norton.

———. (1969). *Ghandi's truth on the origins of militant nonresistance.* New York: Norton.

Eron, L. D., Lefkowitz, M. M., Huesmann, L. R., & Walder, L.O. (1972). Does television violence cause aggression? *American Psychologist* 27: 253–263.

Evans, R. B., & Scott, F.J.D. (1978). The 1913 International Congress of Psychology: The American congress that wasn't. *American Psychologist* 33: 711–722.

Fanon, F. (1962). *The wretched of the earth.* New York: Grove Press.

Feldman, R. S., & Scheibe, K. E. (1972). Determinants of dissent in a psychological experiment. *Journal of Personality* 40: 331–348.

Feshbach, S., & Singer, R. D. (1971). *Television and aggression.* San Francisco: Jossey-Bass.

Fessler, L. (1941). Psychology of nationalism. *Psychoanalytic Review* 28: 372–383.

Ford, C., & Beach, F. (1951). *Patterns of sexual behavior.* New York: Harper & Row.

Franks, L. (1994). Return of the fugitive. *New Yorker* (June 13): 40–59.

Freeman, M. (1993). *Rewriting the self: History, memory, narrative.* London: Routledge.

Freud, S. (1916/1964). *Leonardo da Vinci and a memory of his childhood* (Tyson translation). New York: Norton.

———. (1930/1962). *Civilization and its discontents.* New York: Norton.

Freud, S., & Bullitt, W. C. (1966). *Thomas Woodrow Wilson, twenty-eighth president of the United States: A psychological study.* Boston: Houghton Mifflin.

Friedrich-Cofer, L., & Huston, A. (1986). Television violence and aggression: The debate continues. *Psychological Bulletin* 100: 364–371.

Fromm, E. (1955). *The sane society.* New York: Holt, Rinehart and Winston.

———. (1973). *The anatomy of human destructiveness.* New York: Holt, Rinehart & Winston.

Gallatin, J., & Adelson, J. (1971). Legal guarantees of individual freedom: A cross-national study of the development of political thought. *Journal of Social Issues* 27: 93–108.

García Marquez, G. (1970). *One hundred years of solitude.* New York: Harper & Row.

Gaylin, W. (1970). *In the service of their country: War resisters in prison.* New York: Viking Press.

Geen, R. G., & Stonner, D. (1973). Context effects in observed violence. *Journal of Personality and Social Psychology* 25: 145–150.

Geertz, C. (1980). Blurred genres: The refiguration of social thought. *American Scholar* 49: 165–179.

George, A. L., & George, J. L. (1956). *Woodrow Wilson & Colonel House: A personality study.* New York: John Day.

Gergen, K. (1973). Social psychology as history. *Journal of Personality and Social Psychology* 26: 309–320.

———. (1982). *Toward transformation in social knowledge.* New York: Springer-Verlag.

———. (1984). Self theory: Impasse and evolution. In L. Berkowitz (Ed.), *Advances in Experimental Social Psychology.* New York: Academic Press.

———. (1991). *The saturated self.* New York: Basic Books.

Gergen, K. J., & Gergen, M. (1983). Narratives of the self. In T. R. Sarbin & K. E. Scheibe (Eds.), *Studies in social identity.* New York: Praeger.

Gergen, K. J., & Morawski, J. G. (1980). An alternative metatheory for social psychology. *Review of Personality and Social Psychology* 1: 326–356.

Gesell, A. (1954). The ontogenesis of infant behavior. In L. Carmichael (Ed.), *Manual of child psychology.* New York: Wiley.

Gilligan, C. (1982). *In a different voice: Psychological theory and women's development.* Cambridge, MA: Harvard University Press.

Goffman, E. (1959). *The presentation of self in everyday life.* Garden City, NY: Doubleday Publishers.

———. (1963). *Stigma: Notes on the management of spoiled identity.* New York: Prentice-Hall.

———. (1967). *Interaction ritual.* New York: Anchor Books.

———. (1971). *Relations in public.* New York: Basic books.

———. (1981). *Forms of talk.* Philadelphia: Univ. of Pennsylvania Press.

Goodall, J. (1965). Chimpanzees of the Gombe Stream Reserve. In I. DeVore (Ed.), *Primate behavior.* New York: Holt, Rinehart and Winston.

———. (1971). *In the shadow of man.* Boston: Houghton-Mifflin.

Goslin, D. A. (Ed.). (1969). *Handbook of socialization theory and research.* Chicago: Rand-McNally.

Gough, H. G. (1957). *Manual for the California Psychological Inventory.* Palo Alto, CA: Consulting Psychologists Press.

Gouldner, A. W. (1970). *The coming crisis of western sociology.* New York: Basic Books.

Grandin, T. (1986). *Emergency: Labeled autistic.* Novato, CA: Arena Press.

Greenwald, A. G. (1980). The totalitarian ego. *American Psychologist* 35: 603–618.

Groebel, J., & Hinde, R. A. (1989). *Aggression and war: Their biological and society bases.* New York: Cambridge University Press.

Guetzkow, H. (1955). *Multiple loyalties: a theoretical approach to a problem in international organization.* Pub. No. 4. Princeton, NJ: Center for Research in World Political Institutions.

Guttmann, A. (1978). *From ritual to record.* New York: Columbia University Press.

Haley, J. (1961). Control in brief psychotherapy. *Archives of Psychology* 4: 139–153.

Hall, C. S., & Lindzey, G. (1957). *Theories of personality.* New York: Wiley.

Hall, J. A. (1977). Sincerity and politics: "Existentialists" vs. Goffman and Proust. *Sociological Review* 25: 535–550.

Hallie, P. (1971). Models, burglary and philosophy. *Philosophy and Rhetoric* 4: 215–229.

Haney, C., Banks, C., & Zimbardo, P. (1988). A study of prisoners and guards in a simulated prison. In E. Aronson (Ed.), *Readings about the social animal.* New York: Freeman.

Harlow, H. F. (1971). *Learning to love.* San Francisco: Albion.

Harris, T. (1973). *I'm OK, you're OK.* New York: Avon.

Hartshorne, H., & May, M. A. (1928–30). *Studies in the nature of character.* New York: Macmillan.

Hayes, C.J.H. (1926). *Essays on nationalism.* New York: Macmillan.

Heidegger, M. (1962). *Being and time.* New York: Harper & Row.

———. (1966). *Discourse on thinking.* New York: Harper & Row.

Heider, F. (1958). *The psychology of interpersonal relations.* New York: Wiley.

Heingartner, A., & Hall, J.V. (1974). Affective consequences in adults and children of repeated exposure to auditory stimuli. *Journal of Personality and Social Psychology* 29: 719–723.

Herman, R. D. (1976). *Gambling and gamblers.* Toronto: D.C. Heath.

Hermans, H.J.M., & Kempen, H.J.G. (1993). *The dialogical self.* New York: Academic Press.

Hersch, P. D., & Scheibe, K. E. (1967). On the reliability and validity of internal-external control as a personality dimension. *Journal of Consulting Psychology* 31: 609–614.

Hess, R. D., & Torney, J. V. (1968). *The development of political attitudes in children.* New York: Doubleday.

Hilgard, E. R. (1965). *Hypnotic susceptibility.* New York: Harcourt, Brace, and World.

Hogan, R. (1982). A socioanalytic theory of personality. In M. Page & R. Dienstbier (Eds.), *The Nebraska symposium on motivation.* Lincoln, NE: University of Nebraska Press.

Hogan, R., & Cheek, J. M. (1983). Identity, authenticity and maturity. In T. R. Sarbin and K. E. Scheibe (Eds.), *Studies in social identity.* New York: Praeger.

Huizinga, J. (1949). *Homo ludens: A study of the play element in culture.* London: Routledge and Kegan Paul.

Hunt, J. McV. (1965). Traditional personality theory in the light of recent evidence. *American Scientist* 53: 80–96.

Huntingford, F. A., & Turner, A. K. (1987). *Animal conflict.* London: Chapman & Hall.

Hyman, H. H., & Singer, E. (Eds.) (1968). *Readings in reference group theory and research.* New York: Free Press.

Jahoda, G. (1963). The development of children's ideas about country and nationality: I. The conceptual framework. *British Journal of Educational Psychology* 33: 47–61.

James, W. (1890). *Principles of psychology.* 2 vols. New York: Henry Holt & Co.

_____. (1896/1984). The will to believe. In B. W. Wilshire (Ed.), *William James: The essential writings*. Albany, NY: State University of New York.

_____. (1902/1984). The varieties of religious experience. In B.W. Wilshire (Ed.), *William James: The essential writings*. Albany, NY: SUNY.

_____. (1910/1984). The moral equivalent of war. In B. W. Wilshire (Ed.), *William James: The essential writings*. Albany, NY: State University of New York.

_____. (1911). *Memories and studies*. New York: Longmans.

John, O. P. (1990). The "Big Five" factor taxonomy. In L. A. Pervin (Ed.), *Handbook of personality theory and research*. New York: Guilford Press.

Johnson, R. N. (1972). *Aggression in men and animals*. Philadelphia: W. B. Saunders Co.

Johnston, J., & Bachman, J. G. (1970). *Young men look at military service*. Ann Arbor: Institute for Social Research.

Juhasz, J. B. (1983). Social identity in the context of human and personal identity. In T. R. Sarbin & K. E. Scheibe (Eds.), *Studies in social identity*. New York: Praeger.

Jung, C. G. (1965). *Memories, dreams, reflections*. New York: Vintage Books.

_____. (1958). *Psychology and religion: West and East*. New York: Bollingen.

Kagan, J. (1964). Acquisition and significance of sex-typing and sex role identity. In M. L. Hoffman and L. W. Hoffman (Eds.), *Review of child development research* (Vol. 1). New York: Russell Sage Foundation.

_____. (1984). *The nature of the child*. New York: Basic Books.

Kallick, M., Suits, D., Dielman, T., and Hybels, J. (1979). *A survey of American gambling attitudes and behavior*. Ann Arbor, MI: Institute of Survey Research.

Kanter, R. M. (1972). *Commitment and community*. Cambridge, MA: Harvard University Press.

Kedourie, E. (1961). *Nationalism*, rev. ed. New York: Praeger.

Kelley, H. H. (1967). Attribution theory in social psychology. In D. Levine (Ed.), *Nebraska symposium on motivation* (vol. 15): 192–240. Lincoln, NE: University of Nebraska Press.

Keniston, K. (1965). *The uncommitted*. New York: Harcourt, Brace and World.

_____. (1968). *The young radicals*. New York: Harcourt, Brace and World.

_____. (1970). Youth: A "new" stage of life. *American Scholar* 39: 631–653.

Klama, J. (1988). *Aggression: The myth of the beast within*. New York: Wiley.

Klapp, O. (1969). *Collective search for identity*. New York: Holt, Rinehart and Winston.

_____. (1978). *Openings and closings*. New York: Cambridge University Press.

Kleinberg, O. (1964). *The human dimension in international relations*. New York: Holt, Rinehart and Winston.

Kochman, T. (1969). "Rapping" in the black ghetto, *Transaction* 6: 26–34.

Kogan, N., & Wallach, M. (1964). *Risk taking*. New York: Holt, Rinehart and Winston.

Kohlberg, L. (1963). The development of children's orientation towards a moral order. *Vita Humana* 6: 11–33.

_____. (1969). Stages and sequences: The cognitive-developmental approach to socialization. In D. A. Goslin (Ed.), *Handbook of socialization theory and research*. Chicago: Rand-McNally.

_____ (1971). Stages of moral development as a basis for moral education. In C. M. Beck, A. Crittenden, & D. Sullivan (Eds.), *Moral education: Interdisciplinary approaches*. Toronto: University of Toronto Press.

Kohn, H. (1962). *The age of nationalism*. New York: Harper.

Koestler, A. (1970). Arthur Koestler at 65. *New York Times Magazine* (August 30): 12–26.

Kundera, M. (1984). *The unbearable lightness of being*. New York: Harper & Row.

Lasswell, H. D. (1970). Must science serve political power? *American Psychologist* 25: 117–123.

Lecky, P. (1945). *Self-consistency: A theory of personality*. New York: Island Press.

Lefcourt, H. M. (1966). Internal vs. external control of reinforcement: A review. *Psychological Bulletin* 65: 206–220.

Levchenko, S. (1988). *On the wrong side: my life in the KGB*. New York: Pergamon.

LeVine, R. A. (1969). Culture, personality, and socialization: An evolutionary view. In D. A. Goslin (Ed.), *Handbook of socialization theory and research*. Chicago: Rand-McNally.

Lewin, K. (1951/1975). *Field theory in social science*. Westport, CT: Greenwood Press.

Lewis, M. (1992). *Shame: The self exposed*. New York: Maxwell Macmillan International.

Lifton, R. J. (1956). "Thought reform" of Western civilians in Chinese Communist prisons. *Psychiatry* 19: 173–195.

_____ . (1971). *History and human survival*. New York: Vintage.

Linton, R. (1936). *The study of man: An Introduction*. New York: Appleton Century.

Lofland, J. (1969). *Deviance and identity*. Englewood Cliffs, NJ: Prentice-Hall.

Lorenz, K. (1963). *On aggression*. New York: Bantam.

Lynch, M. D., Norem-Hebeison, A. A., & Gergen, K. J. (Eds.) (1981). *Self-concept: Advances in theory and research*. Cambridge, MA: Ballinger.

MacIntyre, A. (1981). *After virtue*. Notre Dame, IN: University of Notre Dame Press.

MacKinnon, D. W. (1965). Personality and the realization of creative potential. *American Psychologist* 20: 273–281.

MacLeish, A. (1956). *J.B.* Houghton Mifflin Company: Boston.

Mancuso, J. C., and Ceely, S. G. (1980). The self as a memory processing. *Cognitive Theory and Research* 4: 1–25.

Mancuso, J. C., and Sarbin, T. R. (1983). The self-narrative in the enactment of roles. In T. R. Sarbin and K. E. Scheibe (Eds.), *Studies in social identity*. New York: Praeger.

Manis, J. G., & Meltzer, B. N. (Eds.). (1978). *Symbolic interactionism: A reader in social psychology*. Boston: Allyn and Bacon.

Mead, G. H. (1934). *Mind, self, and society from the standpoint of a social behaviorist*. Chicago: University of Chicago Press.

_____ . (1938). *The philosophy of the act*. Chicago: University of Chicago Press.

Michener, J. A. (1976). *Sports in America*. New York: Random House.

Milgram, S. (1963). Behavioral studies of obedience. *Journal of Abnormal and Social Psychology* 67: 371–378.

_____ . (1964). Group pressure and action against a person. *Journal of Abnormal and Social Psychology* 69: 137–143.

Miller, D. R. (1963). The study of social relationships: Situation, identity and social interaction. In S. Koch (Ed.) *Psychology: A study of a science*. New York: McGraw-Hill.

Miller Brewing Company. (1983). *Miller Lite. Report on American attitudes towards sports*. Milwaukee, WI: Author.

Minogue, K. R. (1967). *Nationalism*. New York: Basic Books.

Mischel, T. (Ed.) (1977). *The Self: Psychological and philosophical issues*. Totowa, NJ: Rowman and Littlefield.

Mischel, W. (1968). *Personality and assessment*. New York: Wiley.

──────. (1977). On the future of personality measurement. *American Psychologist* 34: 740–754.

Mischel, W., & Peake, P. K. (1982). Beyond déjà vu in the search for cross-situational consistency. *Psychological Review* 89: 730–755.

Monette, P. (1992). *Becoming a man: Half a life story*. New York: Harcourt Brace Jovanovich.

Morawski, J. G. (1982). History as psychology's epistemological laboratory. Paper presented April 9 at the History Faculty Seminar, Wesleyan University, Middletown, CT.

Mule, S. J. (Ed.) (1981). *Behavior in excess: An examination of the volitional disorders*. New York: Free Press.

Mulford, H. A., & Salisbury, W. W. (1964). Self-conceptions in a general population. *Sociological Quarterly* 5: 35–46.

Mullahy, P. (1970). *Psychoanalysis and interpersonal psychiatry: The contributions of Harry Stack Sullivan*. New York: Science House.

Mussen, P. (1967). Early socialization: Learning and identification. In T. Newcomb (Ed.), *New directions in psychology III*. New York: Holt, Rinehart and Winston.

Nabokov, V. V. (1979). *Speak, memory: An autobiography revisited*. New York: Putnam.

Neel, J. V. (1970). Lessons from a primitive people. *Science* 170: 815–822.

O'Brien, T. (1990). *The things they carried*. New York: Penguin.

O'Neil, J. R. (1993). *The paradox of success*. New York: Putnam.

Orford, J. (1985). *Excessive appetites: A psychological view of addictions*. New York: Wiley.

Orne, M. T., & Evans, F. J. (1965). Social control in the psychological experiment: Antisocial behavior and hypnosis. *Journal of Personality and Social Psychology* 1: 189–200.

Ortega y Gassett, J. (1930/1932). *The revolt of the masses*. New York: Norton.

──────. (1961). *Meditations on Don Quixote*. New York: Norton.

Orwell, G. (1939/1968). Charles Dickens. In Sonia Orwell & I. Angus (Eds.), *The collected essays, journalism, and letters of George Orwell* (vol. 1). New York: Harcourt, Brace and World.

──────. (1940/1968). Review of *Mein Kampf*. In Sonia Orwell & I. Angus (Eds.), *The collected essays, journalism, and letters of George Orwell* (vol. 1). New York: Harcourt, Brace and World.

──────. (1941/1968). The art of Donald McGill. In Sonia Orwell and I. Angus (Eds.), *The collected essays, journalism, and letters of George Orwell* (vol. 2), 155–165. New York: Harcourt, Brace and World.

_____. (1943/1968). London letter to the Partisan Review. In Sonia Orwell & I. Angus (Eds.), *The collected essays, journalism, and letters of George Orwell* (vol. 2). New York: Harcourt, Brace and World.

_____. (1946/1968). As I please. In Sonia Orwell & I. Angus (Eds.), *The collected essays, journalism, and letters of George Orwell* (vol. 4). New York: Harcourt, Brace and World.

_____. (1946) *Animal farm*. New York: Harcourt Brace Jovanovich.

_____. (1949) *Nineteen eighty-four*. New York: Harcourt Brace Jovanovich.

Partridge, E. (1950). *A dictionary of the underworld, British and American*. London: Routledge & Kegan Paul.

Paz, O. (1987). Food of the Gods. *New York Review of Books* 33: 3–7.

Perls, F. (1969). *Gestalt therapy verbatim*. Lafayette, CA: Real People Press.

Perry, H. S. (1982). *Psychiatrist of America: The life of Harry Stack Sullivan*. Cambridge, MA: Belknap Press.

Peters, R. S. (1958). *The concept of motivation*. London: Routledge & Kegan Paul.

Pettigrew, T. F. (1964). *A profile of the Negro American*. Princeton, NJ: Van Nostrand Reinhold Company.

Pfeutze, P. E. (1954). *Self, society, and existence*. New York: Harper.

Piaget, J. (1932). *The moral judgment of the child*. London: Routledge and Kegan Paul.

_____. (1952). *The origins of intelligence in children*. New York: International Universities Press.

Platt, A. M., & Diamond, B. L. (1965). The origins and development of the "wild beast" concept of mental illness and its relation to theories of criminal responsibility. *Journal of the History of the Behavioral Sciences* 1: 355–367.

Pomper, P. (1973). Problems of a naturalistic psychohistory. *History and Theory* 12: 367–388.

Rieff, P. (1968). Cooley and culture. In A. J. Reiss, Jr. (Ed.), *Cooley and sociological analysis*. Ann Arbor: Univ. of Michigan Press.

Rokeach, M. (1964). *The three Christs of Ypsilanti: A psychological study*. New York: Knopf.

Rotenburg, M., and Sarbin, T. R. (1972). Impact of differentially significant others on role involvement: An experiment with prison social types. *Journal of Abnormal Psychology* 77: 97–107.

Rotter, J. B. (1966). Generalized expectancies for internal versus external control of reinforcement. *Psychological Monographs* 80, no. 609.

Russell, B. (1951). *New hopes for a changing world*. London: G. Allen and Unwin.

Sacks, O. (1983). The lost mariner. *New York Review of Books* (February 16): 14–20.

_____. (1993/1994). A neurologist's notebook: An anthropologist on Mars. *The New Yorker* (December 27, 1993/January 3, 1994): 106–125.

Saegert, S., Swap, W., & Zajonc, R. B. (1973). Exposure, context, and interpersonal attraction. *Journal of Personality and Social Psychology* 25: 234–242.

Sampson, E. E. (1993). *Celebrating the other*. Boulder, CO: Westview.

Sarason, S. (1975). Psychology to the Finland station in the heavenly city of the eighteenth-century philosophers. *American Psychologist* 30: 1072–1080.

Sarbin, T. R. (1954). Role theory. In G. Lindzey & E. Aronson (Eds.), *Handbook of social psychology* (vol. 1). Cambridge, MA: Addison-Wesley.

_____. (1967a). On the futility of the proposition that some people be labeled mentally ill. *Journal of Consulting Psychology* 31: 447–453.

————. (1967b). The dangerous individual: An outcome of social identity transformation. *British Journal of Criminology* 10: 355–366.

————. (1968). On the distinction between social roles and social types, with special references to the hippie. *American Journal of Psychiatry* 125: 1024–1031.

————. (1975). Cross-age tutoring and social identity. In V. L. Allen (Ed.) *Tutoring and interage interaction.* Madison: University of Wisconsin Press.

————. (1976). Contextualism: A world view for modern psychology. In J. K. Cole (Ed.), *Nebraska symposium on motivation.* Lincoln: University of Nebraska Press.

————. (1982a). Metaphors of death in systems of conduct reorganization. In V. Allen and K. E. Scheibe (Eds.), *The social context of conduct.* New York: Praeger.

————. (1982b). The Quixotic principle. In V. Allen and K. E. Scheibe (Eds.), *The social context of conduct.* New York: Praeger.

————. (1993). The narrative and the root metaphor for contextualism. In S.C. Hayes, L. J. Hayes, H. W. Reese, & T. R. Sarbin (Eds.), *Varieties of scientific contextualism.* Reno: Context Press.

Sarbin, T. R., & Adler, N. (1971). Communalities in systems of conduct reorganization. *Psychoanalytic Review* 57: 599–616.

Sarbin, T. R., & Allen, V. I. (1968). Role theory. In G. Lindzey & E. Aronson (Eds.), *Handbook of social psychology.* Reading, MA: Addison-Wesley.

Sarbin, T. R., & Coe, W. C. (1972). *Hypnosis: The social psychology of influence communication.* New York: Holt, Rinehart & Winston.

Sarbin, T. R., & Scheibe, K. E. (1980). The transvaluation of social identity. In C. J. Bellone (Ed.), *The normative dimension in public administration.* New York: Marcel Dekker.

————. (Eds.) (1983). *Studies in social identity.* New York: Praeger.

Sarbin, T. R., & Stein, K. B. (1967). *Self-role theory and anti-social conduct.* Progress Report, National Institute of Mental Health.

Scheibe, K. E. (1967). Reflections on Loyalty, *Trinity Alumni Magazine* 8: 12–15.

————. (1970). *Beliefs and values.* New York: Holt, Rinehart & Winston.

————. (1974). Legitimized aggression and the assignment of evil. *American Scholar* 43: 575–592.

————. (1978). The psychologist's advantage and nullification: Limits of human predictability. *American Psychologist* 33: 869–881.

————. (1979). *Mirrors, masks, lies and secrets.* New York: Praeger.

————. (1983). The psychology of national identity. In T. R. Sarbin & K. E. Scheibe (Eds.), *Studies in social identity.* New York: Praeger.

————. (1986). Self narratives and adventure. In T.R. Sarbin (Ed.), *Narrative psychology: The storied nature of human conduct.* New York: Praeger.

Schlenker, B. R. (1980). *Impression management.* Monterey, CA: Brooks/Cole.

Seligman, M.E.P. (1993). *What you can change and what you can't.* New York: Knopf.

Shaver, P. R., & Scheibe, K. E. (1967). Transformation of social identity: A study of chronic mental patients and college volunteers in a summer camp setting. *Journal of Psychology* 66: 19–37.

Shaw, G. B. (1962). *Androcles and the lion.* Baltimore: Penguin Books.

Sherif, M. (1935). An experimental study of stereotypes. *Journal of Abnormal and Social Psychology* 29: 371–375.

———. (1966). *Group conflict and cooperation: Their social psychology*. London: Routledge and Kegan Paul.

Shor, R. E., and Orne, E. C. (1962). *Harvard scale of hypnotic susceptibility*. Palo Alto, CA: Consulting Psychologists Press.

Singer, J. A., and Salovey, P. (1993). *The remembered self*. New York: Free Press.

Sizer, N. F., and Sizer, T. R. (1970). Introduction. In J. M. Gustafon, et al. (Eds.), *Moral education*. Cambridge, MA: Harvard University Press.

Skinner, B. (1948). *Walden Two*. New York: Macmillan.

———. (1971). *Beyond freedom and dignity*. New York: Knopf.

Snyder, L. L. (1968). *The new nationalism*. Ithaca: Cornell University Press.

Spence, D. P. (1982). *Narrative truth and historical truth*. New York: Norton.

Spock, B. (1957). *Baby and child care*. New York: Pocket Books.

Stagner, R. (1946). War and Peace. In P. L. Harriman (Ed.), *Encyclopedia of psychology*. New York: Citadel Press.

Stein, H. F., & Hill, R. F. (1987). The limits of ethnicity. *American Scholar* 46: 181–192.

Steinbeck, J. (1977). *The acts of King Arthur and his noble knights, from the Winchester mss. of Thomas Malory and other stories*. New York: Ballantine.

Stouffer, S. A. (1949). An analysis of conflicting social norms. *American Sociological Review* 14: 707–717.

Strauss, A. (1956). *The social psychology of George Herbert Mead*. Chicago: University of Chicago Press.

Sullivan, H. S. (1950). The illusion of personal individuality. *Psychiatry* 13: 317–332.

———. (1953). *The interpersonal theory of psychiatry*. New York: Norton.

Tajfel, H. (1982). *Social identity and intergroup relations*. Cambridge: Cambridge University Press.

Thorndyke, P. W. (1977). Cognitive structures in comprehension and memory of narrative discourse. *Cognitive Psychology* 9: 97–110.

Tulving, E. (1972). Episodic and semantic memory. In E. Tulving and W. Donaldson (Eds.) *Organization of memory*. NY: Academic.

Turing, A. M. (1963). Can a machine think? In E. A. Feigenbaum & J. Feldman (Eds.) *Computers and thought*. New York: McGraw-Hill.

Tversky, A., & Kahnemann, D. (1973). Availability: A heuristic for judging frequency and probability. *Cognitive Psychology* 5: 207–232.

Tyler, L. E. (1978). *Individuality*. San Francisco: Jossey-Bass.

Vonnegut, K. (1982). *Deadeye Dick*. New York: Delacorte.

Walhke, J. H. (1952). *Loyalty in a democratic state*. Boston, D. C. Heath & Co.

Washburn, S. L., & DeVore, I. (1961). The social life of baboons. *Scientific American* 82: 10–19.

Weber, E. (1971). Gymnastics and sport in fin de siècle France: Opium of the class. *American Historical Review* 76: 70–98.

Wilkinson, J. D. (1985). Remembering World War II: The perspective of the losers. *American Scholar* 54: 329–44.

Wills, G. (1982). *The Kennedy imprisonment: A meditation on power*. Boston: Little, Brown.

Wolfe, T. (1979). *The right stuff*. New York: Farrar, Straus, and Giroux.

Wylie, R. (1974). *The self-concept. Vol. 1, A review of methodological considerations and measuring instruments,* rev. ed. Lincoln: Univ. of Nebraska Press.

————. (1979). *The self-concept. Vol 2, Theory and research on selected topics,* rev. ed. Lincoln: Univ. of Nebraska Press.

Young, T. R. (1971). The politics of sociology: Gouldner, Goffman, and Garfinkel. *American Sociologist* 6: 276–281.

Zajonc, R. B. (1968). The attitudinal effects of mere exposure. *Journal of Personality and Social Psychology, Monograph Supplements* 9: 1–27.

Index

About the Author

KARL E. SCHEIBE is Professor of Psychology at Wesleyan University. He has written extensively in the field.